the HORIZONTAL ORGANIZATION

Frank Ostroff

OXFORD UNIVERSITY PRESS   New York Oxford   1999

the HORIZONTAL ORGANIZATION

What the Organization of the Future Looks Like
and How It Delivers Value to Customers

Oxford University Press

Oxford   New York
Athens   Auckland   Bangkok   Bogotá   Buenos Aires
Calcutta   Cape Town   Chennai   Dar es Salaam   Delhi   Florence
Hong Kong   Istanbul   Karachi   Kuala Lumpur   Madrid
Melbourne   Mexico City   Mumbai   Nairobi   Paris   São Paulo
Singapore   Taipei   Tokyo   Toronto   Warsaw

and associated companies in
Berlin   Ibadan

Published by Oxford University Press, Inc.
198 Madison Avenue, New York, New York 10016

Oxford is a registered trademark of Oxford University Press

Library of Congress Cataloging-in-Publication Data
Ostroff, Frank.
The horizontal organization: What the organization of the future looks like
and how it delivers value to customers / by Frank Ostroff.
p.   cm.
"Throw away your old organization chart and create a new one.
Manage across, not up and down. Use structure to drive results."
Includes bibliographical references.
ISBN 0-19-512138-4
1. Teams in the workplace.   2. Management—Employee participation.   I. Title.
HD66.068   1998   658.4'02—dc21   98-9781

1 3 5 7 9 8 6 4 2

Printed in the United States of America
on acid-free paper

To My Beloved—Wife, Parents, Children, Family

CONTENTS

PREFACE

This book started a number of years ago with a question that I wanted to address: What will the organization of the future look like? I was in management consulting and was working with a number of large and important organizations that were facing a rapidly changing world. If there was an organizational form that would equip them to cope successfully with this change, what would it be?

My answer was what I now call the Horizontal Organization, and over recent years it has been applied in a number of different kinds of firms and organizations with startlingly successful results. Although this book will describe the concept in detail, here is a brief description that will serve as a background to the rest of the book.

Nearly all firms and organizations have as their mission the delivery of something of value to their customers. This can be a product or service, and the customer can be a purchaser of the product or service. But there are some organizations—such as government agencies—that deliver something of value to customers who don't pay directly for it. However, they are just as much customers as those who buy products and services from commercial firms. Clearly, it is to the organizations' advantage if they can deliver maximum value to the customer no matter how the customer is defined. The Horizontal Organization is designed to give organizations the structural form and integrated organizational approach that will allow them to deliver this value to customers.

Thus, the delivery of value to customers is at the heart of the Horizontal Organization. I—and others—call it "delivering the value proposition." Embedded in most organizations are core processes that are meant to deliver the value proposition. But in today's vertically organized firms, the people who make the core process work are almost always grouped according to fragmented functions. Different functional groups, for example, develop products or services, manufacture or produce them, and market them. This fragmentation often hampers the delivery of the value proposition.

The Horizontal Organization organizes around core process groups. All the people who work on a core process are brought together into a group that can easily coordinate its efforts and maximize the value of what it delivers to customers. This group, by incorporating people from a previously vertical organization, results in a much less hierarchical organization, more customer-focused. It is, as its name suggests, a Horizontal Organization.

How does the Horizontal Organization differ from other models that have been offered in recent years? It is more comprehensive in that it incorporates elements of some of the existing concepts, such as process reengineering, individual empowerment, and teams. But it goes beyond them by providing an overall framework for the organization that integrates and makes use of the best of these ideas in a new structure that has been proved in practice.

Is the Horizontal Organization a universal panacea? Not at all. In most cases, the delivery of a value proposition requires a combination of approaches. For example, functions can help in some situations where deep technical expertise is required. My own view is that the organization of the future will very likely be a hybrid, utilizing a variety of approaches in combinations tailored to specific performance challenges. The Horizontal Organization makes an important contribution here by increasing the range, power, and customization of solutions to these performance challenges.

My intention in this book is to help readers understand what the Horizontal Organization is, how it works, how it can be developed, and how to decide where it can be effectively employed in any organization.

October 1998   Frank Ostroff

ACKNOWLEDGMENTS

This book has benefited immeasurably from the support of many folks over many years. I deeply appreciate the help I have gotten from everyone. The goal of the book is to help organizations improve their performance and to make a contribution toward helping improve the lives of those in organizations. To the extent that this book makes these contributions, I hope you will feel good about the part you played and the support you gave to its writing.

For their critical role in the preparation of this book, I am greatly appreciative of the outstanding assistance provided by Wordworks—the editorial contributions of Donna Sammons Carpenter, the project management of G. Patton Wright, and the dedicated, professional work of their colleagues, including Christina Braun, Maurice Coyle, Erik Hansen, Ruth Hlavacek, Susannah Ketchum, Martha Lawler, and Saul Wisnia. I am also appreciative of the encouragement, support, and caring shown by my agent, Helen Rees.

It is a privilege to work with my colleagues in A. T. Kearney and within its Transformation Practice. I have found it exciting to work with those who are engaged in the pursuit of doing Transformation "right." My colleagues include Bart Kocha, Mark Miller, and all the members of the Transformation Practice core team. Others in A. T. Kearney whose support has been important include Martha Peak and Rick Gray in our marketing department. The book's graphics benefited tremendously from the work of those in A. T. Kearney's graphics department, including Holly Gefvert, Caroline Johnson, and Wendy Majkowski.

I am deeply grateful to a number of colleagues and teachers from whom I have learned both professionally and personally. I will always be indebted to Steve Dichter for his mentorship, his caring, and his concern for my development, as well as his inspirational leadership and insights. I am grateful for the help, guidance, and insight that Robert Reich has provided for me over the years. His work on new approaches to organization and management, which I read a number of years ago, was an important early indication that something significant was afoot in how companies were organized and managed. Jon Katzenbach made contributions to my early thinking on the horizontal organization and has always been there for me when I needed him. I am grateful to Doug Smith for his contributions to both the original ideas of the horizontal organization and their expression, as well as his concern for my welfare. I thank Gene Zelazny for both his friendship and insights on the visual depiction of the horizontal organization.

I am especially indebted to Mort Meyerson for having created the opportunity and provided the support to further develop these ideas in new areas. I also appreciate the role Jim Champy played in supporting the development of the ideas.

I deeply appreciate the help and support given to me by Paul Taskier. We are all better off for having people like Paul around who can be counted on to do the Right Thing. Paul is a living example of the "good man."

I have benefited tremendously from the insights and contributions of a number of consultants and academics with whom I have worked. These include Charles Baum, Jonathan Spiegel, Malcolm Sparrow, Roger Boehm, and Cody Phipps.

For providing a collegial and congenial environment and workplace for much of the writing of the book I am very grateful to Colin Campbell and the Georgetown University Public Policy Program. I am also grateful for the support provided by John Crapo, Rich Forshee, and Julie Tea, also of the Public Policy Program.

I thank Sonia Balet and the Faculty of Business Administration of the University of Puerto Rico for giving me a workplace for writing this book during a time of need.

I appreciate the encouraging spirit and insightful advice provided by Hinda Magidson at the inception of the effort to write this book.

I am also appreciative of the design advice provided to me by Tom Phifer. Daniel Kunstler of J. P. Morgan provided important company information.

I am deeply indebted for the help of the companies who participated in the book and their employees who participated in the interviews. The concepts of the horizontal organization has also benefited tremendously from the applications and insights of a number of colleagues and practitioners, including Steve Frangos, Phil Jarrosiak, and the Operation Front Line team.

The folks at Oxford University Press have been an absolute dream to work with. I am particularly grateful for the expertise and support of Herb Addison, my editor at Oxford, who believed in, encouraged, and supported this project over a long period of time. Many others at Oxford also provided important support for the book, including Laura Brown, Mary Ellen Curley, Russell Perreault, Caroline Skinner, and Joellyn Ausanka.

I am deeply grateful for the love and support given by members of my family, as well as my friends: Irving and Barbara Ostroff, Leslie and Glenn White, Jon and Angela Ostroff, David and Ilene Ostroff, Tereso and Nelson Ramírez, Marisol and Gustavo Gelpí, José Ramírez, Violet and Ted Brown, Tod and Sue Brown, Esther and Hal Jacobs, Hy and Colleen Mayerson, Shelli and Marc Ross, Pedro Alonso, Frank, Cece, and Beth Ann Kessler, Ron Partizian, Steve Swire, and Lee Weinberg.

I am eternally grateful for the love and support given to me by my parents, Irving and Estelle. They have watched over me, guided me, and sacrificed for me. I believe it is important for children to honor what their parents have done for them by the life they lead. My mother has now passed, but I hope that both she and my father are proud of how I conduct my life and feel that it honors the values they taught me.

I am deeply grateful to my brothers, Jon and David, and sister, Leslie, for the love, support, and companionship I have received from them over the years.

I am now married, with children of my own. I cannot imagine having a better family of in-laws than the Ramírez family. I am still in awe of the miracle of the role my wife and I have been able to play in giving life to our children, Estelle and Jacobo. To my children, I want to tell you that my love for you is endless and that my most sincere hope is that you go on to be happy in your lives and to help make the world a better place. And to my wife, Tere, I have no deeper Blessing than to have found you. I love you for eternity.

Above all, I am deeply grateful to the Source of all my Blessings.

Part ONE
WHAT THE HORIZONTAL ORGANIZATION IS

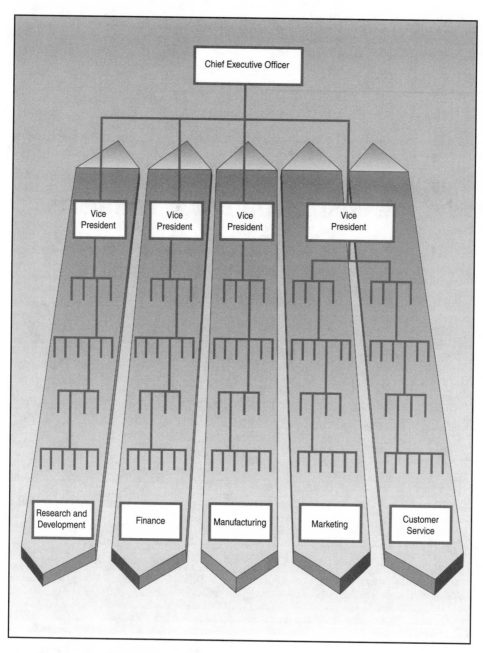

Fig. 1.1 The Vertical Organization

1 WHO NEEDS THE HORIZONTAL ORGANIZATION?

ALMOST EVERYONE

Does this chart look familiar? It should. The diagram illustrates an organizational design that has been the mainstay of business since the Industrial Revolution, helping to promote the efficient production of goods and the administration of government tasks for most of the twentieth century. It is an approach that I call the "vertical hierarchy," which, as the name implies, comprises a tall authority structure with multiple reporting levels and a decision-making apparatus that concentrates authority near the top. "Thinking" is delegated to management; "doing" is accomplished in a collection of functionally distinct departments populated by individuals who are focused on specialized and generally fragmented tasks.

The whole concept of an organization chart—what the French call an *organigramme*—long predates the Industrial Revolution, having been around in one form or another for centuries (diagrams outlining church hierarchy, for example, can be found in medieval churches in Spain). Study one of these skeletal configurations and you quickly see the reason for its longevity: Organization charts provide a tool for understanding how an enterprise operates. They can emphasize certain features and de-emphasize others, quickly allowing the viewer to know what positions exist, how these positions are grouped, how formal authority flows between departments, and who answers to whom.

More than just basic road maps for the interested observer, however, such charts also focus attention on the organizational design's most important building blocks—a distinction that belongs to the individual worker in the traditional vertical scheme. The single worker and his or her job become the foundation of performance in a vertical or functional hierarchy, and managers on higher levels are charged with matching the right people with the right tasks and evaluating and rewarding their performance.[1]

Movement in a vertical organization is either downward or upward. Because separate departments performing separate functions do all the work, the system naturally involves multiple handoffs that devour time and ineluctably focus inward on corporate politics and each department's attainment of internal goals rather than outward on the production of products and services with value that continually satisfies and wins customers.

Verticality is not always a negative force in business, of course. In fact, it is often attributed with maintaining the standard of corporate efficiency. The vertical organization, which assumes a bureaucratic shape dominated by functional departments, was brought to its productive apex by the Industrial Revolution, as manufacturing and industrial production grew more complex and involved the management of more and more workers. In the United States, for instance, the construction of the railroads in the 1840s quickly revealed a desperate need for some means of controlling and managing the work of engineers, builders, schedulers, and others. Because trains often ran on single tracks without adequate signaling, the potential for a disaster was always present.

When a serious head-on collision of two passenger trains occurred in 1841, in Westfield, Massachusetts, a public outcry went up for better management and control. In response, the board of directors of the Western Railroad appointed a committee to make recommendations for managing an increasingly complex operation. In its "Report on Avoiding Collisions and Governing the Employees," the committee faulted the conductor of one of the trains who had disregarded the company's schedule; accordingly, the directors took steps to fix "definite responsibilities for each phase of the company's business, drawing solid lines of authority and command for the railroad's administration, maintenance, and operation."[2]

Directly beneath the president of the Western, the general superintendent managed the work of three roadmasters, each heading a geographical section of the railroad over which he had to operate a handcar every morning during the winter months to ensure that the tracks were clear. At the head of another side of the company, a master of transportation in Springfield, Massachusetts, had responsibility for overseeing a group of managers who administered freight and passenger traffic, maintained the engines, and even bought wood fuel for the locomotives.[3]

In *The Visible Hand*, a study of the rise of business managers in the United States, Alfred Chandler points to the Western Railroad as "the first American business enterprise to operate through a formal administration structure manned by full-time salaried managers."[4] Other railroads followed the example of the Western,[5] so that by the mid-nineteenth century in the United States, near the time of the Civil War, American businesses were formalizing their chain of command and responsibility through the vertical organizational design or chart.

As the hierarchical organization evolved in the early twentieth century, it was deeply influenced by the principles of "scientific management," the foremost explicator of which was Frederick Winslow Taylor. In response to the perceived behavioral problem called "soldiering" (that is, an attitude among workers that they should do the least amount of work in the longest time span), Taylor called for strong measures to reverse this deadly trend in business. Specifically, he saw the primary duty of the manager to increase efficiency by getting the most work out of a worker in the shortest possible time. By "scientifically" measuring productivity and setting high quotas, Taylor proposed an antidote to the "poisonous" type of management called "initiative and incentive," whereby managers bribed workers into doing more by offering them higher wages or promising them promotions.[6] Equipped with stopwatches and notepads, managers conducted time-and-motion studies on workers within disparate functional departments in order to increase productivity. Citing the case of some 600 laborers at the Bethlehem Steel Company, Taylor noted that their improved productivity resulted from an "elaborate organization" guided by managers who were committed to the principles of so-called scientific management.[7]

Not surprisingly, organization designers have experimented with structural configuration over the years, coming up with a number of variations. Surveying the multiplicity of approaches, organizational theorists have long recognized that there is no one "best" structure. They have shown—as part of what is called the "contingency approach" to organizational design—that organizational effectiveness improves when structure fits the particular demands of the situation.[8] But it is increasingly apparent that the long-favored vertical model is, by itself, no longer capable of meeting all the different needs of business. It has been rendered inadequate for today's demanding competitive, technological, and workforce environment by its inherent shortcomings. These include:

- Its internal focus on functional goals rather than an outward-looking concentration on delivering value and winning customers

- The loss of important information as knowledge travels up and down the multiple levels and across the functional departments

- The fragmentation of performance objectives brought about by a multitude of distinct and fragmented functional goals

- The added expense involved in coordinating the overly fragmented work and departments

- The stifling of creativity and initiative of workers at lower levels

That is why leading-edge corporations, such as those featured in this book, are turning to a cross-functional organization designed around end-to-end work flows, an approach I call the "horizontal organization." It is a design ideally suited to a radically different business climate defined by new technology, intense global competition, a constantly changing marketplace, and the expanded aspirations of workers who are demanding increased participation and greater responsibility.

Speed, service, total customer solutions, and flexibility are the watchwords if a company is to thrive in this new economy. The concept of a horizontal organization structured around a small number of end-to-end work, information, and material flows known as *core processes* is tailor-made for helping a company reach its competitive peak. As we will see in chapter 3, the distinction between a core process and an ordinary, simple process is crucial. The former extends across a business and drives the achievement of fundamental performance objectives tied to an organization's strategy. Core processes, which number no more than three or four in the typical organization, are the catalysts that transform an organization from the vertical to the horizontal, channeling all energies toward achieving customer satisfaction.

This chapter will introduce you to the features of the horizontal approach, and explain why it can help make your organization a winner.

A Workplace Beset by Turmoil

Whether we are business executives, middle managers, shop-floor workers, or simply consumers, none of us can ignore the profound changes that have occurred in the workplace over the past two decades. The mind-boggling technological progress that emphasizes computer-based integration, coordination, and communication is apparent everywhere. Unfortunately, so is the troubling disintegration that gnaws away at virtually every area of our lives.

Consider banking transactions in this age of the ubiquitous ATM. The few remaining humans who run the local bank branches oversee one aspect of your business while a maze of invisible back-office departments tends to others. Often no one person has responsibility for every part of a customer's business, and this diffusion of accountability can be a nightmare for the consumer. You probably know, for example, how difficult it is to have checks directed to a new address after you have moved, or to correct an error in your account. The number of people in countless departments who have to make some contribution to the process can turn a simple transaction into endless torture.

What is more, the effects reach well beyond the realm of personal annoyance and aggravation: The bank's inefficiencies devour not only *your* time, but also its own, not to mention its profits and shareholder value. The problem is that your bank—like your insurance company, perhaps, or the airline you travel—is an organization still mired in the vertical mindset of the past.

The vertical organization's focus on internal functional goals means that people are either looking upward, intent on pleasing the boss, or downward, occupied by supervising subordinates. Unfortunately, the most important angle of vision—the view out toward what the whole company should be doing to win customers—is often obstructed by internal concerns. Furthermore, because separate units performing separate tasks do all the work, completing a project naturally requires multiple handoffs that waste valuable time and encourage fragmented, even conflicting, performance objectives, thereby raising costs, decreasing efficiency, and hindering coordination. In addition, the separation of tasks tends to emphasize what is "optimal" for the individual unit or function rather than what is best for the entire organization. All in all, it does not produce a recipe for success in a highly competitive environment.

The vertical hierarchy attained its status and thrived when the business landscape was relatively stable and predictable. So long as markets were steady, competition was primarily domestic, technology meant simple, special-purpose machines such as the typewriter, and labor was abundant and semi-skilled, the vertical hierarchy worked—and worked magnificently.

Change is always inevitable, as we know, but who could have predicted the magnitude of the transformation that has occurred over the past two decades, and how it would forever alter the business landscape? The collapse of borders, the wiring of the world, the need to tailor products to accommodate a diverse marketplace, and a clamor among available workers for more responsibility and job satisfaction—all this came together to make stability and predictability nothing more than a fond memory of a bygone era.[9] With inconstancy becoming the rule, a bureaucracy weighted down by supervisory layer upon supervisory layer and its clumsy inability to coordinate efforts proved incapable of reacting with the speed needed to meet the varied and unrelenting demands of global markets and customers.

To ward off any misconception, I must point out that a vertical, function-based organization can still be an appropriate choice, one that can work where demand for goods exceeds supplies or where worker skills are quite low—in lesser-developed countries, for example—or in situations where success demands technical expertise above all else, or where success depends on high-volume, standardized production. But by and large, the situations where the purely vertical model is appropriate have narrowed considerably. Ironically, this narrowing resides, in part, in what was once the principal source of strength of the vertical organization: namely, the way in which it defines structure.

By dividing large operations into functional departments, the vertical design guarantees fragmented tasks, overspecialization, fiefdoms, turf wars, the urge to control from the top—all the negatives that foster organizational paralysis. Regrettably for late-twentieth-century corporations, verticality spawns a host of handicapped hierarchies at the very moment when business can least afford the resultant loss of speed and efficiency.

A Design for Today . . . and for Tomorrow

With the old order breaking down and organizations and their management staffs enmeshed in seeking new organizational forms, business thinkers have rushed in to fill the void, struggling to conceptualize and articulate what the twenty-first-century organization should look like in order to respond to the competitive, technological, and workforce demands of the new age. Although their efforts were well-intentioned, many early theorists often cloaked their valuable ideas in obscure terminology and metaphors—clusters, orchestras, inverted pyramids, and pizza pies, to name a few[10]—that were more metaphorical than they were actionable.

To be sure, trail-blazing conceptualization is an important first step in explicating fundamental change, but the usefulness of metaphors is limited when addressing the basic issue of how to move from abstract idea to workable design. At the end of the day, the question a manager needs to be able to answer is: How do I put together a performance-based organization for the new era? Metaphors aside, the design solution remains firmly embedded in the way in which labor is divided into tasks and the tasks then coordinated to deliver quickly and efficiently an organization's value proposition, which is the set of benefits that a business offers to convince customers to buy from it and to differentiate itself from its competitors.

In short, structure is still critical to designing an efficient organization for the twenty-first or any other century, and certain essential points must be considered: Who goes where? What do they do? What are the positions and how are they grouped? What is the reporting sequence? What is each person accountable for? In other words, how does authority flow? Now add to these the questions about the organization's actual business: What does the company purport to do best? How does it accomplish that work and deliver its value proposition to the customer?[11] These questions lead managers to the ultimate question: *How does a company's organization propel it forward in its creation and delivery of that value proposition?*

Answering these basic questions while also offering an alternative set of organizational building blocks is the key to meeting the challenges bombarding business. The horizontal organization can help provide answers, and it does so within the framework of a cross-functional, integrated alignment of work and goals, "real-time" problem solving, and the continuous improvement in performance—the hallmarks of competitive advantage in the future.

Exactly what are the fundamental principles of the horizontal organization? Simply stated, horizontal organizations:

- Organize around cross-functional core processes, not tasks or functions

- Install process owners or managers who will take responsibility for the core process in its entirety

- Make teams, not individuals, the cornerstone of organizational design and performance

- Decrease hierarchy by eliminating non-value-added work and by giving team members who are not necessarily senior managers the authority to make decisions directly related to their activities within the process flow

- Integrate with customers and suppliers

- Empower people by giving them the tools, skills, motivation, and authority to make decisions essential to the team's performance

- Use information technology (IT) to help people reach performance objectives and deliver the value proposition to the customer

- Emphasize multiple competencies and train people to handle issues and work productively in cross-functional areas within the new organization

- Promote multiskilling, the ability to think creatively and respond flexibly to new challenges that arise in the work that teams do

- Redesign functional departments or areas to work as "partners in process performance" with the core process groups

- Measure for end-of-process performance objectives (which are driven by the value proposition), as well as customer satisfaction, employee satisfaction, and financial contribution

- Build a corporate culture of openness, cooperation, and collaboration, a culture that focuses on continuous performance improvement and values employee empowerment, responsibility, and well-being

This is the horizontal organization in a nutshell. When properly applied, these mutually-consistent, mutually-reinforcing, aligned principles enable a horizontal organization to perform effectively. They yield an organization capable of responding to today's diverse challenges. What is more, a horizontal organization also leverages and integrates the performance improvement capabilities of many performance enablers introduced in recent years. That is, a horizontal organization reinforces—and is reinforced by—these performance enablers.

Reengineering, total quality management, high-involvement work systems, continuous improvement—wonderful ideas all, but when applied in isolated fashion, they provide only limited performance gains. One of the most appealing features of the horizontal organization, however, is the way in which it ties together the various performance enablers into an integrated, coherent, mutually reinforcing whole rather than presenting them in a laundry list of disconnected "one-offs." A model of the new organization is finally emerging that helps make sense of these enablers and gives each of them a place in the context of an integrated whole where they can actually be seen as reinforcing one another.

Reengineering, for example, produces the efficient and effective processes and work flows that are the necessary foundation of the cross-functional organization.[12] The reengineered processes also facilitate the identification of the skills, activities, and teams needed to achieve overall performance goals. At the same time, the cross-functional, process-based design eliminates the structural boundaries that perpetuate hand-offs, conflicting objectives, and functional groupings of employees, thereby making the reengineering more successful. Most reengineering efforts, even if they are done right, achieve one-time improvements in performance. The horizontal organization, on the other hand, provides the basis both for immediately improving the organization's performance and for promoting continuous improvement over the long term.

As those who have reengineered antiquated core processes and work systems have learned, real transformation involves a dual focus on processes and the organization at large. In a 1993 *Harvard Business Review* article, Gene Hall, Jim Rosenthal, and Judy Wade confirmed that *both* breadth of process and depth of business levers, including roles and responsibilities, measurements and incentives, organization structure, information technology and shared values and skills—meaning consideration of all of the seven S's of structure, systems (information, technology, measurement), skills (people's skills), shared values (behavior), staff, style, and strategy—were crucial for achieving performance improvements at the 20 companies studied for the article.[13] The horizontal organization is the lubricant that facilitates the smooth alignment of all these pieces.

This same kind of symbiotic relationship occurs with high-involvement work systems, too. Whereas empowered workers find that the fragmented and separated departments common to the vertical organization circumscribe their solution space and limit the kinds of activities they can work on, the cross-functional work of redesigned processes within the horizontal organization is ideally suited for empowered teams, about which much has been written recently. When seen in the context of a horizontal organization, teams are not just a good idea, they become an essential component of productivity and continuous improvement. That is because they can combine the human skills and experiences necessary to solve problems not only in real time but in cross-functional flows of work.

Combining multiple skills and experiences as well as integrating activities across a flow of work, these teams engage in real-time problem solving and have the authority, information, training, and motivation to keep process performance on track to meet objectives. They help ensure that the improvements generated by reengineering will be ongoing and continuous. As we will see in chapter 12, one of the hallmarks of the horizontal organization is continuous improvement, an achievement which eludes many reengineering efforts.

By helping each of the performance enablers to enhance and support the others in a mutually reinforcing and cumulative pattern, the horizontal organization dramatically enlarges the performance improvement possibilities envisioned by the creators of the various techniques. It is the missing piece of the map showing where business has been heading over two decades of change. Moreover, each of the 12 principles of the horizontal organization reinforces one another in an aligned, integrated way that covers the broad range of elements that have an impact on business performance. Indeed, these principles can be used to maximize performance. Formulating strategy first and then shaping the organization to deliver the value proposition, management can use the horizontal organization—and all the approaches that it entails—as an executional engine to engender future growth.

Strategy, Structure, Success

A CEO, a middle manager, or anyone else involved in organizational design and change needs a clear picture of who goes where, what each person does, and how different parts of the organization relate to one another. When these structural links are missing or tenuous, managers find a daunting impediment to their attempts to transform the organization. We know, for example, that teams will play an increasingly important role in the twenty-first-century organization. We also know that teams constitute only one piece of the organization's design puzzle. To stop there without trying to understand how the work of teams can be integrated to advance the performance of the corporate whole, or to blindly assume that a large corporation can perform effectively with hundreds of disconnected teams, without any sense of how to ensure that the teams are working in an integrated way that advances the performance of the entire entity, is nothing short of irresponsible. A large corporation simply cannot be 20,000 disconnected teams.

What organizational approach can make sure that all the teams are heading in the same direction? To answer that question, management will need first to formulate an appropriate strategy for the entire organization.[14] They must lay out in detail the value proposition and the one to five core processes that either are already in place or, more likely, will need to be identified, designed, and aligned in order to deliver competitive advantage. In addition, managers must make sure that the contributions of individual teams are fully integrated toward that delivery and that team members are held accountable for performance goals.

For the most part, such organization-wide structure has been sorely missing from transformational efforts in recent decades. The horizontal organization, however, not only presents an actionable picture of the organization of the future, but also provides the architecture needed to pull together all elements of organizational performance into an integrated whole. This need for a corporate architecture to configure the organization of the future cannot be ignored. Without it, would-be wizards are stymied.

Structure is not the only thing needed for transformational organizational design, of course, but its importance must not be overlooked. By itself, structure can inhibit performance because it touches upon a range of issues, from role clarity to accountability to leadership. Structure, by itself, can actually inhibit problem solving and innovative thinking, especially when that structure is rigidly designed so that people in functional areas think only of departmental goals and performance measures rather than asking what is best for the organization as a whole.

To be sure, structure can, and often does, shape what people feel ought to be emphasized in a company's strategy. Specifically, organization can influence strategic choice. How? A company may be examining a number of strategies. If these strategies have equal probabilities of success, it may make sense to select the one the current organization is most capable of executing—that is, the one that would require the least organizational change, disruption, or trauma and, therefore, risk.

Another point: Where a person "sits" in the organizational structure influences what he or she sees as important. The vertical organization provides many examples of what happens to people whose vision becomes more and more narrow as resources allocated to the production and delivery of the value proposition are limited. It is not unreasonable to expect them to fight to protect their "turf" or special interests, often to the exclusion of what is best for the entire organization. The horizontal organization, on the other hand, encourages people to broaden their line of sight in order to understand how their work benefits the entire organization.

Charting the redesigned cross-functional work and assigning people to carry out particular flows of work, for example, serve to define job descriptions and clarify roles. This clarity, in turn, helps people understand what their responsibilities are and what the measures of success are. People throughout the organization can direct their attention to what it takes to achieve competitive advantage and win customers, no longer wasting time in functions that focus on their own internal goals and that may not track with what the company as a whole needs to do to succeed.

A horizontal structure also encourages communication and joint problem solving between areas that need to work together. Core process grouping allows employees from varied disciplines to know and understand one another. It encourages the development of "social bonds," joint decision-making methodologies, and collaborative approaches, thus dissolving the functional barriers that have traditionally thwarted communication. New relationships and new cross-functional responsibilities also promote a broadening of workers' scope, skills, and decision-making abilities.

The very act of drawing an organization chart along cross-functional lines formalizes the new structure and sends a powerful signal, both inside and outside the company, about the importance of cross-functional approaches. People look at the *organigramme* and realize that relationships have changed. Dissolving the old functional associations makes it much harder to slip back into the former way of doing things. Furthermore, a new design means that new leaders can more easily enable change and drive the cross-functional organization to meet new challenges.

The first step in actually designing the new organization requires a thorough understanding of long-term goals because ultimate success requires what Dichter, Gagnon, and Alexander call "a rock-solid linkage" between what the company has to do to win desired customers in its chosen industry and the vehicle that is supposed to deliver that performance.[15] In other words, strategy must precede structure.

To chart a horizontal organization aimed explicitly at executing strategy, you must first:

■ Set a stretch or aspirational goal of where you want the company to be in, say, ten years. (This step seeks to prevent the ad hoc mindset and incremental thinking.)

■ Choose new or existing businesses that support your goal.

- Determine the desired customer segments in your chosen businesses.

- Identify a unique *value proposition*—defined as the set of benefits you offer at a price attractive to customers and consistent with your financial goals—that gives you a competitive edge.

You next determine where your current organization is failing to deliver the value proposition, and then design an engine to bring it about—complete with leading-edge performance enablers that will remedy the shortcomings and propel you to competitive success. After defining the value proposition, you structure the work of the new horizontal organization around the core processes, assigning responsibilities to groups or teams of empowered workers. The activity and work flows of the redesigned processes dictate what skills and training the people who populate those core process groups will need. The resultant organization is one crafted specifically to deliver the distinctive bundle of benefits that sets you apart and causes consumers to seek out your product or service instead of your competitor's.

In a profound way, then, everything in the organization is focused on executing the strategy. You start by determining what success for the company means, then use those criteria to evaluate and design every action and element required by the winning strategy. This amounts to a 180-degree turn from the traditional way of designing an organization around its functions, where there was a disconnect between the strategy and the people at the top who planned it, and those further down the ladder who actually executed it. In the horizontal organization, everyone meets in the middle and the strategy of the company becomes part of the everyday work.

I do not mean to imply that a functional organization is totally incapable of contributing to the delivery of a value proposition. Far from it. Particularly noteworthy is its contribution when a value proposition requires—in whole or in part—the delivery of technical expertise. There are, however, specific characteristics of the horizontal organization's focus on the value proposition that distinguish it from the traditional vertical or functional organization:

- The horizontal organization directs the attention of every team, support group, database, technical expert, and functional group (retained from the vertical organization) toward the production and delivery of the value proposition.

- The value proposition directly drives the design and integration of all these elements, unlike the fragmented efforts of diverse functional groups in the traditional bureaucracy or vertical organization.

- The horizontal approach produces a much more robust, versatile, and finely tuned instrument.

In contrast to the traditional bureaucracy, the horizontal organization does not group people according to monolithic skill bases or hold them accountable for functional goals. While a functional approach can contribute technical expertise to a value proposition, today there is a much larger range of value propositions that require more than simply technical expertise. However, regardless of the value proposition, the predominant approach to organization design to this point has remained largely unresponsive to the cross-functional challenges facing today's companies—insisting on grouping people into functional departments. The horizontal approach, though, vastly expands organizational design "solution space" and allows organizations to be both determined by the value proposition and much more robustly capable of delivering the full range of value propositions (whether that requires horizontal, vertical, or some combination of approaches). To a large extent, and with the advent of the horizontal organization, organizational design can now truly be tailored to individual value propositions and shaped to deliver them. When the value proposition is the starting point—just as it should be for all good organizational design—it directly determines which processes are chosen and what they are designed to achieve, which collections of multi-functional, multi-disciplinary competencies are needed, how people are arranged within the core process groups, and what the performance objectives should be. It even dictates how enabling applications such as information technology systems should be configured.

For example, at the Ford Customer Service Division (FCSD), the core processes and process groups deemed critical were those necessary to deliver on the promise to "fix it right the first time, on time, at a competitive price in convenient locations." That same value proposition was used to identify which processes were critical to its delivery, what the processes were redesigned to achieve, which process groups had to be formed, what skills team members needed, what new accountabilities they would have, and what information-system requirements the division needed.

The horizontal model allows designers to identify individuals with required skills, combine (or not combine) them into teams at the work unit level, and then pull together teams or individuals into core process groups. The combinations are dictated by the redesigned process, which is dictated by the value proposition, which is dictated itself by what is needed to achieve competitive advantage. In other words, structure is derived from strategy to deliver success.

When Solutions, Speed, and Service Count

So who needs the horizontal organization? As I have already noted, it is not right in every instance. But in today's competitive environment, the situations where it can prove valuable are so numerous that I feel confident in stating, as in the chapter subtitle, that "almost everyone" can benefit from the horizontal structure.

Specifically, the horizontal organization can dramatically improve performance for any company with cross-functional performance challenges. It is appropriate for companies that offer what I call "complete solutions"—that is, a product or service that depends on close, reciprocal integration of various areas within the organization such as procurement, inventory, marketing, and so forth.

A horizontal structure would make it much easier for a consulting firm to draw on its cross-disciplinary skills in, say, information technology (IT), change management, and strategy so as to solve a client's specific problem. "Customer-intimate" companies, too, would benefit because they specialize in providing whatever cross-functional expertise is required to satisfy the unique needs of their customers.[16]

In addition, when speed is of the essence or when customer service is a central goal, the horizontal organization will prove invaluable. Speed is an intrinsic byproduct of the horizontal organization because of its cross-functional nature. Core process groups work in parallel and are riveted to a common goal, which eliminates handoffs and unnecessary steps, reduces friction, and encourages joint problem solving—all elements that increase speed.

Speed itself, along with fewer handoffs and a tighter alignment of goals, goes a long way toward improving customer service and increasing satisfaction. But the horizontal organization does not stop there. Process-based teams tap the problem-solving capabilities of their multi-skilled members—and, in some cases, empowered case managers—to craft the integrated solutions that will deliver value and satisfy customers' needs. Frontline workers not only have the skills to solve problems and satisfy customers in real time, they also have a greater sense of responsibility for doing so. After all, the inspiration for organizing horizontally springs from the concept of customer value: the desire to find out what the customer wants and needs and then to do a superior job in delivering it. If all the processes, in other words, are not customer focused, the redesign effort will likely disappoint all stakeholders.

Perhaps the single most useful feature of the horizontal model is the way in which it allows an organization to mix and match both vertical and horizontal elements so as to customize a solution for a particular situation. Even if you determine that it is not feasible for your company to go entirely horizontal, you can still adopt the design in those areas where it is appropriate—creating what can be called a hybrid organization.

For example, when the Xerox Corporation decided back in the early 1990s to reposition itself as "the Document Company," it concluded that it needed, in the words of Chairman and CEO Paul Allaire, "to change the basic architecture of the organization." That meant moving away from the functional, top-down hierarchical arrangement that hindered responsiveness and accountability, and breaking into smaller, market-logical pieces. The result, as observed in greater detail in chapter 8, is a hybrid organization in which basic research and sales operations remain functional, while actual product design and development, manufacturing, and marketing have been restructured into horizontal, cross-functional business groups.

By splitting into five business divisions that are further subdivided into approximately 40 business teams, the $18 billion office-products company has found the best of both worlds: Like a small company it is quick and agile in its accountability and responsiveness to customer needs, but it still has the big-company advantages of scope, efficiency, and technical expertise.

These advantages have been more than apparent on the bottom line, too. Both sales and earnings have risen dramatically since 1992, and Xerox has expanded its market presence with an array of new offerings. From Allaire's vantage point, the hybrid structure is a much more effective way of running an organization.

Elsewhere, such corporate leaders as General Electric (GE), Motorola, and Barclays Bank have adapted the horizontal design to suit their particular needs, developing hybrid structures that suggest the robustness of horizontal organizations. And in the public sector, the U.S. Department of Labor's Occupational Safety and Health Administration (OSHA) has turned to the horizontal model to address long-standing problems in its field operations. These examples will be discussed in detail in later chapters.

By giving organizations a choice of both a horizontal arrangement around core processes and a functionally oriented vertical approach, the design tool kit is enlarged, and design-tailoring possibilities are greatly increased.

Out of the Mist

With companies now able to use both functions and core processes where they are best suited, arranging them so that they can work well together, the picture of the twenty-first-century organization is coming more clearly into focus. Now managers can see how the pieces actually fit together in the redesigned organization. Having a coherent theory also provides a platform for dealing with issues spawned by the advent of a cross-functional business environment. Today we ask questions that ten years ago would never have crossed our minds—for example, how to maintain technical expertise in a cross-disciplinary world. And we are coming up with innovative solutions such as technical pools, best-practice databases, and technical centers of excellence, none of which existed a decade or so ago. Just as the architecture of buildings becomes ever more fantastic with the invention of new methods and materials that offer new possibilities and solutions, the architecture of the business organization is becoming ever more productive and innovative as new tools and methods expand the parameters of design.

Much of what I present with the horizontal organization is completely new. But in developing the theory of the horizontal organization, I also have been prodded by the ideas and creative solutions put forth by others over the past 20 or more years.[17] In the end, I have crafted what I believe to be the optimal form for redirecting corporate energies toward the challenges of today and tomorrow. The horizontal organization unleashes the productive possibilities of new management concepts and refocuses the corporate lens outward on delivering a distinctive value proposition to customers. By integrating performance enablers and reorganizing them around core processes, management is able to draw on the full potential of a company's focused energies to beat competitors and win customers—all the while increasing the satisfaction and participation of its workers.

Just as the vertical hierarchy met the demands and maximized the productive potential created by the Industrial Revolution, the horizontal organization is well suited to dealing with the challenges and capitalizing on the opportunities of the Information Age. The design's adaptiveness—entirely horizontal in some situations or a hybridized combination of horizontal, vertical, and other organizational approaches elsewhere[18]—means that managers need not doubt their ability to succeed in this world of constantly changing demands and global competition. By holistically aligning *all* organizational elements—processes, people, skills—to deliver a company's crucial value proposition, the horizontal model produces a company that is well equipped to process information, make decisions, deliver timely products and services, and sustain satisfying relationships with its markets and suppliers. In short, it is a company perfectly attuned to our times.

Recently, much attention has been paid to the idea of a "balanced scorecard," in which a company's performance is evaluated in terms of shareholder return, customer satisfaction, internal business processes, and employee fulfillment.[19] The holistic approach of the horizontal organization extends the concept of balance beyond measurement and management systems to produce an entirely *balanced organization* with all its elements aligned to deliver the triple promise: Customers win (they get what they want when they need it); management and shareholders win (increased productivity means higher profitability); and employees win (high-involvement work systems counterbalance worker alienation and provide the gratification of participating in a meaningful way in a successful concern).

Make no mistake: The horizontal organization, when applied in the right way in the right situation, can dramatically improve a company's ability to rise to the top in its particular industry (and/or leave others behind). All of the organizations described in this book have generated improvements in operating performance significant enough to impress even the most hard-nosed business and financial analysts.

Besides impressing analysts, bottom-line success has the added benefit of helping organizations be more successful in fulfilling their important missions. It also serves to validate the "faith capital" that employees have invested in the new approach, a benefit that cannot be overstated. Irreparable harm can be done if heroic efforts to change skills and behavior are squandered on a plan that leads to organizational failure. You must deliver on performance to maintain employee commitment. By tying everything to the value proposition, then making sure that you apply the horizontal organization where it is appropriate to achieving that value proposition, you will not abuse the faith and trust that people have vested in the effort. As discussed throughout this book, the 12 principles for designing and institutionalizing the horizontal structure will serve as a basic guide both to the efforts currently underway at various organizations and to your own efforts to deliver a winning value proposition. Those 12 principles are listed at the end of this chapter and discussed more fully in chapters 11-12.

I believe that this new approach offers much to be excited about. With its emphasis on performance, the new horizontal structure can dramatically improve an organization's ability to achieve its mission as well as improve the quality of work life for its employees. Indeed, it has the ability to do both simultaneously. Furthermore, it reinforces what business thinkers sometimes refer to as a "single noble purpose," an overriding goal that people in an organization strive to achieve, one that is challenging, valuable, and exciting to them. The horizontal organization can help your organization achieve its single noble purpose, as well as provide meaning, motivation, and pride to those within it. The result is a passionate commitment from employees and other stakeholders. Grounded in basic business principles, that passion helps ensure that the horizontal redesign makes good on its promise to deliver the value proposition to customers. And that fulfillment, in turn, increases its stock with employees and shareholders. Ultimately, I believe the effects of the horizontal organization will prove to be so dramatic that social institutions—indeed, much of society as a whole—will begin to adapt the structure to fit their own needs.

Succeeding chapters will describe various types of horizontal organizations, illustrated primarily by five well-known companies and one public organization: Ford Motor Company's Customer Service Division (FCSD), the Xerox Corporation, the General Electric plant in Salisbury, North Carolina, the Supply Management Organization of Motorola's Space and Systems Technology Group (SSTG), the Home Finance Division of Barclays Bank, and the U.S. Occupational Health and Safety Administration (OSHA). Ford's Customer Service Division (FCSD) and OSHA provide examples for chapters 2 and 3, which will be followed by a discussion (chapter 4) of the generic horizontal organization. Chapters 5-8 explore in greater detail the architectures of the other four specific organizations. The final portion of the book (chapters 9-12) is devoted to discussing how you can build the horizontal organization that is exactly right for your company's particular needs.

Principles for Designing and Institutionalizing the Horizontal Organization

DESIGN:

- Organize around cross-functional core processes, not tasks or functions.

- Install process owners or managers who will take responsibility for the core process in its entirety.

- Make teams, not individuals, the cornerstone of organizational design and performance.

- Decrease hierarchy by eliminating non-value-added work and by giving team members who are not necessarily senior managers the authority to make decisions directly related to their activities within the value chain.

- Integrate with customers and suppliers.

INSTITUTIONALIZING:

- Empower people by giving them the tools, skills, motivation, and authority to make decisions essential to the team's performance.

- Use information technology (IT) to help people reach performance objectives and deliver the value proposition to the customer.

- Emphasize multiple competencies and train people to handle issues and work productively in cross-functional areas within the new organization.

- Promote multiskilling, the ability to think creatively and respond flexibly to new challenges that arise in the work that teams do.

- Teach people trained primarily in specific functions or departments to work in partnerships with others.

- Measure for end-of-process performance objectives (which are driven by the value proposition), as well as customer satisfaction, employee satisfaction, and financial contribution.

- Build a corporate culture of openness, cooperation, and collaboration, a culture that focuses on continuous performance improvement and values employee empowerment, responsibility, and well-being.

2 EACH HORIZONTAL ORGANIZATION IS UNIQUE

FORD MOTOR AND OSHA SHOW THE WAY

Every horizontal organization is different. To be sure, they have some fundamental traits in common—for example, all derive their essential structures not from narrow functions, but rather from the broader concept of core processes, which in turn are determined by the value proposition. But no two horizontal organizations can ever be exactly alike.

Why? Because *you* customize *your* structure to meet *your* specific problems within *your* distinct parameters—including competitive environment, size, corporate culture, employee skills, and that most-important value proposition, what your organization offers its customers and that affords you advantage over your competition. Presumably, the structure you design should be the optimal one for delivering *your* value proposition and executing *your* company's long-term strategy.

In some situations, the structure more closely resembles what can be referred to as the "pure" model, designed from the ground up primarily around horizontal principles. Most horizontal organizations, however, will probably be hybrids, drawing the best from both the vertical and horizontal and combining the performance capabilities of each. Note, however, that even in those organizations that come closest to being pure-ly horizontal, some functional areas of competency will often remain nec-essary, and some organization-wide "vertical" management processes—such as strategic planning, finance, and human resources—must be re-tained to integrate the efforts of the horizontal operating processes and process groups.

To understand the degrees of distinction between different organi-zational configurations, it helps to think of design as a continuum: At one extreme, most people in an organization—the vast majority—work in process groups, and only a bare minimum of vertical hierarchy exists to carry out fundamental management processes. At the other extreme are organizations that are entirely vertical. Most organizations, however, after careful analysis of their value propositions, capabilities, and skills, will choose a position between these two extremes, creating in effect a "hybrid" structure.

A vertical structure, as previously noted, will continue to be viable in businesses that depend on high-volume, standardized production carried out in simple and stable work environments. Problems arise, however, when production requirements become more complex and are better served by integrating rather than fragmenting tasks, or when the work environment becomes so dynamic that it cannot be predicted or made repetitive.

When demand exceeds supply—as is often the case in emerging econ-omies—and consumers do not have the luxury of being discriminating buyers, verticality will still work well. Consumers in such situations are caught up in just obtaining a product—*any* product—and a company's main task is simply to increase production. A third scenario that lends itself to a functional arrangement occurs when technical expertise is crit-ical to attaining competitive advantage—for example, in a ceramic en-gineering company whose industry position is solely dependent on the superior capabilities of its engineers.

In the years ahead, only a few organizations will probably be found at either extreme; most will reside somewhere in the middle, fully under-standing the potential of both the horizontal and the vertical approaches and taking advantage of both to improve performance. Where functional departments do exist, they will not wall themselves off from the rest of the organization as they once did, concentrating only on their individual goals and performance objectives. They will become "partners in process performance," actively supporting the core process groups by giving them what they need, when they need it to achieve process objectives. In fact, ensuring that a successful partnership exists between the core process groups and those outside them is one of the operating principles of the horizontal organization. Those involved in any redesign effort must address this issue.

Xerox, which is discussed in detail in chapter 8, exemplifies a company that has redesigned itself to take advantage of the best of both worlds—keeping research and sales in a functional mode while putting other areas of the organization on a horizontal track. Equally important, it has instituted mechanisms such as product-quality surveys to make sure that its functional people keep one eye trained on achieving overall performance goals. Together, the once disparate parts are delivering Xerox's promise to provide unique value by offering top-quality software, hardware, and service solutions backed by ongoing customer support and continuing business process improvements. The Xerox 2005 strategic intent statement reads: "Xerox, *The Document Company,* will be the leader in the global document market providing Document Solutions that enhance business productivity."[1] From this follows the company's value proposition of providing proprietary, leading-edge products that quickly and reliably deliver total document solutions of the highest quality.

Like Xerox and the other companies highlighted in this book, the hybrid organization of the future will emphasize multifaceted performance improvements and robust, multidimensional value propositions required to win customers in an ever more demanding competitive environment. In the process, hybrids will tailor their organizations' solutions by selecting those elements of vertical and horizontal principles that best address the particular challenges the organizations face.

In this chapter, we will look closely at the redesigns of Ford Motor Company's Customer Service Division (FCSD) and of the Occupational Safety and Health Administration (OSHA) to see how this facet of horizontal design plays out.

Specialization in the Workplace

Job specialization, the predominant form of the division of labor, is a primordial fact of human life. Indeed, many anthropologists consider the traditional male-female gender roles—the "breadwinner" and "homemaker" differentiations—to be a division of labor that was dictated by the laws of survival for a species in which offspring matured slowly. We can imagine how further divisions of labor might have emerged in early societies: Individuals with unusual skills were designated as the primary doers of certain tasks, with other functions necessary to a group's survival apportioned among the members in some fashion, random or otherwise.

As human beings progressed over the centuries from hunter-gatherers to crop-growers to industrialists, the divisions became more distinct and were formally documented. Henry Mintzberg, in *The Structuring of Organizations,* observes that Eskimo seal hunters divided their boat crews into harpooners, oarsmen, and helmsmen. Tenth-century English textile workers performed specific spinning, weaving, dyeing, and printing jobs.[2] In *The Wealth of Nations,* published in 1776, Adam Smith used the phrase "division of labor" in describing the various tasks involved in making pins:

One man draws out the wire, another straightens it, a third cuts it, a fourth points it, a fifth grinds it at the top for receiving the head; to make the head requires two or three distinct operations; . . . and the important business of making a pin is, in this manner, divided into about eighteen distinct operations, which, in some manufactories, are all performed by distinct hands, though in others the same man will sometimes perform two or three of them.[3]

In France, over a century later, Henri Fayol applied his personal experiences gained from 20 years of managing the coal mining firm of Commentry-Fourchambault (1888-1908) to an analysis of general management and administration. Often called the "father" of modern management, Fayol enumerated 14 principles of administration. Heading his list was the division of labor, which "allows one to reduce the number of objects to which one's attention and efforts must be directed."[4] Although Fayol did not take into account the "human factor" in evaluating highly repetitive work and the need for increased specialization, he was an early advocate for assigning tasks to *groups* of people in order to increase productivity and quality. Division of labor, Fayol wrote, "is recognised as the best method of utilising the powers of individuals and groups of people. It can be applied not only to technical jobs, but to any kind of work which employs a fairly large number of people."[5]

The driving force behind specialization, of course, was increased productivity. Production became not only more efficient, but also more uniform as workers devised methods to ensure that output maintained a prescribed standard. In the early twentieth century, as enterprises advanced in scale and size, they adopted the vertical structure recommended by Frederick Winslow Taylor, who sought to apply scientific principles to the philosophy and practice of business management. Taylor emphasized a strict division of labor, with work precisely segmented into functional departments, each devoted to making part of a product or providing the administrative infrastructure.

Stringently applied, Taylor's principles of scientific management often produced jobs with limited breadth and depth. That is, the task was narrowly defined, and the worker had almost no control over how to do the work itself. Each part of the divided enterprise concerned itself with isolated fragments of the work process, which, often by choice, became detached from the external environment.[6]

Thus, in the belief that effective management required a perspective broader than that of the worker, vertical organizations took away the worker's control over the work process. And, indeed, when a job is highly specialized and the task is very narrowly defined, the worker's perspective shrinks as well, making it hard for him or her to relate to what others involved in the process are doing. Specialization, then, reinforces the need for a hierarchy to supervise and standardize. Limiting the breadth of a job virtually assures that its depth must be limited as well.[7]

The Case of Ford Motor Company

Nowhere was the vertical, specialized model of organization more firmly entrenched than in the House that Henry Ford Built—the Ford Motor Company. It was Henry Ford, after all, who perfected assembly line techniques to the point where, early in this century, one of his Model Ts rolled off the assembly line every ten seconds. The company eventually produced more than 15 million Model Ts, growing into a hugely successful enterprise, and one of America's "Big Three" automakers.

But as the century neared its end, Ford as a company encountered a perplexing problem: Sales were climbing, but so was criticism about after-sales service at its dealerships. Any dissatisfaction with service is troubling in itself, but the inextricable link between a car buyer's ongoing relationship with a dealer and the likelihood of that customer buying again made the Ford service complaints all the more disturbing: Customer service shortcomings posed a threat to Ford Motor Company's all-important new-car sales figures.

The root cause of the discontent? Performance goals among the various operations comprising the Ford Customer Service Division (FCSD) failed to focus attention where it belonged: satisfying the customer.

For example, a single operation such as technical support might be able to deliver on its functional objective of getting training material to the dealers, but that, by itself, would not necessarily lead to customer satisfaction—which was most critically dependent on getting the customer's car fixed right the first time, on time. Would the material be up-to-date, accurate, and comprehensible (even to the point of being in the proper language for non-U.S. dealers)? Would it be provided in the most useful form—paper, electronic, or otherwise? Would it be provided when it was needed? Would that information describe procedures in a way that would help the technicians do a better job of making the repairs? Would there be a continual exchange between the service technicians at the dealers as new information and better methodologies were developed?

Various other direct and indirect processes had to be aligned in order to achieve that customer-driven objective: making sure the customer's appointment was properly scheduled and the order written up correctly, having the right tools and the right parts available at the dealership, which, in turn, meant that purchasers had to buy the right part in the first place and that someone had to make sure it was delivered to the dealer's service location.

At the beginning of 1995, when the company launched its "Ford 2000" initiative to become the world's leading automotive enterprise in the twenty-first century, the need for a more efficient and integrated approach to service became even more pressing. Throughout FCSD, people from a variety of functional operations worked on individual pieces of the customer service process, and they worked in different ways, at different speeds, and at different levels of quality. Processes across the regions had been developed independently; they reflected different reasons for being, making it impossible for FCSD to deliver best-in-class service. Further complicating this picture, the company expanded operations worldwide, building and marketing cars as well as servicing customers in practically every corner of the globe, thus forcing FCSD to make quick and dramatic transformations in its core processes.

Looking to remedy the situation, Ron Goldsberry, vice president and general manager of global customer service operations, and a Ford 2000 transition team determined that the old chimney-like structure was not capable of focusing on an overall objective and then bringing together all the resources needed to deliver the value proposition. Goldsberry turned to the horizontal organization, he says, because he believed it provided the "best opportunity" for accomplishing the three-pronged goal of bringing speed, quality, and efficiency to the customer transaction and establishing Ford as the leader among automakers for superior after-sales service. In addition, Goldsberry and the Ford 2000 transition team saw an opportunity, not coincidentally, of providing "an ownership experience so good that customers would naturally return for future vehicle purchases and service needs."

Having set a stretch goal, Goldsberry and other team members next identified the division's value proposition, which they termed, "Fix it right the first time, on time, at a competitive price in convenient locations." Summing up the competitive value that FCSD sought to provide, those words became the division's mantra. From there, the division mapped out all of its direct and indirect processes—an analysis that it had never done before—in order to decide which of the processes were critical to achieving its objectives. Goldsberry points out that a side benefit of this scrutiny is the elimination of waste: Settling on what is most important also serves to identify processes that are of no importance in delivering the value proposition, thereby allowing you to eliminate them and reallocate resources.

Key Processes Identified

The thorough analysis of FCSD's activities pinpointed four core processes as critical to delivering the desired value proposition. The four end-to-end work, information, and material flows that extend across Ford's business and drive the achievement of its fundamental performance objectives are:

■ *Business Development,* which analyzes the competitive environment and sets price targets to ensure that repairs can be done correctly at a price that is competitively balanced for both customer and company

■ *Parts Supply and Logistics,* which is responsible for acquiring parts from manufacturers and distributing them to the dealerships in a fast, efficient, low-cost manner

■ *Vehicle Service and Programs,* which gathers information about current-model problems and how to repair them, then disseminates that data to service departments; it also feeds this acquired knowledge back into future-model design

■ *Technical Support,* which ensures that every service department is staffed with competent, trained technicians who are provided in a timely fashion with the technical information they need in the form they require

Once the team identified core processes, the company formally restructured the division around them, setting up numerous teams to handle operations or activities in North America, South America, Europe, and Asia-Pacific, as well as in new markets. Each of the four core process groups has an "owner," who is responsible for overseeing the work of the teams and making sure that they meet overall process objectives. Goldsberry, as vice president, is in charge of the entire FCSD global operation, which involves 12,000 employees serving nearly 15,000 dealers worldwide.

Next, the transition team determined where responsibilities overlapped and cross-functional work could occur. It then proposed a specific work plan for every individual in each process. Here's how the four core process groups contribute.

Business Development   Whether in Toledo or Taiwan, FCSD had been treating every parts and repair issue with equal weight instead of emphasizing those repairs that would further the value proposition. Moreover, because pricing policies in the United States and abroad did not consistently focus on providing the greatest value to Ford customers, dealerships were losing out to independent shops. Consequently, many customers visited dealerships for warranty purposes only; with the quality and reliability of new vehicles improving, those sales began falling off, too. Poor sales and an excessively complex set of noninterchangeable parts meant that FCSD and Ford dealers ended up with overstocked, obsolete inventories, the costs of which had to be passed on to consumers, further exacerbating the pricing problem. In short, FCSD needed to make improvements in time, cost, and delivery at each stage of the supplier-to-customer process.

Horst Hoyler, the leader of the process owner team for the Business Development group, now directs his team to look for opportunities to improve relationships between Ford and its customers. "In every market where we do business," Hoyler says, "we've found that automotive service customers have the same basic wants and needs. They need their vehicles fixed right the first time, on time, and at a price they're willing to pay. They want to be treated with respect and courtesy, and they want convenience." The group has set extremely high standards, including a "fix-it-right-the-first-time-on-time" measure of at least 95 percent of all orders.

To improve service and win back customers for Ford, Business Development is charged with thoroughly understanding each region's competitive environment. It must set targets for each piece of the value chain that will allow FCSD to deliver a satisfactory repair, in an acceptable amount of time, at a competitive price. To that end, it has designed a process that integrates the key elements of repairs—parts, delivery, labor, and pricing—while assuring high quality. The business development process group also includes traditional functional areas like marketing and sales. The entire process group, including its subgroups, is one of four horizontal core process groups depicted in Fig. 2.1.

To meet the company's overall financial goals, Ford dealers needed to capture a greater share of the retail parts and service market, especially business from owners of older vehicles. Ford dealers in the United States had a particularly low share of the overall retail after-service market. In-

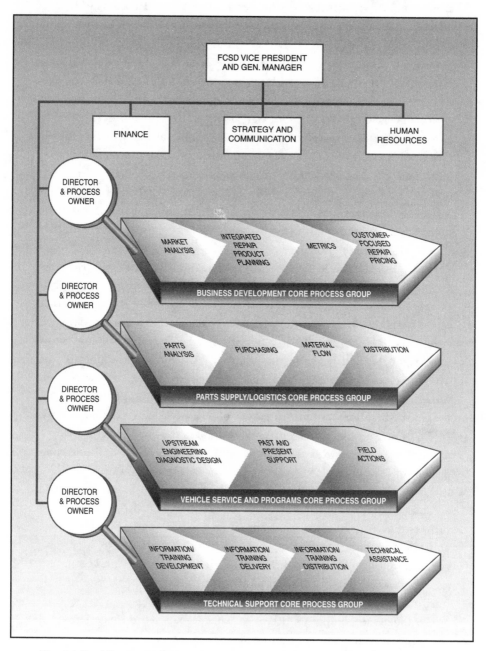

Fig. 2.1 Ford Customer Service Division

deed, whereas 87 percent of Ford owners in Germany remained loyal to a dealership during the first year of vehicle ownership, that measure stood at only 39 percent in the United States. After ten years of ownership, 40 percent of German owners were still loyal, while a mere 4 percent stood by their dealers in the United States.[8] At the same time, however, dealers were not competitively positioned to service owners of older models because repair costs exceeded the residual cost of the vehicles. There was also the threat from after-market repair chains such as Pep Boys and Auto Zones to worry about.

Business Development devised several ways to deal with these problems. First of all, team members now look at each repair process as a product, then they put together all the pieces necessary to deliver that product. For example, say the objective is to deliver a brake repair job at a price of $89 (or whatever the competitive benchmark is in each particular market). Business Development determines the price at which parts must be purchased or manufactured, delivered, and installed so that the total package costs $89 and still allows all people in the value chain to make the right amount of money. As part of the process, the group also seeks to provide product consistency in the specialization of parts, labor, tools, and repair methods. They prioritize repair planning and make it market-driven, meaning that the team determines the price according to its value for the customer rather than its difficulty for the repair shop.

Once a repair product is designed, the next step is execution. To improve overall customer service and employee efficiency and to facilitate consistency, Business Development consults with dealerships for 40 weeks, revamping their operating practices and setting up sustainment tools.

The third leg of the process is to measure whether the repair product is effective. The two key metrics are customer satisfaction and efficiency. Are the customers happy with the way that FCSD handles repairs or improvements? Do they like the way they are treated? Are they being adequately informed about the type of repair and the price? Has efficiency improved within the dealership? How much time is idle? What causes the delay? (Workers waiting for parts or looking for tools? Poor scheduling?) How fast is inventory turning at the dealerships? Those are the kinds of questions that Horst Hoyler or his team of senior managers can use in evaluating performance of the core process group. Because more people now accept responsibility for ensuring that the process runs smoothly, accountability increases for ensuring that such glitches are rectified immediately.

In addition, Business Development encourages the sharing of best practices from around the world, increasing FCSD's competitive advantage in a number of countries. For example, the FCSD team took ideas on how to deal with customers from various cultures and piloted them in Europe and North America, helping Ford and Lincoln-Mercury dealers achieve best-in-class customer satisfaction.

As Goldsberry puts it, the entire Business Development process can now be viewed as a three-stage benchmarking process: Products are designed, then executed, then measured. By putting uniform metrics in place at dealerships and aligning these with corporate standards, the group is closing the performance gap between Ford and its competitors.

Parts Supply and Logistics According to Ron Turecki, leader of the process owner team, the job of FCSD's global Parts Supply and Logistics process group is to "deliver the right part, to the right place, at the right time, and at the right price—as defined by the customer." The FCS2000 transition team initially found many problems in this area, including unstable, unmeasured depot-to-dealer order fulfillment, minimal concern for after-sales requirements, and no objective ratings in purchase cost efficiency, delivery, quality, and technical support. High distribution costs resulted largely from inventory handoffs, low turn rates, and excessively long replenishment cycles. Ford dealers used any number of systems for entering and processing orders. As a result, FCSD could not consistently deliver the right part to its dealerships on time or at a price customers were willing to pay.

As one solution, the Parts Supply and Logistics core process group designed a new order entry and processing method that all Ford dealers can use. No matter what part of the world an order comes from, a dealer can now receive and process it directly and accurately. To improve order fulfillment results, the group stabilized the order cycle and reduced turnaround times.

Teams replaced inventory management with a process that monitors supplier-to-dealer flow and increases communication from dealers to FCSD to suppliers. By providing its suppliers of vehicle parts with customer feedback, FCSD encourages them to consider customers' after-sales needs in their initial designs. If team members see, for example, that an engine is not easily accessible for certain repairs, they can require a re-design so that future customers will not incur unnecessarily high labor costs.

Furthermore, the team has developed global standards for all Ford suppliers so that everyone in the supply chain uses the "same set of wrenches," so to speak. The standards affect performance, delivery, qual-ity, and technical support. They even apply to a repair manual that pro-vides near exact translation equivalents.

Early results in Parts Supply and Logistics are extremely promising. Improved cycle time, lower per-piece costs, and significant gains in re-plenishment time all point to success for the horizontal makeover.

Vehicle Service and Programs   Members of FCSD's Vehicle Service and Programs core process group collaborate regularly with designers of Ford vehicles to make sure that the customer's "voice" is heard at every stage of production. Team initiatives for this process already existed in Europe and North America before the makeover, but analysis of future trends showed that more integration was necessary. As a result, the team's activities and best practices were made flexible enough to cover Ford's operations worldwide.

According to Tony Kaduk, leader of the process owner team, "We have to align ourselves better with product development if we are going to change product design. We have to voice the customers' requests while the engineers are still working on paper as opposed to real hardware." In this statement Kaduk describes what Vehicle Service and Programs must do to improve its contributions to FCSD's value proposition.

The most innovative part of the new process, for instance, involves an "upstream customer service" program, which consists of two teams: One takes responsibility for upstream support on future vehicle programs; the other is responsible for current and past model support, including recalls. The teams have developed a common process to report customer con-cerns and capture any unique market requirements. If the need for a product recall arises, the process team makes sure the recall and repair are handled efficiently.

In addition, the Vehicle Service and Programs process group actively seeks customers' complaints in order to discover when products and parts fail. Gathering data from dealers, hot lines, and warranty records, the team provides information that is used to anticipate customer service concerns and to feed into future model design.

Technical Support   A company can have the best parts, delivery, and design teams in the world, but none of that matters if its technicians do not have the skills, capabilities, and tools they need to service, maintain, and repair the products. The Technical Support core process group at FCSD is clearly aligned with the division's shared objective of fixing it right the first time, on time. As leader of the process owner team, Jim McDonald sees the value proposition of the Technical Support process group in these terms: "Our job is supporting, training, and providing information to dealership technicians all over the world so that they can meet those customer expectations."

It has not always been so. In the past, when Technical Support published inaccurate information in its parts catalogs, it unintentionally added costs that had to be spread across the entire value chain, forcing dealership technicians to struggle to reach cost-containment goals. An inordinate number of repair schedule options complicated the repair process for technicians and parts personnel; in the United States, for example, 600 defined operations covered 90 percent of all warranty repairs, yet FCSD included over 3,250 repair options. Repair manuals were geographically proprietary—that is, they were published either in Europe or North America, and were thus incompatible with each other and largely inaccessible to personnel in other areas. Technical Support employees could not share data efficiently because global translation efforts were driven by funding rather than market needs, and local markets had to handle their own translation needs. The lack of a global training system hampered efforts to monitor technicians or acknowledge a job well done.

With the advent of a common technical information process that can support simultaneous global vehicle launches in an accurate, timely manner, much has changed in FCSD's Technical Support organization. Besides producing more comprehensible manuals, the team has devised a global training program to assess, monitor, and improve the skills of dealership technicians. FCSD now requires competency testing in certain areas before technicians can become certified. To ensure that proper training is taking place, team members travel the world visiting dealerships and arranging for video satellite instruction when face-to-face teaching is impossible.

What is more, formal links have been established with suppliers so that many Technical Support employees in effect "live" at supplier locations. This arrangement facilitates product development—for example, by integrating its computer systems with a translation company, the Technical Support process group can simultaneously incorporate any change in a service manual into all manuals, regardless of company or language. The end result: lower costs and more timely information. Although they cannot be seen in the depiction of Technical Support (Fig. 2.1), a number of design principles underpin this process. While these will be discussed later in the book, we can note here the use, for example, of information technology to help people reach performance objectives in delivering the value proposition, the empowerment of people through information sharing, training, and the granting of authority to make decisions, and the integration with customers and suppliers to improve the process.

Making Sure FCSD Measures Up

In its quest to provide the best set of services and repair values to its customers, FCSD measures itself on four dimensions: growth, efficiency, customer satisfaction and loyalty, and employee satisfaction. In the end, the dimensions are all interrelated.

"We think growth is the great rallying cry," explains Chris Torres, manager of business strategy and communications. "If we're doing everything right, we should be growing." But growth, of course, means increased market share and revenues, and "you can't grow unless you're efficient," he observes. Judging FCSD's efficiency involves all the usual financial yardsticks: return on sales, return on assets, number of inventory turns, and so forth.

Financial strength is, in turn, dependent on customer satisfaction and loyalty. A major portion of the division has been horizontally restructured specifically to improve customer satisfaction. With a 20 percent improvement in overall satisfaction results and a 90 percent improvement in the area of "quicker service fix," the division would seem to be meeting its goals, although Goldsberry expects these numbers to increase even faster over the long term. But Torres considers loyalty to be the true measure of customer satisfaction. Is the new-car buyer coming back for service and, eventually, for another new car? That is the mindset the organization aims for, as well as the relationship that ultimately will propel growth. The fact that FCSD has been able to reduce its prices on selected repairs by up to 60 percent cannot help but encourage just that kind of customer loyalty.

The final dimension of success, employee satisfaction, is, in some ways, the cornerstone for all the others.

When people understand the mission and are committed to it, it's unbelievable what kinds of talent are unleashed.

Chris Torres, manager of business strategy

Happy employees who are satisfied with their own performance and with their role in the organization are more likely to have an emotional stake in the organization and its objectives. It might be inferred from the 25 percent improvement in customer-handling scores that workers are happier in their service roles. Such evidence further indicates that FCSD is attuned to its workers' needs.

FCSD uses training, coaching, and annual "pulse" surveys to assure that employees are as effective as possible in providing stellar service. The pulse survey measures how employees feel about such matters as their training and development, work load and stress, reward and recognition, and management. The survey allows Ford staffers to express their pleasure (or displeasure) with how well their immediate supervisor helps them achieve a quality work experience. Better communication enhances the quality of work for everyone, thus helping to ensure a better product or service for the customer.

Indicative of the horizontal organization's positive impact on employees are the results of the pulse survey. The parts of the division that have gone horizontal score significantly higher than other areas of FCSD, which as illustrated in Fig. 2.1 have remained vertical (specifically, finance, strategy and communication, and human resources). Horizontal employees are 15 percent more satisfied with their work groups and teamwork activities than are their counterparts in other FCSD areas that have remained vertical; in terms of rewards and recognition, the difference is 12 percent;

and employees in horizontal processes rate their overall job satisfaction 13 percent higher than their counterparts in other FCSD areas.

Recognizing that the personal satisfaction of workers can go a long way toward determining the quality of their performance, FCSD puts heavy emphasis on cross-functional teams. The satisfaction of an employee in the Parts Supply and Logistics Group is improved by knowing that he or she plays a major role in the division's value chain, while at the same time experiencing a first-hand connection to people on other teams. "Breaking down the chimneys to get the right corporate solution is key," Torres says. "We're all on the same page, and need to think like it."

Impact on Hiring and Worker Evaluations

How people are chosen to fill new jobs has changed significantly since FCSD restructured. A personnel development committee that includes functional and core process managers as well as human resources representatives reviews all openings to determine who is best qualified to fit each position. The committee comes up with a list of required skills for the job, then recommends four or five candidates based on their qualifications. Each is evaluated in the various skill areas, and the candidate with the highest overall mark gets the job—pending an interview and final approval from the manager involved.

What people can do becomes more important than simply the functions—the chairs they sat in before.

Sally Wacker, capabilities development specialist

"It used to be kind of an old-boy network, where one manager would call another and just say, 'I've got an opening. Have you got anybody?' " recalls Sally Wacker, capabilities development specialist at FCSD. Promotions often depended more on who you knew than what you did, thus excluding qualified candidates. "Now a whole group of people gets to review openings, and decisions are based more on skills," Wacker says. People move because they are able to communicate effectively and work well with others, skills essential for the horizontal organization.

Because the horizontal structure breaks down barriers between different departments, there is much more cross-functional movement taking place. Previously, workers mastered and remastered the same functional skills to move up an increasingly narrow vertical chimney. Eliminating much of the vertical hierarchy encourages people to be multitalented. Cross-functionality increases the likelihood that they will receive additional compensation. And when a highly regarded FCSD employee lacks some of the expertise necessary for a promotion or salary increase, the personnel development committee attempts to find the right combination of team assignments and training to help that person develop the needed skills.

Although human resources (as well as the finance and strategy and communications units) retains a functional structure, FCSD has redesigned staffing, incentives, measurements, and career and development approaches to ensure that the function works as a partner-in-process performance to support the core process objectives. This, we recall, is one of the 12 principles for designing a successful horizontal organization, and it will be discussed more fully in chapter 12. For the present illustration, however, it is important to establish that core process teams cannot operate in isolation from the traditionally vertical parts of the organization: Those who are not themselves directly involved in horizontal teams must nonetheless learn to "partner" effectively with their colleagues in core process groups.

At FCSD, for instance, human resources staff members provide their expertise in addressing business problems at the earliest stages. They are encouraged to voice their concerns. This input not only gives the larger team more information and insight for use in the decision-making process, it also allows the human resources representatives to develop a fuller understanding of a project. Having become partners in the process, they are much more likely to hire the right people for the right jobs.

"Before the transformation, technical and business plans would have been developed without any consideration of whether FCSD had employees with the skills to do a good job," says Wacker. Now the human resource department is being included in the early stages of planning. "We're getting better at assessing the skills we have," Wacker notes, "and at asking questions up front to help us focus on what we need and how we can get it." Human resources is becoming a change agent and a partner in designing the organization.

To support changing management roles, FCSD has determined necessary leadership skills and behaviors—such as integrity, trust, empowerment, and communication. The division has set up a process of peer-to-peer and subordinate surveys to assess managers' skills and to develop an action plan to address any shortcomings.

Wacker explains that a leader deemed deficient in listening skills, for example, might set up an action plan that calls for ongoing feedback from peers for a specified period, say six months. That means that at the end of each team meeting, other members will evaluate the manager on clarity of communication and amount of attention given to opposing opinions. To make sure that the action plans have teeth in them, managers are held accountable not just for setting up the plans but for following through on honest change commitments. Those assessments are not obvious from a casual glance at an organization chart such as the one depicted in Fig. 2.1, but it is important to understand that they are inherent in successfully institutionalizing the design of the future company. The organization, in other words, is never to be equated with the chart itself, any more than one should confuse an X ray with a patient or a portrait with its subject.

On one level after another, Ford Customer Service is proving the robustness of the horizontal organization. Benchmarking his division within Ford Motor Company overall, Ron Goldsberry says it has significantly outachieved other segments of the company's internal operations, and "this is very much a long-term solution."

Elsewhere, in both the public and private sectors, others are realizing the multiple benefits of this new concept in organizational design. Even the most skeptical of readers will be pleasantly surprised by the changes taking place in the reinvention of the United States government and its bureaucracies long known for their hardened attitudes toward change, efficiency, and effectiveness. The Occupational Safety and Health Administration (OSHA), a regulatory agency within the U.S. Department of Labor, serves as a leading model for public-sector performance-based transformation, similar to what we have seen at Ford's Customer Service

Division in the private sector. OSHA is also a benchmark example of going deep into the basic organization and operating model of a public sector agency to dramatically improve performance—serving to illustrate that transformation in the organization and performance of public sector agencies is possible.

A Horizontal Transformation at OSHA

At the other end of the spectrum from a well-known corporate giant with shareholder and market accountability and a wealth of global resources is the case of a beleaguered federal government agency. The transformation of OSHA, particularly at a time when the public's faith in the competency of the government as a whole is shaky,[9] could not have come soon enough.

OSHA was created in 1970 by an act of Congress that authorized the U.S. Secretary of Labor to set workplace safety and health standards, inspect workplaces for compliance, and issue citations and penalties for noncompliance. The act also enabled states to set up their own safety and health programs. Today, 23 states operate such programs with 50 percent funding and oversight from the federal office. Around two-thirds of OSHA's approximately 2,200 employees work out of some 67 federal field offices in ten regions across the United States. As a regulatory agency within the U.S. Department of Labor, OSHA is headquartered in Washington, D.C. From there it issues regulations while the Compliance and Safety Health Officers (CSHOs) in regions throughout the country travel to different companies, conduct investigations of work sites, issue citations for violations, and conduct education and outreach activities on workplace safety and health issues.

The toll that accidents and illnesses exact in the American workplace is staggering: Occupational injuries cause around 6,200 deaths a year, and work-related illnesses kill another 50,000 people. (For perspective, that is equivalent to a plane crash with 150 casualties every day of the year. More people in the United States die each year from work-related injuries and illnesses than are killed in highway accidents.) In monetary terms, the reported 6.6 million workplace injuries in 1996 cost some $60 billion in annual workers' compensation, and the National Safety Council estimates that additional indirect expenses such as those tied to training and loss of productivity raise the total to $110 billion—and that's just for accidents alone.[10]

Prior to OSHA's redesign, many of its field employees had frontline responsibilities but very little empirical knowledge of where the injuries, illnesses, and deaths were concentrated, and no data-based, systematic way of focusing their efforts on the high-risk areas. OSHA relied most heavily on the threat of inspections and fines to force safety improvements—a one-size-fits-all approach—without attempting to understand underlying causes so that it could tailor its actions to address specific problems effectively. What is more, the army of crucial onsite inspectors was distressingly small relative to the number of companies and industries that had to be inspected.

Under attack from one quarter or another almost from the beginning, the agency found that its travails only increased as new health care challenges presented themselves in the 1980s. Ergonomically incorrect work spaces and equipment were widely recognized as a source of health problems in many industries, and workers in health care institutions and elsewhere feared exposure to biological infections such as hepatitis B and AIDS. Poorly equipped to deal with such widespread dangers to begin with, OSHA found itself caught in a catch-22 situation: The Reagan administration, intent on recasting the priorities of government, actually decreased funding just as the public's expectations of the agency's responsibilities were increasing.

And the turn of the decade brought no respite for OSHA's dedicated but overextended staff as observers called the agency to task for its slowness and its tendency to react to workplace tragedies rather than to prevent them. Even OSHA personnel had the distinct feeling that they were forever locking the barn door after the horse was already out. Additionally and problematically, OSHA measured its success on the basis of its activities, linking success to the number of inspections the agency performed and the amount of fines it collected. Success was not defined in terms of results—the number of injuries, illnesses, and deaths the agency prevented. OSHA employees derided this system as "the numbers game."

Nay-saying from the other side of the fence were members of the business community who felt that OSHA was "nickel-and-diming" them over petty matters having little or no relation to preventing casualties. Typical of the bureaucratic behavior was the enforcement of a rule requiring every workplace to post an OSHA form stating the number of accidents reported in the previous 12 months. Asking companies to post safety histories does not seem like an unreasonable request, but what raised the ire of companies was the fact that failure to post the form drew a citation from inspectors even if the number of accidents reported was zero. When CSHOs did find serious problems, they did not have adequate resources or support to make sure problems were fixed or to provide adequate help to those companies wanting to prevent safety problems in the first place by implementing effective safety management programs.

Entangled by sometimes senseless bureaucracy and suffering from the constraints of a classic vertical structure, the agency was poorly informed about safety conditions in many areas. Accordingly, it too often wasted its limited resources on symptoms rather than on improvements to its research and reporting methods to determine where the worst safety problems were occurring, why they were occurring, and what could be done to increase the agency's role in preventing them. Agency people chafed under arcane rules and customs that blocked information flow, delayed responses, and prevented them from carrying out the meaningful and motivating work of saving lives and reducing workplace injuries and illnesses—the job they were originally meant to do. Supervisors spent inordinate amounts of energy on internal staffing problems rather than external safety problems.

I think there was a general belief that we needed to focus or become more coordinated. There were a lot of times when different parts of the organization were working on entirely different priorities. So the resources we had weren't being effectively used because they were not applied in a coordinated fashion.

Leo Carey, co-leader of the OSHA redesign team

As this litany of woes indicates, OSHA's transformation into a higher-performing organization came about out of sheer necessity. Joe Dear, who was appointed in 1993 to head up OSHA as the Assistant Secretary of Labor for Occupational Safety and Health, frankly admitted (as did many others inside and outside the agency) that OSHA was "failing." Although its mission was vitally important and its people were thoroughly dedicated to their work, the agency was in real danger of losing its political capital, without which it could not protect its statutory authority to operate and secure appropriations. The recognition that OSHA might not survive prompted a radical redesign of its enforcement operations.

A Push From the Top

According to Leo Carey, former head of reinvention at OSHA and co-leader of the redesign team, the changes that led to OSHA's transformation actually began with the 1992 election. Vice President Al Gore had authored a book entitled *Reinventing Government*,[11] and early in the new administration, President Clinton and he began pushing this initiative, targeting an overhaul of agencies such as OSHA.

As part of these efforts, Secretary of Labor Robert Reich met with OSHA employees to hear suggestions on how the organization might be improved. They discussed eliminating bureaucratic layers within the organization, reducing the number of supervisors, and even reducing the influence wielded by OSHA's national headquarters and management staff. Then when Dear came on board, he, like Carey, saw that the organization's fundamental problem was too much responsibility and too little means. "Something like 100 million working men and women employed at over 6.3 million establishments had rights under the Occupational Safety and Health Act," says Dear. "OSHA's budget in 1996 was $326 million, and it had a staff of 2,200 people. So there was an incredible gap between the mission and the resources available to the agency."

Launched during Dear's tenure, the redesign aspired to eliminate all preventable injuries, illnesses, and deaths from the American workplace within ten years.[12] OSHA recognized, of course, the essential impossibility of eliminating *all* preventable injuries, illnesses, and deaths. But at the same time, this tall order was one that could galvanize the energies of OSHA employees and that would resonate with them—after all, they got out of bed and went to work in the morning to save lives, not to fill out forms and push paper. Although audacious, the aspiration would require the agency to determine how it could dramatically improve its ability to prevent injuries and respond quickly and effectively when injuries and illnesses did threaten or actually occur. Similar to any private-sector organization seeking a dramatic improvement in performance and contemplating a horizontal redesign as part of that transformation,[13] OSHA had to identify its overall goals and value proposition. It had to determine if and why its existing organizational approach would be unable to deliver the desired performance. It had to design and develop a new approach—if required—including a determination of which core processes were necessary for delivering the desired value.[14]

For an agency created specifically to administer the Occupational Safety and Health Act of 1970 (amended 1990) through regulation, enforcement, and education, its unique value could be summed up by restating its statutory mission—that is, to do a superior job of effectively and efficiently assuring "safe and healthful working conditions for working men and women."[15] OSHA then identified strategic, or preventive, problem solving and problem response processes as being critical to delivering that value proposition. Key activities within these processes involved determining and ranking the areas of greatest injury, illness, and death; analyzing root causes; tailoring specific solutions; and, where possible, amplifying agency resources by enlisting industry or labor union cooperation.

Knowing he was unlikely to get a budget or staff increase, Dear focused on trying to change and enhance performance among OSHA's current personnel. One problem he found was that many employees believed that, as government workers, they had no recourse to change the variables affecting their performance. Political opposition to making changes ran high because the primary stakeholders of OSHA, those responsible for its political support and protection, were largely wedded to its original approach and structure. Their solution to safety problems was pure and simple: Establish regulations, then enforce them. Dear, however, attempted to expand OSHA's approach to safety and health not only by continuing to establish regulations and enforcing them, but also by maximizing the efficiency with which OSHA used its limited resources. He focused OSHA's efforts on those most pressing safety and health problems, identifying and analyzing their root causes, and taking strong action against "bad actors" as well as assisting other companies in developing and implementing their own safety management programs. He also sought to work in concert with industry associations, unions, and other government agencies to solve problems.

Internally, OSHA's people had been battered and bruised by years of political administration. Individuals who had attempted to assert leadership for change generally were punished. The culture was rigid, hierarchical, bureaucratic, slow, protective. People were unwilling to step forward.

Joe Dear, former assistant secretary of labor
for Occupational Safety and Health, and head of OSHA.

Dear estimates that about 25 percent of OSHA employees were "change ready." Another 25 percent or so strongly opposed any tinkering with the agency's original approach or its original command-and-control structure. The latter were either old-timers who did not want to make waves or people who assumed that only top-management changes (or more money) could cure the organization's woes. The other 50 percent of OSHA employees were ambivalent about taking action, believing either that Dear would not be around long enough to enact real change (the average assistant secretary lasts 18 months), or that this transformation would lose steam (they had seen other assistant secretaries attempt other changes), or that there would never be enough funding for new technology and training anyway.

Still, Dear went ahead with his plan to free OSHA from its inefficient and ineffective structure. Concentrating on improving productivity of the field staff as quickly as possible, he formed a joint labor-management redesign team made up of OSHA managers and members of its employee union. The redesign team wanted to improve significantly OSHA's ability to reduce workplace injury and illness by funneling resources into helping companies determine what their most serious risks to health were and how to correct them. Knowing that OSHA could never hope to inspect *all* industries and companies (indeed, the AFL-CIO had estimated that it would take OSHA with its current resources more than 87 years to inspect every U.S. business), the redesign team sought to implement methodologies and techniques that companies could use in analyzing root causes and developing appropriate solutions. In short, Dear and the redesign team emphasized prevention and reduction of injuries, illnesses, and deaths, not penalty, then went about building an organizational approach that would support that value proposition.

Learning from Past Success

An important component of any redesign is to look at where an organization was successful before and under what conditions. Studying the 18 years from 1975 to 1993, Dear's design team found that workplace injury and illness rates decreased most markedly in areas where OSHA had made a focused effort to develop and enforce standards: specifically in the construction, manufacturing, and oil and gas extraction industries, which accounted for 84 percent of the agency's compliance inspections during the period. The team also discovered, however, that despite those documented successes, OSHA has not traditionally used data to define and prioritize specific health and safety problems and then intervene appropriately to solve them—a particularly difficult problem given OSHA's limited resources. As Dear put it, nobody ever sat down and said, "The problem we're going to attack is how to protect construction workers from falls. We're going to do this by developing a new standard, then going out and enforcing it." Similarly, there was never a view towards the future, no attempt, for example, to set a goal of reducing fatal falls by a certain percentage over a specified time period.

The group postulated that once OSHA's redesign was in place, resources could be allocated at the local and national levels specifically to define problems and conduct interventions, carry out education, form partnerships, and measure the impact of those efforts.

As Dear saw it, the way to improve OSHA was to liberate the talent, energy, knowledge, and skill of its people. An approach that touched all facets of the agency had the greatest potential for finding ways to unlock those qualities, giving people a stake in the change and the opportunity to design it themselves. Even short-term performance improvements could do wonders for a worker's sense of personal empowerment, and the momentum gained from such incidents would flow through the entire organization. Smarter work would lead to better results.

OSHA's old strategy for field offices was primarily inspection-based, with a little outreach thrown in. Two or three work groups organized according to functional expertise—either industrial hygienists focused on chemical exposure, radiation, and noise, or safety specialists focused on manufacturing and construction sites. Supervisors dictated assignments. Since its inception in the early 1970s, the organization comprised various

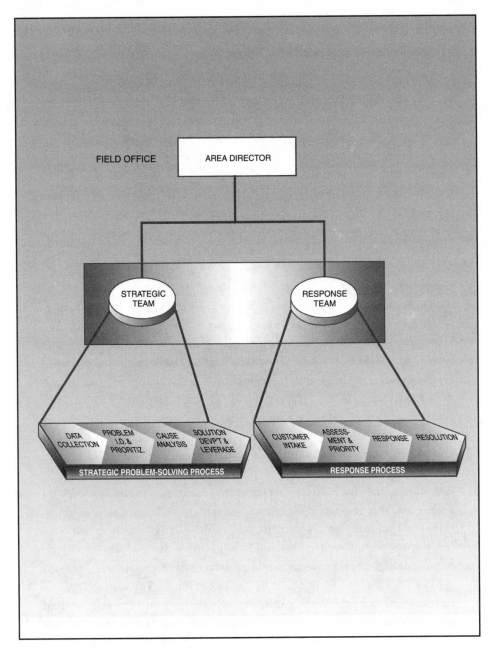

Fig. 2.2 Occupational Safety and Health Administration (OSHA)—Field Office

Note: The first three stages—data collection, problem identification and prioritization, and cause analysis—are parts of a process that are often carried out in other parts of the organization as well, both at the national and the regional levels.

"silo" functions such as compliance, enforcement, training, consultation services, and information technology. There was no guarantee that one section knew or cared much what the others were doing.

With the redesign, the agency turned to new ways of collecting data, namely by identifying, defining, and prioritizing problems, then developing solutions that maximized leverage and extended reach both by compelling compliance and by encouraging cooperative efforts to decrease the number of workplace injuries. As part of its horizontal remodeling, OSHA spends more time on preventing problems—as opposed to a primarily reaction-based approach of dealing with problems only as they arose. OSHA officials still respond, of course, to reports of hazards, but that response is now much faster because of the process redesign and the elimination of non-value added steps in the reaction process. There is also the specific assignment of response teams to investigate workplace dangers at 38 of OSHA's 67 field offices.

Those teams are part of the newly redesigned OSHA field offices illustrated in the organizational chart shown in Fig. 2.2. The new horizontal structure retains the authority of each field office under an area director, who heads the office teams. A proactive strategic team takes responsibility for the problem-solving processes, including data collection, identifying and prioritizing problems, analyzing causes, and developing solutions. Handling customer intake, assessment, and incident resolution, a response team takes responsibility for responding in a timely and effective manner to reports of actual dangers to worker safety and health in the workplace. What is more, the teams are cross-trained and cross-functional: Both safety specialists and industrial hygienists work together on the same teams. (Again, although such qualities as cross-functional training, empowerment, and multi-skilling do not show up on the organizational chart depicted in Fig. 2.2, without them horizontal organizational improvements would be impossible.)

The process leaders of those two teams maintain constant communication to ensure that their teams set goals that are in sync and focused on resolving problems effectively. Empowered team members accept greater responsibility for handling their caseloads. They take care of many daily operations at the field offices, work that used to be done by the area directors and assistant directors. Freed from some of their previous management and hand-holding duties, those directors now devote more time working with the community in outreach activities, forging relationships with businesses, chambers of commerce, and other local organizations to promote safety and health issues.

The Fruits of Change

OSHA's Atlanta office illustrates many of the improvements inspired by the horizontal structure. For example, after identifying a problem that existed between the Argonaut Insurance Company and Horizon Steel, a local steel construction business, the new OSHA teams worked in partnership with the companies to devise a practical solution. Here's what happened.

A number of Horizon workers had been seriously injured in falls on the job, forcing Argonaut to consider withdrawing as Horizon's insurer because it could not afford the enormous increases in workers' compensation costs. In response, OSHA assigned a CSHO who had no enforcement jurisdiction—and thus could not issue citations—to do a walkaround of the Horizon facility and point out hazards. In exchange for this nontraditional approach, Horizon had to agree to implement a "100 percent fall protection program," whereby all Horizon personnel would wear harnesses when working on buildings. Such protection measures usually are not instituted in the industry because workers resist them strenuously, but OSHA convinced management to insist that its workers wear the harnesses.

The results were dramatic. Three workers who fell from heights above 50 feet all walked away unharmed. What is more, workers' compensation costs at Horizon immediately dropped 96 percent. By coming up with a creative solution, OSHA's Atlanta office saved lives and cut the insurer's costs without compromising any regulations—a triple win.

OSHA's handling of workers' complaints has also improved dramatically since the agency adopted a horizontal structure. In the past, mounds of paperwork from thousands of workers complaining of unsafe or unhealthy working conditions overwhelmed the CSHOs, who faithfully examined the companies in question but often not until 30 to 60 days after the OSHA officials received complaints. In the case of "informal complaints" (letters or calls from nonworkers or unknown sources), OSHA staffers wrote letters to the companies, waited for responses (if any), and then inspected 10 percent of those companies that bothered to respond. To call this system cumbersome and inefficient hardly suffices.

Under the new structure, however, OSHA teams are able to respond immediately to all informal complaints made by workers. They call companies within 24 hours after complaints arrive, fax copies of complaint letters, then allow five working days for the companies to respond to OSHA's directive that the problem or hazard be removed. Based on the acceptability of the response and further communication with dissatisfied employees, OSHA response teams decide whether legal and policy guidelines justify a full investigation. Decision-making authority lies with the teams themselves, who are the principal building blocks of the horizontal structure.

Since OSHA implemented its horizontal design, teams have reduced the time it takes to respond to informal complaints by 90 percent. Positive assessments of the new structure continue to roll in: Workers are gratified to know that their complaints receive immediate attention; employers are happy to be able to talk with OSHA representatives in a non-adversarial manner and take corrective measures; and OSHA does not waste valuable time doing useless inspections of things like dirty bathrooms. Now, in many cases, a single phone call usually corrects the problem, and the speed with which OSHA teams resolve relatively minor complaints frees up their schedules to take on more serious issues affecting workplace safety.

"The end result of redesign for OSHA is an organization much more open to its customers, much more open to new ideas, and one that literally saves lives with its new approach," says Dear.

Apparently, Vice President Gore agrees. The Vice President met with the redesign team for OSHA's field organization and presented them a Hammer award in recognition of their outstanding contributions for helping "reinvent government."

Good news can have a wondrous effect, particularly in beleaguered circles. Under the old structure, OSHA workers, for instance, felt trapped in a routine of checking off boxes during an inspection. Simply completing the inspection was the order of the day, and field-office employees found their work little better than that of robots. In the new horizontal organization, according to Bob Kulick, director of reinvention for OSHA, field workers are taking a more active role in helping people change their behaviors at work sites. "Compliance officers," he notes, "while still able to be 'tough enforcers,' now see it as a major part of their jobs to educate employers in how to develop effective safety and health programs, eliminate hazards, reduce injuries, and look for further opportunities to work cooperatively to improve safety and health in the workplace." Similarly, traditional supervisors, no longer burdened with conducting lengthy reviews of employees, are now better cast as the teams' facilitators. Team members, Kulick adds, "have been empowered to conduct their own self-reviews."

Given such visible improvement, it is clear why OSHA received a budget *increase* for fiscal 1996 rather than the cut it expected. In addition, hundreds of appreciative letters from both employers and employees have poured in to OSHA.

Looking to the Larger Purpose

While much has already been accomplished, much still remains to be done. For example, redesign still needs to be "rolled out" to the 29 remaining offices. The agency needs to implement a results-based measurement system that will systematically and accurately measure OSHA's impact in curtailing injury, illness, and death rates. And an on-going senior management steering committee needs to be put in place to provide oversight and leadership for future changes at the agency. Charles Jeffress, the new assistant secretary for OSHA, has stated that he is fully committed to finishing the work begun by Dear and the redesign team, as well as building commitment to the new horizontal structure. As Joel Sacks, former acting director of reinvention at OSHA, puts it, "Clearly redesign has gotten off to a great start, and there have been successes, but there is a need for on-going commitment and focus throughout the organization in order for roll-out to be completed and redesign to be successfully institutionalized throughout OSHA."

OSHA's accomplishments provide dramatic proof that a government agency can transform itself and turn its performance around, while helping its employees derive greater satisfaction from their work. OSHA exemplifies the kind of performance-based transformation that is crucial if we are to solve the very real problem of poor operating performance that now plagues our government institutions.

Internal focus, fragmented objectives, overly complex procedures, insular bureaucratic levels—all these elements of the vertical hierarchy significantly inhibit performance and frustrate government employees who sincerely want to do a better job and help their agencies succeed. On a larger scale, this under-performance seriously undermines the faith of the American public in the federal government's general attempts to do the "right thing." In fact, as Vice President Gore pointed out in his commencement address at Harvard, such confidence has dropped from 60 percent in 1965 to 10 percent in 1994.[16] And for good reason: Despite their often critical missions—and the fact that most government employees are skilled and dedicated to those missions—many government agencies simply are not delivering what they could or should.

The bureaucratic approach, with its multiple levels and extensive system of checks, is to be commended for providing a bulwark against corrupt practices. But when the bureaucratic approach predominates to the extent it does in most government agencies, it can and often does inhibit performance. Remedying the situation requires major changes in all of the dimensions that drive performance—strategy, structure, style, systems, shared values, and skills. The redesign of OSHA's field offices illustrates this kind of holistic undertaking and demonstrates that a horizontal makeover can deliver just what citizens yearn for: responsive and effective government.

Bureaucratic shortcomings are not the sole province of the public sector, of course, despite the chorus of complaints about ineptitude. Red tape, role redundancy, misalignment of people and skills—all these and more can be found inside any number of large, vertically structured, private-sector corporations. Some well-known organizations that have embraced reform provide examples to be examined in chapters 5-8.

As we look at these companies, you will notice that each one is different and that each organizational chart reflects a different set of priorities centered on each one's value proposition. All these organizations, however, share a desire to enhance the core processes for producing their respective value-added products or services. Those value propositions, after all, help solidify each company's relationships with all stakeholders. Because the horizontal model does not demand an either/or choice, but instead expands design "solution space," you will see how those companies have blended horizontal and vertical elements to arrive at the configuration that best suits their goals.

The challenge for you and your organization, then, is to seek your unique balance from among the available design approaches so as to deliver optimum performance. To accomplish that goal, you must become familiar with the design principles that govern the horizontal organization. Otherwise, 50 years of exposure to only the standard organization charts will prevail, making it impossible for you to arrive at the ideal mix.

Before embarking on design, however, it is useful to examine the distinctive features of and some popular misconceptions about the horizontal organization. The discussion in chapter 3 illustrates how the concept works in conjunction with leading management principles to define and strengthen the organization of the twenty-first century.

3 HORIZONTAL IS NOT THE SAME AS FLAT

DISTINCTIVE FEATURES OF THE HORIZONTAL ORGANIZATION

The initial encounter with the horizontal method of structuring invariably creates confusion about what the resultant organization looks like and how it works. "Isn't a horizontal organization simply a vertical organization turned on its side?" I am often asked. "Aren't you just slotting reengineered processes into an existing vertical structure?" And for that matter, "How does the horizontal concept differ from reengineering? Is *horizontal* a synonym for *flat?*"

Such questions are hardly surprising, given that our experience has, for so long, been limited to the hierarchically structured, functionally oriented vertical design. It is difficult for us to visualize an organization cut loose from the traditional vertical constraints. But the answers to these and other questions can be found by examining key features of the horizontal model. To reiterate, no two horizontal structures are ever *exactly* alike because each is designed to deliver a distinctive value proposition, but certain characteristics that are not found in a vertical organization are common to every horizontally structured one. For example:

- Core process groups cluster employees according to the sets of multiple skills needed to meet process-based performance objectives and deliver a value proposition.

- Teams—not individuals grouped in hierarchical departments—constitute the fundamental units of the organization and are encouraged to be self-managing.[1]

- Process owners, either teams or individuals, are responsible for leading and managing entire core processes from end to end.

- The focus is largely external rather than "internal" in the sense that each department seeks to satisfy measures of productivity that it has set for itself. In contrast, the horizontal organization sets its sights on delivering a winning value proposition to customers.

These features clearly differentiate the horizontal structure from the vertical, no matter the viewing angle—sideways, right side up, or upside down.

Core Process Grouping Sets the Stage

The first of these distinctive elements—clustering people around whole processes, not individual tasks—sets the stage for all that follows.

The idea of grouping is not new, of course, being one of the fundamental ways of coordinating the various types of work that take place within an organization. As Henry Mintzberg points out in *The Structuring of Organizations,* grouping strengthens coordination within a particular unit by:

- Providing a system of common supervision

- Requiring resource sharing

- Creating common measures of performance

- Encouraging mutual adjustment among workers[2]

The new twist that the horizontal design brings to modern business is the way it coordinates the work of people around core processes. In the traditional arrangement, departmentalizing has typically revolved around functions or tasks performed, such as manufacturing, engineering, finance.[3] People who perform the same range of tasks and use a homogeneous set of skills are assigned to the same functional department. One of the main advantages of traditional functions is the cultivation of technical expertise.

Core process groups, on the other hand, are very different from functions: They encompass end-to-end work, information, and material flows that extend across many functional areas in a business and that are crucial to meeting previously defined performance objectives aligned with the value proposition. In core process groups, people are positioned according to a natural flow of work determined by the more complex redesigned processes and directly related to the needs of customers. The jobs within the group incorporate many more tasks and often require a multidisciplinary set of skills, in contrast to the tightly defined roles prescribed by a single, specialized, functional activity. In addition, core processes along with the organization's skills are the operations that define an organization's primary capabilities, that distinguish that organization from others in its field, and that direct the use of its strategic assets.[4] The work itself is more integrated, unlike the narrow, fragmented tasks typical of a functional orientation.

Grouping by core process eliminates the inefficient cycle of handoffs that occurs when work must bounce around between various departments so that each can carry out its particular role. Anyone who has ever worked in a functional setting knows the routine: Because the work seldom moves in any kind of natural order, speed is forfeited, confusion reigns, and the potential for losing information grows apace. Issues best handled through joint, real-time problem solving end up getting less attention than they deserve as each department operates only from its own perspective. Snafus invariably crop up when one hand does not know what the other is doing: Orders are misplaced or wrongly canceled; production bogs down because crucial parts are not available; conflicting goals put the organization at odds with the customer (recall the example of Ford's Customer Service Division in chapter 2).

Winning the Customer Takes Precedence

Core process groups have external, customer-driven objectives based on delivering value propositions, not the internal concerns that so often take center stage in a vertical setup. So rather than being at odds with the customer, core process grouping facilitates a tight alignment with what the customer wants and needs.

This unwavering emphasis on winning the customer is one of the major reasons why the horizontal design is the right design for tomorrow as well as today. In any discussion of what it will take to inhabit the twenty-first-century universe of winning companies, certain characteristics elicit nearly unanimous agreement. Leading the list is an almost single-minded dedication to the customer.

Instant communication and technological marvels have given today's consumers more options than ever before. In this intensely competitive environment—where success is measured with a global yardstick—failure to make customers the center of a company's orbit exacts a heavy toll. The horizontal organization is the perfect vehicle, however, because from the outset it sets its sights on doing a superior job of delivering value to the customer and measures its performance accordingly. The measures of achievement, in other words, focus on whether customer expectations are being met and how satisfied customers are with the product or service.

The horizontal organization seeks to satisfy both "internal" and "external" customers. In effect, it removes much of the opposition between these two groups. Those customers internal to the organization receive the information and products they need, when they need them, in order to deliver the value proposition to customers external to the organization. (Medical personnel inside a hospital, for instance, are customers of certain products and services such as X rays or physical therapy, which they then incorporate into the valuable service they offer their patients.) If internal customers keep performance goals on track, they can set as their primary goal the complete satisfaction of external customers and have confidence that delivering the value proposition will assure bottom-line success.

How does this philosophy play out in the day-to-day operation? The work flow becomes the catalyst for channeling all energies toward delivering a superior value proposition to the customer. It links the activities of employees to the needs and capabilities of both customers and suppliers so that all three are aligned in the company's quest to achieve its competitive advantage. Frontline people are equipped with the skills to understand not only how their own processes contribute to the delivery of the value proposition, but also how the individual work flows are related one to another.

Because the work of a process is usually too much for any one person, work is broken into team-sized chunks, with the amount of work determined by the size of the team. Teams can range from 2 to 25 people, but the typical team comprises 15 to 20 members. Merely labeling a group as a "team" does not make it one, however. The true team brings together people with complementary skills who are committed to a common purpose—not just a common assignment—and who have specific and measurable performance goals for which they hold themselves mutually accountable.[5]

The people who populate the teams, and ultimately the core process group, are chosen because they can perform the tasks and either have, or can develop, the skills needed to carry out the work of the process now redesigned to enhance the value proposition. They are then formed into teams according to how the work flows. Sometimes one team can perform an entire core process end to end. However, there is often more work or subprocesses than any one team can handle. Accordingly, a chain of teams is organized to perform the sequential work of the core process and constitute the core process group.

Teams in the horizontal organization also assume real managerial responsibilities. When teams are organized around work flows, it is only logical to make them self-managing. After all, who knows better where the bottlenecks are and how the process can be improved than those frontline workers who are responsible for it from beginning to end? Giving these people the key components of empowerment—that is, authority, information, training, and motivation—enables them to solve problems in real time and keep process performance on track.

Hierarchy of a Different Kind

Hierarchy is not completely abolished in the horizontal organization, however. The core process groups report to process owners—typically teams of leaders or sometimes individuals (teams are preferred)—who are responsible for meeting the specific performance objectives of each process. The owners dedicate themselves to building capabilities, teamwork, and open communication across the work flows. They make sure that problems are resolved and obstacles removed before the work of the process is impaired.

There is still some hierarchy overlooking the whole company as well. A certain amount of hierarchy will always be necessary because human capabilities are naturally limited: No one can know and do everything, nor will everyone in an organization always agree about what ought to be done. Consequently, all organizations—large or small, wealthy or limited—need leaders to make decisions for others.[6] The hierarchy retained after a transformation to a horizontal enterprise continues, for example, to shape the company's overall strategic direction, identifying and articulating its value proposition, providing the road map for business development and organizational change, and overseeing the redefinition of cross-functional processes. Those leaders must keep their eyes trained on developments in the external environment, assessing threats and opportunities wherever they arise.

That said, hierarchy can be kept to a minimum so long as the horizontal arrangement links the various work flows directly to one another. Related but fragmented tasks are combined, and non-value-adding activities—such as repetitive inspections and unnecessary meetings—are abolished. The result is a flatter but still hierarchical arrangement of teams that replaces the steeper, more vertical hierarchies of traditional functional management.[7]

Flatter, not flat, is an important distinction to make in describing the horizontal organization. There are certainly fewer levels of hierarchy, but the organization will not be totally flat, nor should it be. Accountability and a value-adding hierarchy that directly contributes to achieving performance goals will still be evident in any organization structured around core processes.

Although managers retain control, their emphasis shifts to leading teams, coaching employees, and facilitating relationships among customers, suppliers, and the organization. They allocate time differently now than they did in the past, developing capabilities in others, discovering new resources, improving processes, eliminating bottlenecks, and looking for innovative ways to deliver value. Moreover, if those managers become process owners, they evaluate situations, make decisions, and apportion resources with an eye toward continuous performance improvement. For employees, this rebalancing of power means that information and training are provided just in time on a need-to-perform basis. Career paths follow work flows, and advancement goes to people who master multiple jobs, team skills, and continuous improvement. Compensation rewards both individual skill development and team performance in support of process goals.[8]

The horizontal model's incorporation of the principles of empowerment, process structure, multi-skilling, and process and customer-based performance measurement and feedback has a wonderfully uplifting effect on employees that counters the alienation engendered by the mind-numbing specialization prevalent in the vertical organization. An explanation of why this approach so enriches the workplace is offered by Hackman and Oldham in their book, *Work Redesign*. The authors cite five specific "core job dimensions"[9] that can alter an employee's psychological state and thus promote greater job satisfaction:

- *Skill variety*, or breadth, meaning the number of different activities required to do the job (appointment scheduling, record keeping, word processing, and so forth)

- *Task identity*, or depth, which refers to how much end-to-end responsibility is involved. (Is the worker charged with making one whole item or completing one entire process from beginning to end?)

- *Task significance*, or the perceived impact the job has on others

- *Autonomy*, or the empowerment that people have in planning and carrying out their own work activities

- *Feedback*, or information shared with employees about how effective they are in performing their tasks[10]

This model has been the focus of many empirical tests, most of which support many aspects of the model.[11]

Jobs with those characteristics are jobs that people enjoy, care about, and are committed to. Taking increased responsibility for the outcome of their activities, people are motivated to provide high-quality performance, all of which translates into lower absenteeism, reduced turnover, and, ultimately, success for the organization as a whole.

The important point to make in discussing organizational design is that every one of these five crucial characteristics is implemented and supported by the principles underpinning the horizontal organization. By utilizing high-involvement work systems, empowered workers grouped in teams, just-in-time feedback, and multidimensional training practices, the horizontal design creates a more humane work environment and gives newfound meaning to work itself.

Consider, for example, the experience at OSHA. Before the redesign, OSHA inspectors were simply evaluated on how many inspections they did and how many dollars worth of fines they levied. Today, all organizational elements of the field offices' performance—the strategy, the processes, the organizational structure—have been redesigned to enable the agency to reduce injuries, illnesses, and deaths. High-involvement work systems now empower workers to do a better job of reducing injuries. As worker satisfaction increases at OSHA, so do motivation and performance. As a newly designed horizontal organization, OSHA is moving toward measuring field officers on the impact of the safety measures they recommend and on the success they have at reducing injury, illness, and death in the U.S. workplace. The inspectors' work is no longer just a numbers game; they work in teams on whole tasks to deliver performance with real impact on achieving OSHA's aspirations and the safety and health of the people of the United States.

To see the reaction of these field workers, people who had worked in the system for 20 years, and now for the first time it was almost as if they themselves had been reinvented. They felt reinvigorated. They told me that this was why they had come to work as OSHA in the first place—to make a difference in how people worked, to make the workplace better and safer, to save lives.

Nelson Reyneri, former director of reinvention at OSHA

What about Reengineering?

Over the past several decades, a number of performance enablers have been advanced and adopted by both large and small companies in an effort to improve their performance and to make themselves more competitive. The horizontal organization maximizes the gains from many of these enablers, such as the advanced use of information technology to provide computer-based coordination and communication, just-in-time inventory control, and the like. It rests upon the broad shoulders of such concepts as reengineering, cross-functional teams, and high-involvement work systems. Of course, the theory and practice of horizontal organizations add insights of their own, which will be evident from the discussion of particular organizations in chapters 2 and 5-8, but it is significant to note that without its important antecedents, the horizontal organization would never have evolved and commanded the attention it is receiving.

Few proposals have had the far-reaching effects that reengineering has had. In *The Reengineering Revolution,* Michael Hammer and Steven Stanton define reengineering as "the fundamental rethinking and radical redesign of business processes to bring about dramatic improvements in performance."[12] A key concept behind the horizontal organization as well, performance improvement provides one of the primary means by which managers can measure the success of the business transformation. In reengineering processes, managers seek immediate and dramatic improvement. The horizontal model, however, looks to improve performance *and* to institutionalize the capability for continuing those performance gains while enhancing the quality of life for employees. And by focusing on the relationship between strategy and organization, the horizontal organization helps amplify many of the gains made by reengineering by making sure that performance improvements are directed at leverage points that matter most to a company's competitive success.

The horizontal model both utilizes reengineering to change how processes work and supports the dramatic improvements that reengineering engenders. But more to the point, it explicitly draws on reengineering within the core process group to achieve the value proposition to guide organization design. The horizontal organization depends on the reengineered process to help identify what skills an organization needs, for figuring out how to use individual talents, and for determining who should work together on teams.

In neatly synergistic fashion, the horizontal design in turn supplies what the organization utilizing reengineering needs to scale the heights of success. It makes sure that the makeover does not begin and end with merely a redesign of processes but also incorporates the required organizational changes, including developing the requisite behaviors and skills to make sure that performance improvement is continuous and ongoing rather than just a one-shot occurrence. Research on how to implement reengineering most effectively has stressed the need to address concurrently all elements of organization performance including structure, systems, skills, shared values, staff, style, and strategy.[13] The horizontal organization does just that.

An additional distinguishing characteristic of the horizontal organization is that at its inception, the question that the horizontal organization attempted to answer was what the organization of the future might look like and how it would work. Thus, from the outset it specifically aligned all seven of the factors that affect performance and geared them toward delivering the value proposition.[14]

I would be remiss, however, if I did not remind readers that companies adopting horizontal structures cannot possibly attain peak operating performance unless they have in place the basic requirements for any high-achieving company. These include a demanding, aspirations-driven senior leadership, a focus on key customers and markets, a strong performance ethic, world-class capabilities in at least one dimension critical to delivering the value proposition, and other fundamentals such as an effective balance sheet and capital structure management and adequate investment in research and development.[15] That is a tall order. But it is better to know in advance that merely moving your people and functions around will not transform an old jalopy into a Ferrari.

All this may be so familiar as to seem obvious, but all too often in the race for the most recent cure, the fundamentals may be overlooked. If that is true of your business, you must address these issues before—or at least concurrently with—the adoption of a horizontal approach.

Rethinking Downsizing

While sometimes necessary, downsizing is often of limited effectiveness and done thoughtlessly.[16] Given the trauma suffered by those on the receiving end as well as the tremendous social costs involved,[17] it is important to conduct any downsizing activities as thoughtfully as possible and avoid them when feasible. Indeed, companies need to exercise more creative thinking about alternatives to downsizing that they can use.[18]

Organizing horizontally does not mean or require downsizing. Yes, horizontal organizations reduce bureaucracy and eliminate non-value added work; but properly conceived and implemented horizontal organizations develop new roles for current and future employees as well as new processes that provide value to the customer and help support long-term success. The horizontal organization does not just reduce bureaucracy and non-value added work. Problems have arisen at many organizations that make drastic cuts without thinking about what the new organization should look like and without determining which skills, talents, and assets are needed to compete effectively and help assure long-range success. A horizontal framework, however, promotes new roles for employees that improve their sense of worth, and it develops new activities and processes that add value and deliver a winning value proposition.

The employees interviewed for this book speak in glowing terms of the new roles that they play in their horizontal organizations. Many of them now serve as process owners or members of teams responsible for identifying best practices, sharing knowledge and skills across the organization,[19] leading projects, supporting integration efforts with suppliers and customers, promoting continuous improvement and process redesign.

Particularly disconcerting about the waves of downsizing that have marked this decade is the remarkable thinning of the ranks of middle managers and business professionals. Michael Hammer predicted "a probable reduction of over 50 percent in the number of people with 'managerial' job titles."[20] Too much indiscriminate cutting, however, has already sliced away valuable muscle along with the fat. Certain companies have effectively forfeited their ability to sustain competitive advantage because they inadvertently or unthinkingly weeded out both the better workers and the mid-level leadership necessary to generate change and fuel future growth without thinking through what critical skills are necessary for going forward.[21]

The horizontal approach is totally at odds with the quick-hit, wholesale slash-and-burn maneuvers that, by their very nature, preclude taking the time to decide which personnel and skill sets are fundamental to achieving competitive advantage and long-term aspiration—let alone actively working to preserve and replenish those elements. One of the first steps in horizontal design, as a matter of fact, is to figure out the winning value proposition and then exactly who and what are needed to deliver that value proposition. Then the designers set about developing a clear, actionable picture of how to proceed.

While skills and roles may be different in the horizontal organization, leaders should direct their energy to training current employees to handle additional responsibilities. This training should not overlook those people from other parts of the organization who can fill gaps in processes and expertise that appear elsewhere. A fundamental rule in a horizontal makeover is that people should not be treated like disposable machinery. Employees who already have the skills the company needs to win in the future should be retained, and those who are willing to work to gain those skills should be supported with all the encouragement management can muster. Of course, in some situations external recruiting will also be required.

The emphasis on support and retraining speaks to the humane nature of the horizontal model. This new approach reflects a desire to reinstate the social contract between companies and employees that many observers believe has been severed in recent corporate dismemberments. Certainly people can still be let go if they perform poorly or if they simply cannot adjust to a fresh approach to accomplishing the work of the organization, but companies do have a responsibility to retrain where possible and to try to find new opportunities for people who must be discharged.

In terms of leadership, such a philosophy instills loyalty and grooms leaders who will make necessary accommodations to implement needed change. Being assured of retention and reward in the new organization increases their courage to participate in the revamping and their willingness to commit to the transformation. What is more, since long-term success ultimately depends on institutionalizing a new way of thinking in the ranks of management, companies can make great strides toward assuring that outcome by rewarding those leaders who promote and support the change in the first place.

It is not enough just to say that the horizontal model is at odds with mindless downsizing; in actuality, it can be a platform for *new* growth.

Many of today's most successful, fast-growing companies, having organized horizontally in whole or in part, are geared to successfully execute strategy and to support growth. They are attuned to the demands of new technology and actively work to keep employees up-to-date. These cutting-edge companies do not saw off limbs without any idea of what the surviving entity wants to be or should be, nor do they operate without any understanding of what types of skills and people are necessary to go forward.

A problem typical of, but certainly not limited to, a downsized organization is a serious *mismatch* of skills. Constantly changing technology demands constantly upgrading skills. Companies whose ranks have been thoughtlessly depleted can quickly find themselves short of the brainpower needed to meet the challenge. The multiskilling expected and promoted in the horizontally structured organization, however, more easily accommodates an environment that is in flux.

Can Expertise Survive?

Any mention of multiskilling or cross-functional approaches inevitably raises the question of how functional or technical expertise can survive in such a setting. The answer lies in the versatility of the horizontal model. As you will recall from the preceding chapter, the design does not require an either/or choice between horizontal and vertical. A hybrid combination that draws on the performance capabilities of each easily permits the retention of a functional structure where technical expertise is crucial or where a critical mass is needed for economies of scale. For example, an insurance company might make case managers responsible for the end-to-end customer-service process, while forming dedicated teams to handle specialized or technically difficult regulatory problems.

Other approaches also exist to help maintain technical expertise. Best-practice "diffusion teams" such as those at Motorola's Space Systems and Technology Group can help ensure that cross-functional teams are up to date on the latest technologies and approaches; they also provide the expertise and best approaches for dealing with complex activities such as collaborating with suppliers and customers in the design of products, marketing and distributing products, and satisfying increasingly discriminating customers. Specialists who are part of functional "pools" can provide needed expertise to cross-functional teams on an "as-needed" basis, and then return to the pools to refresh or develop new knowledge. Online courses and training can help ensure that teams are kept up to date on the latest technology and best practices.

Networks are another option for providing expertise that can be quickly accessed—not just documentation but real people with concrete experience handling similar types of situations. Many companies already use best-practice databases and networks that include computerized information categorized according to different kinds of challenges, as well as online access to other people with pertinent knowledge. Networking behavior also allows employees to work collaboratively to solve immediate problems, form ad hoc teams, or access the needed technical knowledge, expertise, or documents.

In the case of OSHA, the technical challenges in the field were not so daunting that people needed to remain divided into functional specialties. Rather, members of the cross-functional teams maintain requisite technical proficiency by attending conferences and training sessions, accessing best-practice networks, and keeping up with the current technical literature. Of course, in some situations technical expertise will be so challenging that highly specialized individuals must work on an ongoing basis alongside others who are regularly dealing with related technical challenges. In such situations, people usually remain assigned to functions (for example, as we will see in chapter 8, Xerox has retained its researchers in vertical groups).

At Xerox, everybody up and down the line sees the post-installation surveys we ask our customers to complete. Even our research people see these responses, as well as those (the PhDs) who are designing and developing our products.

Paul Allaire, CEO of the Xerox Corporation

Under such circumstances, people must remain in functions, but orient themselves not just to the internal performance goals of functions but to enabling/supporting the performance of the core process groups and the company/organization as a whole. Now they must learn to view themselves as "partners in process performance." They will be evaluated on how responsive they are to the needs of their internal customers, the core process groups: Do they give the processes what they need when they need it?

In answer to the question of whether technical expertise can survive in a horizontal organization, the answer is a resounding *yes!* Not only can it survive, but it can also thrive.

A Virtuous Circle

Organizations that are performance-focused are the ones that will lead the way into the new millennium. These survivors will continue to provide meaningful work, and in so doing, they will create what I like to think of as a "virtuous circle": an enriched environment that taps individual skills and creativity to produce ever greater performance in an endless round of progress and productivity.

But unless companies have both a picture of the new organization and a well-thought-out, integrated theory of how it is going to work, it will be frighteningly easy to retreat to the familiar, to the model that worked in years past. Once people are sheltered from the petty tyrannies and turf wars of the vertical culture, they will find working horizontally to be liberating and enlivening.

The next chapter will discuss in greater detail the design principles behind the horizontal organization in its generic form. With those principles firmly in mind, you will begin to see how the generic chart evolves into the actual and distinctly different images of actual organizations discussed in chapters 5-8.

4 THE HORIZONTAL ORGANIZATION EMPOWERS PEOPLE

HOW EMPLOYEES CONTROL THE COMPANY'S CORE PROCESSES

Max Weber, the nineteenth-century German sociologist renowned for his study of social and economic organizations, came down foursquare on the side of the vertical organization headed by a single individual: "The monocratic variety of bureaucracy," Weber wrote, is "capable of attaining the highest degree of efficiency and is . . . the most rational known means of carrying out imperative control over human beings."[1] Weber's observation grew naturally out of his study of a range of hierarchical organizations, from political and economic institutions to military forces to ecclesiastical orders. Nevertheless, his examination was, by virtue of its place in the flow of history, rather limited: Few, if any, enterprises then existed that could offer Weber an alternative to the traditional vertical organization.

Weber's notions of bureaucracy, however, were innovative for his day. Whereas the vast majority of hierarchies were built on the principles of nepotism, favoritism, even political corruption, Weber proposed a bureaucratic system comprising people who had proven themselves deserving of authority and who had the technical expertise the system needed to flourish.

As organizations in the early part of the twentieth century combined Weber's meritocracy with Taylor's principles of scientific management, a new organizational architecture began to take shape. Henry Mintzberg calls this the "machine bureaucracy," a highly productive means of organizing and managing that, as previously discussed, has become the dominant model for organizations even in the late twentieth century.[2] In the right situations, as mentioned previously, the machine bureaucracy offers extraordinary efficiency and productivity. Characterized by inflexibility and slow to react to market forces, however, machine bureaucracies such as the one Henry Ford built cannot keep pace with the changes taking place today on a global scale. The horizontal organization, however, in which the emphasis shifts from top down to focusing across at customers, from compliance with executive orders to meaningful participation in the production of customer satisfaction, quality, and team excellence, is much more attuned to today's radically different business world.

Part III of this book concentrates on showing you how to adapt the horizontal model to fit your specific needs. To lay the groundwork for that transformation, this chapter illustrates, so far as possible, what the new kind of organization designed around core processes looks like. It uses generic charts to represent a horizontally structured organization in general terms. An organization chart is just a picture, of course, and cannot depict the skills and behaviors necessary for organizational effectiveness. It should *never* be mistaken for the organization itself. Despite its shortcomings and oversimplifications, it does serve a number of useful functions. By examining these charts, for instance, you can get a better sense of how some of the key elements of the horizontal approach, as outlined in chapter 1, fit together to provide an actionable design for the organization of the future. Actually seeing the design principles at work will help you to draw the chart that best describes or defines your own horizontally structured organization.

Why the Organization Chart?

An organization chart is merely the visual representation of an organization's features; obviously, one cannot really "see" the internal structure of an enterprise. But like an X ray that shows the vertebrae of the spine or the body's skeletal system of joints and levers, the chart diagrams the various parts of the organization and shows how they are interrelated, how individuals are grouped, and how tasks, authority, and responsibility are allocated. It is a useful tool for avoiding confusion and for developing a shared understanding of the organization among those who populate it.

But perhaps its most interesting and useful feature for organization designers is the way it allows them to play "what if"—that is, to problem-solve on paper by trying out various structural permutations and people placements. For leaders seeking to transform their organizations by adopting the horizontal model, being able to work with a horizontal chart helps free those engaged in organization design from the restrictions of the vertical "template" that is too often "hard-wired" on their subconscious. No more do tall authority structures with their multiple reporting levels and top-down decision making or functional departments have to predominate. Now leaders can begin to visualize what a flatter, customer-driven, team-based, empowered organization looks like and understand how it might be structured.

At the same time, I must emphasize that the horizontal organization entails much more than a series of boxes and connecting lines on a piece of paper. Not all of the 12 design principles (outlined briefly in chapter 1 and discussed in greater detail in chapters 11-12) will be visible in a tangible way on the chart. For example, no drawing can show how empowered workers exhibit frontline problem-solving and continuous improvement skills, how they develop them, or how the whole organization is measured according to balanced performance objectives. The crucial role that information technology plays within a horizontal organization is unchartable as well.

Be that as it may, certain structural similarities will be apparent whether the chart is a generic one, like the ones in this chapter, or whether it is drawn to illustrate the horizontal organization in one of its various incarnations, as exemplified by the case studies discussed in this book. The horizontal organization can potentially be applied:

- Across more than one company

- At the enterprise level, such as over an entire corporation

- Across multiple business units within a corporation

- Within an individual business unit

- Over a core process group within a business unit

- At the operating-unit level (say, a factory or office) within a business unit

The core process group (CPG) is, of course, the centerpiece of every horizontal organization, and it is clearly visible on the organization chart (although the reengineering of processes and the strategy behind it are largely invisible). The CPG provides the architectural framework that makes it possible for a large organization with potentially thousands of teams to work in a unified fashion. Without the concept of core processes, it is virtually impossible to coordinate all the activities that are required to produce a product or service. Instead of departmentalizing people into functions, it is more logical and efficient to departmentalize them into core process groups.

Core processes take raw materials (or raw data or still-simmering ideas) and turn them into an end product or service that has significant value for a customer. A core process might include actions that range from procuring needed raw materials, to consulting with suppliers and customers on new-product design, to involving customer service representatives in measuring how satisfied customers are with the product. The overall core process, in other words, extends far beyond the physical limits of the conveyor belt or the production room. It reaches around corners and down corridors and across floors. And in many organizations, the core process even extends beyond the boundaries of the physical plant to embrace suppliers and customers in the design and marketing of products and services.

Each organization's core processes are unique to that entity, of course, because they are designed specifically to deliver the organization's value proposition. The manufacturer of steel cases or the provider of financial services or the communications giant will each engage people in the unique and not-so-unique sets of activities required to make its product or provide its service.

Before you can begin to design your own organization and form formal organizational departments around core processes, you must first

determine what your core processes are. To do this, you have to start wi
a painstaking analysis of your objectives and your operations, as described
in chapter 9. Many managers run into problems when attempting to reengineer processes because they fail to ask the hard questions about where
they want the company to go, what businesses they want it to be in, what
customers they hope to win, and what value proposition they can offer
to capture those customers. The answers are not always so obvious. Stories
are legion about companies that have jumped onto the Internet bandwagon before doing the necessary homework and strategy setting, only
to discover too late that they were not adequately prepared.

A thorough analysis of the operations of most any large organization,
public or private, will uncover probably no more than three or four core
processes that capture the essence of the business, its strategic objectives,
and the customer segments it seeks to attract. Although the details of one
company's core processes differ in important ways from those of another
company (even in the same industry), certain primary features of processes themselves can be isolated and described to illustrate how a horizontal organization is charted and how the work flows.

A Generic Picture of the Horizontal Organization

Facing stiff opposition, either imagined or real, a change-management
team may be tempted to take what seems to be the easy, nonconfronta-
tional approach to transforming a company into a horizontal organization. Why not simply turn the traditional stovepipe functions or departments (finance, R&D, and marketing) on their sides? This is analogous
to digging a tunnel in hopes of striking oil. The problem is that this so-
called solution is at odds with the concept of core process groups, without
which there can be no horizontal transformation. It fails to take into
account that core process groups are typically flatter than functions and
actually cut across multiple functions, requiring a team or teams of people with cross-disciplinary skills in order to reach the end-of-process objective. For example, a company wishing to deliver the highest-quality
audio product to its customers at a competitive price must bring R&D
experts into direct contact with suppliers, customers, manufacturing personnel, and others in the factory to determine the most cost-effective
means of assembling and testing product.

In place of (or, in some cases, in addition to) the departmentalization found in the vertical hierarchy, groups or teams of employees representing various functions assume responsibility in a horizontal organization for an entire process from its beginning point to its end result (or, in cases where the process is especially complex, for a selection of steps involved in that process). A core process group may comprise case managers, members of a single team, or even hundreds of teams. A typical core process group might include managers and staff from finance, R&D, manufacturing, marketing, and customer service, but their overall objective is no longer confined to the narrow parameters of their former functions.

For example, theoretically minded inventors from the R&D department might move out of their closed-door offices to join fellow team members on the shop floor where the manufacturing occurs or in the laboratory where a new product is assembled and tested. There they meet others whose expertise may lie in creating great marketing campaigns, or in dealing effectively with customers, or in searching for the least expensive, most reliable suppliers. Together they become members of the same organization department and are held jointly responsible for making sure that the end product achieves and maintains the characteristics of cost, quality, and timeliness that the company has set for its production. In this theoretical example, one can see how the various design principles—core process grouping, teaming, performance-based measurement, empowerment, and cooperative culture—come together in the horizontal organization.

The objective in charting the organization is to group people together in cross-disciplinary ways so as to achieve the overall goals of the process. That grouping cannot be dictated by convenience of location or by individual personalities; instead, leaders must try to group people according to the exact mixture of skills necessary to realize the primary objectives of the core process and deliver the organization's value proposition.

Fig. 4.1 depicts a core process group that cuts through several of the traditional functions of a vertical hierarchy. Some departments, like Strategy or Research and Development, as indicated in Fig. 4.1, that are not incorporated into core process groups and remain vertical, are still charged with working as "partners in process." This relationship between the vertical and horizontal parts of a hybrid organization cannot be charted, but it is addressed in the horizontal design principles.

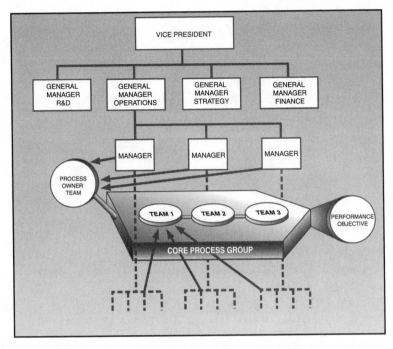

Fig. 4.1 A Generic Horizontal Organization with One Core Process Group

Note that at the top of the organizational chart in Fig. 4.1, there are still a few layers of vertical authority, here assigned to general managers. These positions of high-level hierarchical authority are held by people who guide the organization's operations, determine overall performance goals for multiple core process groups where applicable (as depicted in Fig. 4.2), and set the company's future strategy for attaining those goals.

What is more, these managers must make sure that the core process groups are not operating at cross-purposes and that the selected processes are indeed the ones that are needed to produce the product or service in a way that will satisfy the desired customer. In addition, as leaders well know, some day-to-day responsibilities do not always lend themselves to the team approach. Rewarding or disciplining people for their behavior, for example, are duties often best handled by an individual rather than by committee. And lest we forget, somebody has to sign the checks!

The third tier of the generic chart shown in Fig. 4.1, however, illus-

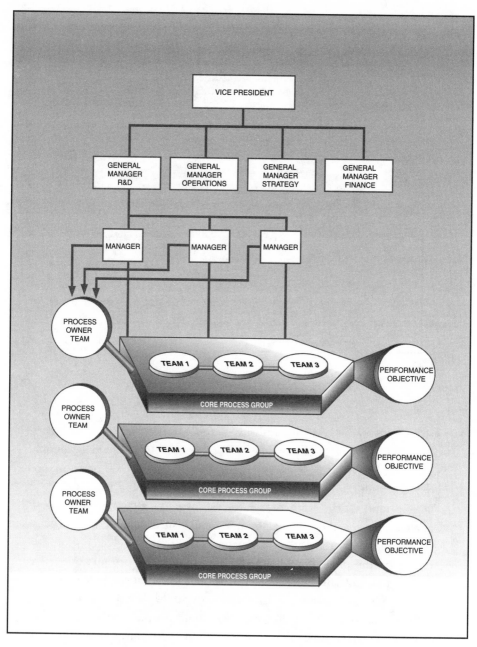

Fig. 4.2 A Generic Horizontal Organization with Multiple Core Process Groups

trates a major departure from a traditional hierarchy. It depicts what traditionally would be another level of managerial supervision, but now these managers are assigned, as indicated by the three arrows, to a flatter position: that is, they become members of the process owner team. In this position, they are slightly above that of the core process group itself (their elevated position is suggested by the 45° line extending to the core process group). Although they are "owners" of the process, in many cases they also serve as members of the core process group. That is, these process owners report to the top managers, but join frontline workers from the various departments to form the three teams that comprise the core process group. Each team takes responsibility for achieving a set of performance objectives critical to the core process.

The generic charts in Figs. 4.1 and 4.2 assume that the organization in question operates 24 hours a day and employs three shifts, or teams, of workers. People take positions on the team corresponding to their shift. At the beginning of the first shift, the process owners meet with members of Team 1 to set priorities for production, determine availability of resources, and anticipate problems that may arise during the day. At 3:00 P.M., Team 2 takes over the core process group's work, accepting the set of priorities established by the owners or altering the schedule if an emergency order is received. This second team hands off its work to Team 3 at 11:00 P.M., which continues the work of the process and orders parts or raw materials as necessary to prepare the way for Team 1 to resume the work the next morning. Representatives from Team 3 then meet with the process owners to update the progress on meeting the core process group's objectives.

I hasten to point out that the membership of these teams is not absolutely fixed. People can move on and off a team when their expertise is required to reach performance objectives or when other team members are absent. In some organizations employees may rotate from shift to shift, again as needs dictate or as workers wish to vary their schedules; however, in most horizontal organizations it may be more reasonable to ask frontline employees to move from team to team within the same shift. For special projects or when top managers determine that a new performance objective is needed, the teams can be radically reconfigured. Furthermore, in organizations with thousands of employees, multiple linked teams can be assigned within each shift to coordinate the work of a single core process.

Vestiges of the vertical organization are suggested in the dotted lines of Fig. 4.1 that extend from the managerial positions to the frontline workers. In the traditional vertical chart (see Fig. 1.1), those workers were represented by the fork tines extending below mid- and low-level managerial positions, but in the generic chart, they are mere shadows of their former selves. (Fig. 4.1 indicates the incorporation of three representative employees into Team 1, but it should be understood that frontline workers can become members of any team that needs their special skills or expertise.) Core process grouping more fully utilizes these frontline workers as team players who are much less narrowly focused on internal functions. In the modern horizontal organization, with its emphasis on empowerment, multiskilling, and evaluation based on process-engendered performance goals, these people do work that is more gratifying and more clearly directed to achieving a value proposition and winning customers.

An Actionable Alternative

The initial significance of the generic horizontal chart is evident in the way it provides an actionable alternative to what most of us have long believed was the only way to organize an enterprise. With late-twentieth-century theorists suggesting all sorts of organizational schemata but without providing a reasonable approach as to how they should actually be put in place, too many leaders have been in the dark as to who goes where and, even more important, *why* this or that arrangement is the best. Eventually, without a visual clue as to how the pieces of the new organization should fit together, they have ended up retreating back to the old vertical standby. This has been an actual impediment to leaders who wish to transform their organization, but who lack an actionable picture of what the transformed organization might actually look like. Among the many virtues of the horizontal organizational chart is that it finally shows leaders how to link people to cross-functional process objectives rather than to internal functional goals and how to use empowered, multidisciplinary work teams effectively.

Organizing a company horizontally by core process groups helps direct information to the people who need it at the time they must have it. At Team 1's daily meeting, for example, managers and employees map out precisely what they will need to meet the group's objectives for that day, the upcoming week, or the next three months. Information—in substantial measure provided by appropriately designed information technology systems—about availability of raw materials, suppliers' inventories, and customers' specific requests remains in full view before all members of the core process group. Whereas such information has a tendency in a vertical hierarchy to become distorted (or to fall through the cracks completely) as it passes from one level to another, this does not happen in a horizontal organization. In more sophisticated versions of the horizontal approach, as we will see in chapters 5-8, suppliers and customers actually participate on some teams, working hand in hand with employees to design products that meet their specific needs. Information from suppliers and the customers could hardly be more direct or pertinent.

A horizontal organization also overcomes problems related to fragmentation. When traditional hierarchies promote internal functional goals and reward employees for individual achievement, there is no guarantee that those departmental goals will add up to a product or service that actually delivers a value proposition and meets customers' needs. More than likely, each stovepipe will simply blow its own smoke. And what good is it to redesign work processes in a cross-functional manner, only to suboptimize the performance improvements possible? This happens when people remain departmentalized in functions, and handoffs and conflicting objectives remain between the different functional departments.

Because the horizontal approach of organizing around processes brings together people from various departments or functions, fragmentation becomes much less of a threat to a company's unity of purpose. In fact, when top managers set direction and coordinate the efforts of multiple core process groups, the fragmentation so familiar in vertical hierarchies disappears. The newfound unity of purpose, in turn, reduces coordination costs. A horizontal organization also avoids the costs that inevitably accompany an excessive number of handoffs, which pass work or parts of products from one department to another. Without the need to re-do, re-format, re-train, and re-program, the company can realize significant savings in short order.

Perhaps most important, when empowered employees have the information, training, and authority to make process decisions, they begin to see that their input has real results, that they are part of a company-wide effort to achieve articulated goals, and that they are responsible for building quality into the products and services they offer customers. Job satisfaction necessarily improves when people understand what value their contributions have in overall performance.

Although it does not show up on an organization chart, this improvement of the quality of employees' lives is of no small significance. Several years ago, I spoke with a 62-year-old grandmother who worked on an empowered team with what was then the Martin Marietta Astronautics Group (now part of the Lockheed Corporation). When asked whether the new system had changed anything, she put it this way: "Yes, first of all, we're winning. Second, for the first time in my life, I've got meaning and I participate. My input means something. I make a contribution and have say over what is done."

One team member, an employee of the General Electric plant in Fort Edwards, New York, responded this way to the same question: "Yes," she said, "I no longer go home from work crying."

Because it offers more people the opportunity to share the responsibility for getting work done and achieving the value proposition, the horizontal organization answers one of the age-old problems inherent in Weber's machine bureaucracy, especially when imbued with Taylor's scientific management principles. That model for organizational structure assumed that most frontline workers had nothing to contribute (other than their back-breaking labor) and would take no interest in making decisions or judgments about a business process, a customer's needs, or a value proposition.[3] The horizontal organization, in contrast, abhors the vacuum of this assumption. It presents an argument, in real-life situations, for worker empowerment through shared information, direct contact with suppliers and customers, involvement in decision-making authorities, self-supervision, and accountability.

This empowerment, of course, represents a major departure from the way we used to conduct business. Accordingly, core process groups within many horizontal organizations experience regular changes in personnel and in performance objectives. It should be expected that managers would reorder priorities or assign new ones when the company's markets or products or competition changes. They may then reassign individual workers who have the special skills needed to meet the new objectives, or they may bring new members onto the team if customers change product specifications or suppliers cannot meet delivery deadlines.

Although there is some danger that core process groups will become insular, managers or process owners can keep rotating personnel from one team to another to prevent it. Workers gain a broader perspective from multiskilling, working collaboratively with others inside the organization as well as with customers and suppliers. They come to understand better the company's objectives, as well as those of core processes, and they develop skills in frontline problem solving. Thus, they become more adaptable and ready to respond to changing conditions. Training employees to acquire new skills, then giving them a chance to use these skills in creating, building, testing, and marketing new products can also help energize them to achieve their best results.

In sum, the horizontal organization integrates the best efforts of numerous people on cross-functional teams. Centering their skills and expertise on a single core process, these employees take greater control over that process and the product they create. By structuring the organization around a small number of integrated core processes, those three or four core process managers help eliminate barriers and handoffs while providing the space and means for frontline people to engage in creative problem-solving. Thus empowered, those workers willingly accept more responsibility for improving process objectives and building into their products the highest possible level of quality.

If Weber is correct in his assertion that the monocratic hierarchy is the most efficient structure for *controlling people*, the obverse has greater validity for our times: The horizontal organization is the most efficient means for *people to control* the products of the organization. As we will see in the four organizations examined in chapters 5-8, when the right employees take control of a company's core processes, the outcome is an extraordinary increase in efficiency, energy, and involvement.

Part TWO
HOW THE HORIZONTAL ORGANIZATION WORKS

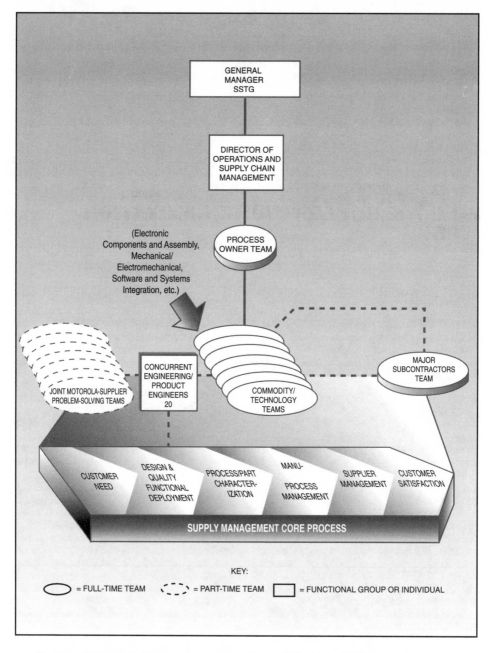

Fig. 5.1 Motorola's Space and Systems Technology Group (SSTG)—
Supply Management Organization

5 ORGANIZING AROUND A CORE PROCESS

THE SUPPLY MANAGEMENT ORGANIZATION OF MOTOROLA'S
SPACE AND SYSTEMS TECHNOLOGY GROUP

When astronaut Neil Armstrong relayed his first words from the moon in 1969, he used a Motorola-designed and -manufactured transponder. That transmission came through with remarkably little static despite its having to travel some 200,000 miles. Twenty years later, however, the Motorola Space and Systems Technology Group (SSTG) might just as well have considered communicating from the moon, given the amount of static that interrupted the interchange between employees, suppliers, and customers. Vertically organized, the SSTG was too fragmented and inefficient in its procurement of supplies.

SSTG is one of four businesses within Motorola's Communication enterprise which also includes paging, land-mobile products (e.g., radios), and cellular phones. The group produces high-end satellites for telecommunications and data management customers, as well as test equipment for communications products such as cellular radios and telephones. It is also a major military supplier of tactical radios and secure products, and its communications systems division specializes in battlefield imagery. Besides the U.S. Department of Defense and NASA, Motorola SSTG serves various commercial users including the Iridium LLC and the Raytheon Company.

Prior to the 1989-1990 redesign of the supply management operation, procuring materials within SSTG—then known as the Government Electronics Group (GEG)—was a complicated, predominantly vertical, functionally divided affair. Some 12 departments in various separate groups within GEG were each engaged in locating suppliers, taking bids, obtaining supplies, and ensuring quality. This fragmentation resulted in an enormous and inefficient bureaucracy, making a task as simple as the selection of a supplier for a new product a complicated and time-consuming undertaking that required the involvement and approval of many different department heads.

Moreover, because the entire group was separated by function, its various departments and divisions seldom had common goals. If the engineering department designed an electrical part, for example, it was not required to make sure that a supplier could actually produce the part efficiently and with high quality. Another department assumed that responsibility. Quality engineers were expected to police operations and intercept bad parts before they got to the production floor—not *solve* the problems, mind you, just *find* them! Once found, those problems could be analyzed for root causes, which Motorola workers could correct and prevent from reoccurring.

Buyers took responsibility for obtaining specified supplies in the correct quantity at the lowest possible price. Looking "upward" at supervisors and department managers rather than "out" to customers, those buyers had little concern for issues of quality and timeliness. By the same token, design engineers were obligated only to supply the design of a new product. Whether the company could get needed parts at the right time or the right price or whether the parts required for a design would themselves cause quality or manufacturing problems rarely, if ever, entered their thinking. There was no cross-functional responsibility or optimization of cross-functional objectives, no sharing of skills or perspectives, and little concern anywhere for how individual functional actions would affect either upstream or downstream efforts to deliver the value proposition. In short, no one was really responsible for overall performance.

The old supply procurement approach was mired in hierarchy. A decision or order would filter down from the group's general manager to the divisional general manager to the operations manager to the materials manager to the section manager, and so on down the ladder to the lowest buyer level—seven to nine levels overall. This organizational hierarchy made it especially difficult for frontline employees to voice their opinions and suggestions, or to act in real-time to solve problems. Seven hundred workers performed various supply management tasks, but coherence and cross-functional teamwork were virtually nonexistent. Not surprisingly, the communication lines between the supply management organization and its suppliers crackled with static. Something had to be done.

The SSTG'S Value Proposition

The first step was for Motorola to determine where it wanted the group to go, what it wanted to offer customers—that is, the division needed to define its value proposition. After analyzing its strengths, weaknesses, and long-term goals, the company concluded that it had a "commitment to employ leading-edge technology to provide total customer solutions with the highest possible quality, reliability, and speed to market"—and to do that by fully integrating its suppliers and subcontractors into the process. With this value proposition clearly spelled out, Motorola identified supply management as a core operating process within the group— that is, this process was critical to providing the desired value to customers. Taking supply management horizontal by viewing it as an end-to-end, cross-functional process and designing a new organization around it seemed like the best way to achieve the company's goals.

"Ownership" of this process is assigned to a team of four commodity process and technology managers headed by Larry Burleson, a vice president of SSTG and the director of operations and supply chain management. The actual responsibility for carrying out the end-to-end work— including supply management—of the newly integrated process and for meeting its time, cost, and quality objectives is vested in commodity teams that report to the team of process owners. In the Motorola SSTG supply management organization, these commodity teams comprise purchasing agents, buyers, supplier managers, and various types of engineers—commodity, component, product, quality, and so on.

The teams are not just groups of people who work side by side on the same shift; rather they are highly empowered employees who receive the necessary internal information (via team meetings and online sharing of project data and knowledge) and, most important, have the authority to make timely decisions as to which purchases they should make and which suppliers can provide the most appropriate components. To reach this level of empowerment, supply management employees are encouraged to acquire multiple skills through Motorola in-house training sessions and actual course work at Motorola University. This kind of organizational support helps ensure that employees have the skills to improve their performance and the ability to deliver the all-important value proposition more effectively.

Aptly illustrating the power and promise of this integrated approach is a real-life example in which a problem with faulty parts was spotted and corrected by an empowered team. Alerted to a problem indicated by rising defect rates, the supply management teams went about systematically searching for the root causes. As Cindi Wong, a purchasing agent with the Motorola supply management electromechanical commodity team, recounts it, investigators discovered parts with bent leads, which rendered them useless. In the ensuing root-cause analysis, a Motorola components engineer led the supply management team in determining that the culprit was the supplier's packaging process.

Under the old dispensation, Motorola employees would have come up against familiar barriers that frustrate communications with suppliers. With the new horizontal approach, however, in which teams of suppliers work jointly with the commodity teams at a Motorola facility, many of those barriers fall, and teams are able to correct defects quickly and efficiently.

In this particular event, the Motorola team devised a new way to package the delicate part—complete with a drawing of what type of packaging should have been used and even how the supplier should have positioned the part in the box in order to ensure its safe shipment. Delighted to receive this expert help, the supplier found that a very costly problem was resolved quickly and efficiently because the multiskilled Motorola team did not need to wade through multiple layers of administrative approval before it could act. Even better, the supply management organization's defect rate went down and the group made good on the value proposition it promised its customers.

This packaging solution illustrates a problem-solving approach to working with a supplier in order to enhance the value proposition, saving customers both time and money they would have spent in repairs or replacements. Empowering SSTG employees with control of the supply management process proves to be much more than paying lip service to fashionable trends and persnickety customers. In the supply management organization of the Space and Systems Technology Group, the shift to the horizontal organization represents a significant rearrangement of the business landscape.

Organizing a Core Process Horizontally

Fig. 5.1 at the beginning of this chapter presents a schematic view of the supply management organization's new horizontal structure. Managers of various commodity teams (e.g., electronic components and assembly, mechanical/electromechanical, and software and systems integration) combine forces with managers of production to streamline standard off-the-shelf purchases and engineering. They coordinate the activities and carry out the steps of the end-to-end supply management core process. These commodity teams—along with teams for streamline purchasing, systems and software, and operations support—are arrayed beneath the process owner team, which comprises vice president and director of operations and supply chain management Burleson and the three commodity managers.

"Our overall strategy is to take our internal capabilities or competencies and add them together with the core competencies of our suppliers for competitive advantage and differentiation," explains Burleson. "In order to win customers, we try to provide the highest quality at the lowest total cost, with the added value being our problem-solving capabilities. That's where we stand out, and where this horizontal structure most helps us."

To prepare employees for cross-functional decision making and empowered problem solving, Motorola gives each of its teams a tool kit that includes the Ishikawa "fish-bone" diagrams, and it trains them in areas such as cost-risk assessment, setting objectives, and problem-solving methodologies. Team members and leaders alike are required to take 40 hours of training a year. Classes range from "Workforce Diversity," which everyone takes, to "Manager of Managers." Instruction runs the gamut from technology to strategy to interpersonal relations, and some classes such as Pro-Engineer are available on CD-ROM.

Knowing how to get people to speak instead of listen to you is very important. You need to get that two-way conversation going.

Larry Burleson, SSTG vice president
and director of operations and supply chain management

The company puts such emphasis on cross-training that even non-engineer types such as purchasing agents and supply managers undergo technical instruction. Giving those employees a better understanding of the company's high-tech products allows them to take a more active part in issue resolution (even if they do not completely understand all the scientific and mechanical intricacies of a particular product).

Fig. 5.1 suggests how the new horizontal design has dramatically reduced the inefficiency of the old hierarchy. Organizing around the supply management process, implementing cross-functional work flows, and vesting decision making in empowered teams are directly responsible for paring eight or nine managerial levels down to three. Now when an empowered Motorola supply management team needs a supplier or has to change suppliers for an existing product, it can go ahead on its own to find one. Team members communicate freely with development and quality engineers, visit various suppliers, then make their decision based on the first-hand information. Even their own team manager need not be informed until after a change is made.

In the popular imagination, "freedom" connotes the absence of responsibility. At Motorola, however, the supply management teams demonstrate that the reverse holds true: Increased freedom to act brings with it added responsibility and accountability. Equipped with the information, training, authority, and motivation that distinguish true empowerment from merely symbolic sanction, the Motorola teams are evaluated on how well they are using those tools to achieve process objectives and continually improve their performance.

In order to monitor how well its actions support SSTG's overall strategy, each team continually receives information that tracks its performance along a number of dimensions critical to success in delivering the value proposition. Tracked daily, weekly, or monthly, as the case may be, those measures include defect rates, delivery requirements (on-time deliveries), cycle time, and costs. Beneath the goals appears a roster of organizational imperatives—strategies and specific actions that Motorola needs to accomplish by predetermined completion dates.

The new horizontal structure rewards teams that meet those performance imperatives helping to guarantee the high quality of Motorola products. Team members attribute much of their personal growth, not to mention merit raises and promotions, to evaluations that they receive from process owners and other managers each quarter. In addition, annual peer evaluations point out in nonthreatening ways how teams members can improve both their own work and the products they make. Evaluations from supervisors and peers focus on overall team performance goals and on what individual members are doing to meet them. An employee working on a software commodity team might be evaluated, for example, on how well the entire team writes up a procedure and develops metrics for rating software suppliers, as well as on how effectively he or she personally works with suppliers and other team members. The focus is always on enhancing personal growth and development, as well as specific individual behaviors deemed important to the team's high level of performance.

Working on a team allows me to draw resources together and focus on the precise task at hand. I've become much more time-conscious and efficient. The new horizontal organization is much less bureaucratic . . . I have a greater sense that I can control my own destiny.

Brett Traube, supplier manager of the electrical commodity team

---

More efficient work habits enhance employees' sense of personal and team accomplishment, a central feature of the horizontal organization.

As an added benefit, managers can now reallocate time and resources formerly spent on supervision. That is not to say that management cannot or will not intervene if team performance goes off track or if other performance barriers arise. But now the self-directed teams assume many of the former managerial tasks: They fix their own work schedules, evaluate their peers, and set their own performance goals. Management is then freed up to pursue other activities that add value such as improving processes, setting strategy, and understanding customer needs.

Each one of us can use the skills that we have rather than working in a micromanaged environment. We can flow in our ideas of how to improve a certain step or process, then actually have a chance to implement those ideas into the process.

Cindi Wong, purchasing agent with the
electromechanical commodity team

Suppliers Are Part of the Process

A joint effort between the supply management organization and its suppliers at the early stages of design and production inevitably improves quality, performance, and customer satisfaction. Another virtue of the horizontal structure is that it enables the supply management organization to involve suppliers directly in core processes. This relationship is illustrated in Fig. 5.1 by the dotted line that joins joint Motorola-supplier problem-solving teams, product engineers, commodity teams, and major subcontractor teams: All four work together on the supply management core process, maintaining end-to-end control over the various segments of that process and ensuring its quality.

Chosen suppliers work directly with Motorola employees and meet face-to-face with end users or intermediate customers, tackling production issues such as improving cycle time and devising more coherent plans to manage risk. Motorola representatives explain every facet of the company's requirements and often send "quality notes" to suppliers—messages on purchase orders that alert suppliers to points in the process where they might need to handle parts with particular sensitivity or schedule an inspection with Motorola before completion of a project.

In the area of design, information technology systems allow a Motorola team to e-mail a design database directly to a supplier for review. Within a matter of hours—not weeks as would have been the case only five years ago—the supplier's changes can be returned and the design updated accordingly. The interchange gives suppliers a better understanding of the manufacturing process and allows them to plan their own operations with an eye toward accommodating Motorola's future needs.

Every month, Motorola sends each primary supplier a summary documenting metrics dating back as far as one year. In addition, the company evaluates each supplier's quality (in terms of defective parts per million and rates each according to delivery criteria for the 12-month period. Motorola and its suppliers reach mutual agreement on goals for quality, price, and design, and those goals become a part of Motorola's continuous improvement process, which it calls "Six Sigma."[1] Now widely adapted by companies of every stripe, Six Sigma has become synonymous with the most exacting standards of quality that are practical and achievable. Such an assessment of supplier performance enables Motorola SSTG and its suppliers to integrate their problem-solving capabilities to track how effectively they are meeting objectives, then to develop ways they can work collaboratively to improve their collective performance.

The company disseminates those evaluations each month to every team in the supply management core process group, noting anomalies and assigning a team's purchasing agent and commodity engineer to investigate any problems. "The plan is developed with suppliers, and we have buy-in from them each step of the way," explains Brett Traube, supplier manager for the electrical commodity team. "Together, we study root causes of a potential problem. Is it a software problem? Is it a test problem that's reducing the yield? Are the tests incorrect? The situations vary, but the focus is always on identifying opportunities for improvement."

Motorola's suppliers provide such high-tech parts as semiconductors, printed wiring boards, microelectronics, capacitors, and resistors—components that change rapidly as technology makes new advances. Merely trying to keep up with those changes requires a team commitment because no one person could hope to master all of them. The supply management organization's cross-functional, horizontal structure allows it to have immediate access to the experts who are an integral part of the teams before, during, and after the components are designed into a system. In the resulting synergy, Motorola experts work with suppliers not only to anticipate a problem before it occurs, but also to bring about a speedy resolution when a problem is found. Although not always visible to customers, this open and cooperative culture extending across Motorola's boundaries adds great value to the company's products.

The Iridium Project

Motorola's Satellite Communications Group (SCG), part of Motorola's SSTG, is a prime example of how horizontal design principles come together in a cross-disciplinary environment to deliver a complex total solution effectively and efficiently. Designed to provide global wireless voice, paging, facsimile, and data services by late 1998, the Iridium project called for Motorola SCG to build, launch, integrate, and control a 66-satellite constellation. Not only were the numbers daunting, they were simply unheard of. As Burleson points out, "Prior to this, there was no such thing as a satellite factory. The traditional method was to build satellites one at a time." In 11 months Motorola launched 65 satellites. Motorola used 45 percent of the world's satellite launch capacity with nine launches in three countries. The closest to this performance was the Global Positioning System with 24 satellites in four years.

In gearing up to take on such a monumental task, the SSTG supply management organization had to evaluate carefully its supplier processes and figure out how to reduce costs to one-tenth of their historic levels while also meeting requirements for quality, durability, and reliability. Reliability engineers, quality-control specialists, buyers, commodity engineers, as well as representatives from the subcontractors, all brought special expertise to the decision-making process as they worked to marry the needs of the project with what the supplier base could offer.

This multidisciplinary expertise was particularly crucial because this project involved a major shift in the way things had been done in the past: Commercial, off-the-shelf parts were to be used, for example, rather than parts specifically crafted for the project. Since plastic parts would be flown into space for the first time, everyone involved needed to know that decision makers were bringing to the table the best available multidisciplinary knowledge and information about processes, parts reliability, cost, suppliers' delivery time, and cycle time. A satellite whirling around the earth at 17,000 miles an hour is not easily repaired, so with a lot of Motorola money at stake, it was imperative that the best decisions be made on the ground.

All Iridium team members armed themselves with a checklist of technical and business requirements and the tool kit of problem-solving skills (such as cost-risk analysis) that Motorola gives to every employee. "We spent a long time with our teams in training. . . . We knew [problem solving] was something they were comfortable with," says Sandra Hopkins, manager of streamline purchasing and head of systems and software procurement for SSTG. The team members drew on their individual expertise and the historical data on suppliers and designs available to them through Motorola's information technology system.

The IT system also proved extremely useful when team members needed to know the characteristics of particular parts. Purchasing agents and supply management engineers gathered facts on cost, lead time, and performance characteristics from suppliers, and then immediately disseminated them via e-mail to all other team members. This capability made for a much speedier and more effective decision-making process.

Without the cooperative involvement of suppliers and multidisciplined, cross-functional SSTG teams, the company would never have been able to meet the performance requirements involved in building and launching the Iridium satellites, the first five of which roared into space in May 1997.[2]

The Proof in the Pudding

Although the cross-functional commodity teams have helped transform Motorola SSTG's supply management organization into a cost-efficient and productive operation, as the Iridium project indicates, Burleson and other leaders believe there are some areas where a function-based, vertical structure is still preferable to the horizontal. Physical design and highly specialized areas such as microwave development, for example, are best left as functions within traditional departments, in order to provide the requisite technical expertise. Nevertheless, these functions cooperate in furthering the performance of the overall organization.

Not surprisingly, the team members and leaders interviewed at Motorola were unanimous in their praise for the horizontal organization. They derived their satisfaction with their status as highly empowered employees with a newfound sense of growth and expanded opportunities to integrate and apply expertise. As Hopkins puts it, "Now I have the best of both worlds: purchasing knowledge and the technical knowledge to make the decisions." Burleson adds, "She's been doing gigantic things in process improvement." For Kris Krishnaswamy, engineering and quality manager, having empowered teams working on specific problems has freed him to concentrate on key technical issues and strategic matters that need his attention. Team members, too, voiced appreciation for their ability to solve problems in a more timely manner without waiting for managerial approvals.

It's just a lot easier to manage the supplier, work with customers. . . . Folks are working together. They're communicating together, and they're all after a main goal. We're not pulling against each other. It's a big difference.

Karen Chapman, supplier manager on the mechanical commodity team

---

The success of Motorola's reorganization finds its measure not only in workers' increased perception of their empowerment and their new enthusiasm, but also in the reduction of supply management costs. The supply management operation has cut costs 60 percent as a result of implementing the main elements of the horizontal organization. At the same time, the percentage of rejected parts has dropped from 20 percent in 1989 to less than 1 percent today. Delivery performance, which once showed a 40 percent delinquency rate, now checks in with just 8 percent of total deliveries arriving behind schedule.

As the Motorola SSTG supply management organization case study makes abundantly clear, the 12 principles of horizontal organization are not one-time tools to be discarded once the structure is in place. They are interwoven throughout the entire organization and, in fact, come to define what the organization is and how it works on a day-to-day basis. The makeover has meant that all supply management employees are now responsible for actually carrying out what the value proposition proclaims: to "employ leading-edge technology to provide total customer solutions with the highest possible quality, reliability, and speed to market." The integration of horizontal design principles with performance enablers has changed Motorola team members from mere problem finders into truly empowered problem solvers. "That isn't my job" is an excuse you will no longer hear at Motorola.

6 ORGANIZING A HORIZONTAL OPERATING UNIT

GE SALISBURY

The General Electric plant at Salisbury, North Carolina, produces electrical lighting panel boards designed for industrial and commercial applications. Although more complex, these panels are similar to the box of circuit breakers or fuses you likely have in your basement.

Up through the mid-1980s, GE Salisbury manufactured the panel boards in a costly and rather inefficient job shop manufacturing process. Organized vertically, GE Salisbury required at least a six-week lead time to manufacture and ship an electrical lighting panel board.

Complicating matters were the realities of the production process: Bottlenecks played havoc with schedules and made synchronization of manufacturing subprocesses an enormous challenge, particularly in a traditionally vertical, fragmented organization. When all was said and done, the product line costs were too high, service commitments to customers were not consistently met, and they were losing market share.

In 1984, however, GE Salisbury began an extensive transformation to restructure and consolidate the lighting panel construction process into a new horizontal structure that would link multiskilled teams and make them responsible for the entire build-to-order process. "We decided the only way that GE Salisbury could survive was to expand the flexibility of our workforce and integrate their efforts with a better technology to manufacture the panel boards," says Phil Jarrosiak, former manager of human resources at GE and one of the original architects of the new organization. Jarrosiak was joined by Roger Gasaway, at the time the manager of the GE Salisbury plant and currently general manager of manufacturing at GE ED&C (Electrical Distribution and Control).

Under the direction of these leaders, the changeover to a cross-functional, team-based organizational approach began to take shape. New technology was investigated that could help team members achieve the production and performance results required to establish the plant's competitive position. But more than just bringing in the nuts and bolts of technological systems, these leaders undertook the arduous task of instilling a new philosophy among all employees, one that emphasized teamwork, responsibility, continuous improvement, and empowerment. As a result of their efforts, GE Salisbury completed its transformation to a horizontal organization by 1991 (although some fine-tuning of management and production continues today), and the plant has become a model for a highly involved and empowered workforce.

"A transformation this extensive of an existing plant was virtually unheard of at the time," says Gasaway. "Skeptics gave it little chance of success, but the GE environment and philosophy established by CEO Jack Welch encouraged us to take the risk. And we did."

The performance and productivity improvements have been nothing short of remarkable. Production bottlenecks rarely disrupt the flow at the plant these days, and the six weeks' cycle time for lighting panel boards has been drastically reduced: Typically, the process teams build the electrical panels in a 2.5-day cycle, although they can regularly complete the manufacturing process in only one day, if an emergency order arrives.

The GE operating unit at the Salisbury plant comprises two fundamental fabrication processes: Employees construct a steel box to house the electrical components; then, they assemble and test the electrical parts that form the internal circuitry. But because no two GE customers have identical needs, there the uniformity ends. Each panel box with its contents is configured and built to order, and the Salisbury plant can build as many as 70,000 variations on the basic design.

Since its transformation to a horizontal operating unit, the Salisbury plant has established an industry-wide reputation for its ability to fine-tune its manufacturing process to fit the specific needs of its customers—namely, to make the highest quality product precisely to customer requirements and to do so in a way that is economical, efficient, and competitive. Moreover, in the first years after the facility switched to a horizontal operation, variable costs declined and have continued to drop.

Transferring ownership to the shop floor has helped create a culture based on pride, responsibility, cooperation, and self-management. The teams understand both personal and company goals, and drive the changes needed to get there.

Dan MacDonnell
GE Salisbury plant manager

Inventory turns have increased sixfold, while output and operating margins have both doubled. GE product quality has also improved. Customer complaints have fallen from 2 percent to 0.02 percent, with plans in place to reduce it even further through GE's aggressive Six Sigma initiatives.

Production numbers, however, constitute only a part of the picture. Employees report a much higher degree of satisfaction with their work now as opposed to what it was ten or more years ago; turnover is lower, and frontline workers and management are united in their effort to stay well ahead of the competition.

How did GE Salisbury achieve such striking results? The answer to that question is complex, embracing not only a full assessment of the company's key capabilities, but also a deep commitment to competitive excellence on the part of both management and the front line. At the heart of the transformation are the process-oriented teams, horizontally organized against a backdrop of employee empowerment and design efficiency. And apparent in a multitude of ways (even when not easily visible in an organization chart) are the other principles of horizontal organization. They work singly and in combination to enhance performance on a daily basis.

GE Salisbury's multiskilled, highly empowered teams receive information about sales, backlogs, inventory, staffing needs, productivity, costs, quality, and various other data related to objectives critical to delivering the value proposition at intervals ranging from every eight hours to every month, depending on what kind of goals are involved; in this case, the customer service objective was included in a monthly review. These teams fully understand that they are strictly accountable for performance results, so once they were informed of the problem, they called into play their company-provided training in problem-solving and analysis to produce some workable suggestions.

One team zeroed in on the sequencing of various parts in the production process—by changing the sequence, a customer's order could be completed more quickly. Both of these team-devised solutions contributed significantly to achieving GE Salisbury's intent to deliver the product precisely as the customer wants it, promptly and cost-effectively.

The Value Proposition

Before it could form any teams for the build-to-order process or undertake a transformational makeover, however, the GE Salisbury operating unit had to define its value proposition. After assessing its own capabilities, as well as those of competitors, the organization came up with the following objective encapsulating the promise of the value the plant offers its customers: To produce lighting panel boards "of the highest possible quality, in the shortest possible cycle time, at a competitive price, and with the best possible service." With that goal in mind, employees were then able to pinpoint the build-to-order process as critical to delivering its value proposition, design it to achieve that value proposition, and then to organize the plant and themselves around it.

As depicted in Fig. 6.1, GE Salisbury's horizontal organizational chart highlights the concerted work of four teams in the build-to-order process. These are represented in the chart as "links" in a chain, suggesting that they work in concert with each other. Each team comprises 10 to 15 people, but the actual composition changes every eight hours as employees from the next shift take over. For purposes of this discussion, the teams are identified as follows:

- The electrical components team (Team 1) assembles and tests the lighting panel (this team now includes a former team devoted to shipping).

- The fabrication team (Team 2) cuts, builds, welds, and paints the parts that form the steel boxes.

- The maintenance team (Team 3) performs heavy equipment maintenance that cannot be done as part of the production process.

- The "production control" team (Team 4) takes responsibility for receiving the orders, planning and coordinating production, purchasing, working with suppliers and customers, solving customer complaints, and keeping track of inventories.

On the right side of Fig. 6.1 appears a group of "associate advisors," former managers who now bring their expertise to the teams on an advisory basis and serve more or less as guides and coaches on problems that may arise. Because they are individuals, they appear in Fig. 6.1 within a rectangle, and their "as needed" relationship to the team is indicated by the dotted line extending to the linked operating teams.

Solid lines extend from the linked operating teams to the wedge representing the actual parts of the build-to-order process that leads to the delivery of the value proposition. These lines suggest both the teams' new authority and control of the entire process as well as the span of their responsibility.

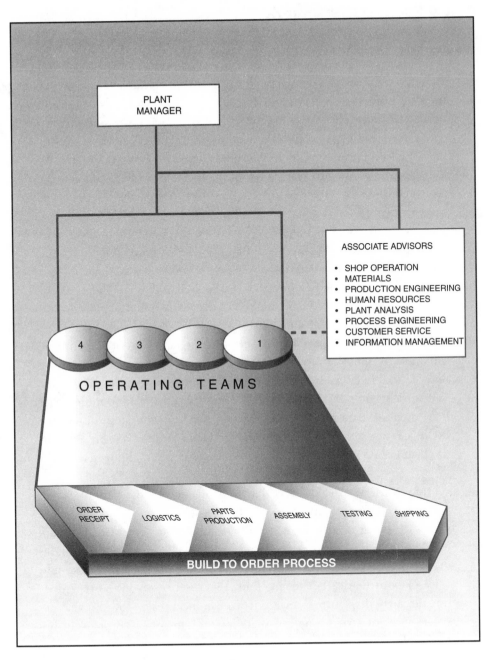

Fig. 6.1   General Electric—Salisbury Plant

A New Focus on Teamwork

As Fig. 6.1 suggests, hierarchy could hardly be flatter at GE Salisbury. Team 4 acts as the process owner and, in addition to the duties cited above, is responsible for making sure that the frontline teams stay on track in terms of speed, cost, quality, and flexibility so as to meet overall process objectives linked to the delivery of the value proposition.

Teams 1 and 2, perhaps more than any of the others, directly perform the actual production in the build-to-order process. Both Teams 1 and 2 share information with Team 4 about logistics, but only Teams 1 and 2 are responsible for parts production, and only Team 1 actually assembles the electrical panel boxes.

A number of factors help to ensure a smooth integration of the work of the two fabrication teams, including regularly scheduled joint production meetings, job rotation, cross-training of employees, and a work flow that has been designed to proceed in a sequence that facilitates coordination of the teams' efforts despite the fact that different time frames are involved. At GE Salisbury, these highly involved teams assume responsibility for setting their own performance targets in alignment with the value proposition (within and in support of strategy and performance guidelines set by ED&C, of course); they determine production and work schedules, as well as the assignment of overtime duties; they hold themselves responsible for plant-wide safety, communications, and housekeeping concerns; they identify problems and devise corrective action; and they can even purchase equipment within budgeted guidelines.

Due to the varying product demands dictated by the customers, GE Salisbury cross-trains employees to move easily from one team to another when a backlog occurs. By one estimate, some 90 percent of frontline employees know how to perform approximately 90 percent of the tasks in the Salisbury facility. Furthermore, they understand the tasks and roles of both fabrication teams; thus, the absence of one worker does not threaten the entire process. If a machine breaks down, a maintenance team of cross-trained workers is ready to solve the problem immediately.

Much of the training at GE Salisbury comes in the form of community college course work that provides employees with the foundation to work effectively in high involvement teams and hone their specialized skills. They take courses in basic team survival skills, team development skills, meeting skills, interpersonal skills, and communication techniques. Team members also receive technical training and instruction in problem-solving methodologies. The bulk of the training comes in an employee's first two years, although follow-up training occurs in areas such as safety, Six Sigma quality, and continuous improvement. For their part, associate advisors receive additional instruction in conflict resolution, problem solving, coaching, and setting performance objectives, among other things.

Team 4 consists of ten cross-trained, broadly skilled members who rotate among various roles: One person acts as the master scheduler; three people are in charge of purchasing; four handle customer service; and two work on logistics. Collaborating with eight associate advisors, Team 4 takes responsibility for seeing that the entire build-to-order process flows without bottlenecks from the first contact with a customer to the satisfactory installation of the electrical lighting boards at that customer's site.

A process that could become a logistical nightmare is kept running smoothly because Team 4 calls together the key players every eight hours. At 7:00 A.M., 3:00 P.M., and 11:00 P.M., production representatives from each team meet with two members of Team 4. Together they make plans for the next eight hours of production and ensure that component parts are ready for assembly.

What makes these teams so efficient and productive is their common commitment to the build-to-order process. True, the employees must have the skills and training to allow them to rotate between jobs at a moment's notice and to meet any challenge that arises on the factory floor. But just as important is their sense of ownership of and pride in the production process in which they participate.

Of course, the esprit de corps exhibited by the teams at GE Salisbury did not fall like an apple from the tree. It took hard work to achieve, and it must continually be renewed to keep the factory at peak capacity. In the first few years after the horizontal organization was introduced, some GE Salisbury employees found the team approach too demanding, and they left to pursue other jobs; still others had to undergo extensive training to bring them up to the standards set by their peers.

Tim Deal, production scheduler, recounts how the team rallied around an employee who was having difficulty with his work and coming up to standards. A team facilitator, a training coordinator, and the production representative met with the individual to begin identifying root causes for his problems, absenteeism, and difficulty in working productively with a group. The employee was receptive to this analysis and undertook on-the-job training. He eventually improved his job performance to the point where he was either meeting or exceeding the team's average production.

Employees can receive on-the-job training in the production of lighting panel boards. And all employees rotate between job assignments to avoid burnout and to promote cross-training throughout the production process. This job rotation is essential in meeting GE Salisbury's performance goals.

A critical part of the original concept—and one that I believe is still integral to the high performance levels that have been achieved at Salisbury—is that the people who are on the floor, on the job, doing their work eight hours a day, are the people who know best what the needs are, what the problems are, and how best to go about correcting them, making improvements.

Phil Jarrosiak, architect of the GE Salisbury reorganization

From the employees' point of view, the team approach is empowering in that it reassigns overall responsibility for the smooth functioning of the process to the workers themselves rather than to managers who exist in a hierarchical vacuum. Decision making—whether it is a question of material supply (as when the company needs to replenish its inventory of raw material) or of personnel (such as the need to reassign four workers from the assembly team to the fabrication team)—becomes a responsibility jointly shared by the production reps and the team members. Some issues such as disciplinary actions and approval for large-scale purchases still reside within the managerial ranks, but at GE Salisbury, people know that even those issues are open for discussion and that their suggestions will be taken seriously by those in authority.

Management's New Role

It almost goes without saying that the role of management takes on new dimensions in an environment like that at GE Salisbury. The former plant manager reported that his position had "drastically changed," and he described himself as the "local on-site representative of the two key customers of the facility." Besides the customer who buys and utilizes the end product, current plant manager Dan MacDonnell thinks of GE as a customer as well because it "sources from us the activity of building this product" and expects some financial return. The plant manager has to "negotiate between GE and the outside customer, and all of his responsibilities are, in effect, related to meeting customer requirements."

Within that broader scope, however, the GE plant manager also performs certain traditional leadership roles such as integrating plant and corporate financial goals, motivating employees and overseeing disciplinary actions, negotiating with customers and suppliers, and making investment decisions.

Dennis Milbrandt, associate advisor of shop operations and a process leader at the GE Salisbury plant, points up the contrasts between his role now and his former role as a manager for 23 years in a traditional vertical hierarchy. The primary difference lies in the willingness to relinquish authority, he says. "You have to be willing to let go, empower people, for instance, to contact vendors on their own, ask them to fly in from Italy to North Carolina to discuss a new technique for welding or improving components." Initially, many frontline workers think themselves incapable of contacting a vendor about a fabrication process, but with training and assurance that the company values their contributions, most process team members willingly take up the challenge. "After all," Milbrandt adds, "they are the experts who work on the equipment, so it makes sense that they, not I, should make the contact."

On the other hand, many traditional managers balk when they have to give up that much authority. Fearing that their own jobs will be eliminated, they imagine that frontline workers will not be up to the task of negotiating, planning, ordering, and dealing directly with customers and suppliers. After a time, however, they find that when given the appropriate training, information, and motivation, employees can handle many of these responsibilities, thereby freeing managers from the administrative burdens and allowing them to concentrate on matters that bring additional value to the company and its customers. Since the Salisbury plant has gone horizontal, for example, Milbrandt spends much more time learning what his customers need and developing ideas for improving customer service, running continuous improvement projects, coaching, and budgeting. He spends much less time strictly overseeing the work that employees do.

Harold Driver, an automated equipment operator as well as a production representative, agrees. In fact, he speaks of "retraining management" to teach them effective team skills such as coaching, listening, and working one-on-one with team members. As Driver observes, "A lot of talk about team concepts will never get the job done. If managers or process owners are not fully committed to those concepts, if they are not open-minded enough to give the teams a chance to work, then the whole transformation will fail." And here is a twist on the usual concept of training: Driver says a team often experiences a setback when a new manager takes over because the people on the frontline have to train the new manager both in how the process works and in how the teams operate.

A View of the Operating Process

Modern information technology plays a significant role in the Salisbury plant's ability to operate horizontally. In fact, the build-to-order process begins when a field sales engineer takes an order at a customer's site, enters it into a laptop computer, and transmits it to the plant in Salisbury.

The order arrives with all parameters specified: amperage, number of circuits, voltage, size and shape of panel box, and perhaps hundreds of other specifications each customer makes. Once logged in, the order proceeds to the production team, which evaluates its priority and sets a production schedule (a high-priority item can enter production immediately and be completed and shipped within 24 hours).

In the horizontal organization, everybody owns the end result and works in a fully coordinated environment. A linchpin in this coordination is the daily production meeting, where members from the various teams report their standing in relation to the daily production schedule to meet the customer requirements. Given this goal, the teams set about to decide how best to allocate personnel and materials for the next three shifts. In addition, team members share information about ideal production rates, sales dollars generated in a particular month, and, most important, customers' orders and the special needs each customer has.

Helping employees to keep abreast of the process is an electric scoreboard, fully visible to all on the shop floor. Here are recorded such things as the progress made on that day's orders and the number of panels completed. The teams have also added e-mail capability to keep one another informed about customers' expectations, the number of new orders, and any backlog. If one team—say, the box fabrication group—begins to fall behind in the schedule, the teams can quickly readjust themselves and send one or more members to join the problem group to take up the slack. "This is the advantage of multiskilling," says Milbrandt.

I would rather be on a team. If you have a problem, you have other people who will come and help you.

Opal Parnell, automated equipment operator

The build-to-order process continues to work smoothly because team members have authority to keep it that way and because they have developed a supportive culture that emphasizes trust, openness, and cooperation. They evaluate their peers' performance, order parts for the machinery as well as materials for the process, work with customers and suppliers, and test the quality of the products they make.

Let one emphasize, however, that none of these newfound responsibilities came easily into acceptance. All met initially with some resistance.

When the principles of the horizontal organization were first put to work, there were some people, even some who had seniority, who decided that they did not want to accept the new responsibilities. Thus, they either retired or found work elsewhere. Gradually, they've been able to recruit new people who are willing to take on more responsibility, work with others in a team setting, and make the decisions necessary for the process to run smoothly. Today, they all see that this is a large part of what makes the job so satisfying for workers.

The GE Salisbury experience offers a corrective to Weber's ideal of a highly productive bureaucracy that arises from the impersonal face of an organization structured along strictly hierarchical lines. Team members at the North Carolina plant exhibit an uncommon commitment to maintaining and continuously improving the high quality of their product. Evidence of their success lies not only in the premier place that GE Salisbury holds vis-à-vis other competitor companies, but also in the extraordinary degree of customer satisfaction that has been achieved.

The design principles of the horizontal organization are often well suited to a manufacturing process, even one as complex as that at the GE Salisbury plant where team members work to satisfy hundreds of customers with thousands of specific needs. As we will see in the next chapter, those same design principles also successfully underpin the horizontal organization of the Home Finance Division of Barclays Bank around an integrated sales and service delivery process. No matter which side of the Atlantic (or the Pacific) you explore, you will see the positive results of organizations, both public and private, that have taken the bold, courageous moves toward the horizontal organization.

7 ORGANIZING A DIVISION AROUND A SALES AND SERVICE DELIVERY PROCESS

BARCLAYS BANK'S HOME FINANCE DIVISION

In today's financial marketplace, banks no longer have a monopoly on the lending business. Just about anybody with a little extra money can, and does, offer credit. Automobile manufacturers, retailers, insurance conglomerates—a consumer can borrow money from most any business that comes to mind, and long-standing institutions like Barclays Bank have found that it is increasingly difficult to distinguish products in a marketplace of look-alikes.

Indeed, customers take the path of least "insistence." They choose the lender who offers the lowest interest rate or the biggest discount, and then jump to someone else just as soon as the short-term interest bargain lapses. The loyal customer is something of a rarity in this industry. As Michael Ockenden, managing director of Barclays Bank's Home Finance Division, puts it, "People come to you for price and leave you for price."

For mortgage lending in particular, the situation in the United Kingdom is clouded by the public mind-set: When the British think of buying a home, they think of the building society, an institution comparable to thrifts in the United States, but with a near lock on mortgage lending. "People just are not generally aware that banks do mortgages," says Ockenden.

It was in this crowded arena that Barclays first sought to achieve a standard of operational excellence in the early 1990s. Like many of its competitors, the Barclays Bank home mortgage operation was, to say the least, inefficient. Multiple layers of hierarchy, an inconsistent, fragmented approach to customers, unnecessary steps, delays, and hand-offs, as well as a lack of commitment, planning, and follow-through meant that it could take months to get the initial mortgage approved, three to four additional weeks to get a formal offer on the table, and still more time to clear the title and process the insurance. When all was said and done, moving from one house to another took four or five months. So in mid-1992, Barclays set out to differentiate itself by launching its "Being the Best" initiative.

Communication channels were opened up, clear business objectives were laid out, and the business processes were redesigned to improve efficiency and quality of service. Not surprisingly, turnaround times did improve. Borrowers received approvals within three days and a formal offer within a week. Yet, because mortgage lending is not a repeat business in the sense that people pop in every week to take out a loan (average time from one purchase to the next is seven years), operational excellence was, by itself, insufficient to capture a larger share of this price-dominated market.

Thus, Barclays decided to leverage its newfound strengths of speed, accuracy, and quality by developing an intensely customer-focused, integrated operation that would aim to become the preferred place for home financing by offering a value-added package. With that goal in mind, Barclays Home Finance Division (HFD) was formed in April 1995 as a strategic business unit within the Personal Sector of the Barclays Group.

The Value Proposition

Armed with research showing that moving from one house to another ranks third behind death and divorce in terms of the amount of stress it generates, Barclays determined that it could achieve its objective of "being the best" and winning customers by delivering "a total solution that de-stresses the home ownership process." Using that unique value proposition as its guide and recognizing that structure has to follow strategy, Barclays HFD undertook the task of organizing itself horizontally around an end-to-end mortgage sales and service delivery process.

"We were 45,000 people in various disconnected groups or functions, each with its own strategy and business objectives, but we had nothing that integrated the various parts of the Home Finance Division," Ockenden recalls of the former functionally organized home mortgage operation. The loose confederation of geographically separated enterprises was organized chiefly around traditional business functions that included:

- Underwriting, the initial processing that received mortgage applications and began a lengthy investigation of creditworthiness

- Risk management, a division based in London that set the parameters for lending (while actual risk approval was taking place in over 2,000 local facilities)

- Marketing, a business function centered in Coventry that handled other products besides mortgages

- Processing and information technology, a Manchester-based function

- People management, which was controlled from London

The actual delivery of service in the old operation included initial processing, which meant taking applications as they came through the door and dealing with them to the point where they were actually established as a loan. The loan was then handed off to mortgage services, which was concerned with maintaining the account and making sure that it was not redeemed or moved elsewhere. Mortgage services also provided customer support and help, such as answering any questions. Finally, a third area—referred to as customer assistance—actually dealt with defaults. Each of those areas required employees with very different and specific skill sets. As Gregory O'Mahony, project manager for enterprise design, observes, "There was little or no flexibility for managers and our people to work within each of those stovepipes. It was very difficult to balance the supply to the demand."

Today, Barclays has made significant steps toward formally reorganizing around a cross-functional, end-to-end sales and service delivery process in which one salesperson working with a team handles a home loan from start to finish. At this point, multifunctional, multiskilled service delivery teams comprising sanction officers, risk advisers, and administrators who handle account opening and maintenance are set up in four different regions. Eventually, the teams will include salespeople (also called "mortgage specialists") and customer assistants, and will operate in 12 regions all across Britain.

An intriguing part of the Barclays HFD vision is the value-added "extras" available to mortgage customers with their loans. Recognizing that there was practically a 100 percent inverse correlation between a product's price and market share (that is, a 5 percent rise in price has a predictable 5 percent decrease in market share), Barclays focuses on differentiating its product by the range and integration of services offered to attract and retain customers. After analyzing the elements that make home ownership so emotionally trying, it now offers title guarantee, legal services, and moving assistance. If the customer wishes, the HFD can even switch on the utilities at the customer's new location, arrange to have the grass mowed and the garden tended, or write into the loan a provision for painting the house in five years. It is the customer's choice: Select the services, and the costs will be written into the monthly mortgage payment.

Also intriguing is the way Barclays HFD now designs payments around individual needs. Young families appreciate the option of skipping a mortgage payment in August after a summer vacation or in December when holiday giving strains pocketbooks. Loyalty is rewarded, too. After five years of faithful mortgage payments, customers become eligible for a six-month hiatus; a ten-year record with Barclays HFD gives customers the option of skipping an *entire year* of mortgage payments. These added options appeal to customers who recognize that predicaments such as job loss or major medical expenses can disrupt even the most stable lives, or to those who may wish to take a sabbatical or change careers. In short, in an industry where *distress* is the expectation, Barclays HFD, by delivering a range of services, is de-stressing the process of home ownership from beginning to end.

This part of the HFD value proposition could never have been achieved by the fragmented functions of the old vertical structure. Under the new structure, however, the team's cross-functionality enables it to deliver this range of services. As we will see in the next section, team members from various areas of mortgage financing bring their expertise to bear on each customer's special needs or requests.

Early Results of Organizing Horizontally

Currently the sixth-largest mortgage business in the United Kingdom, the company is meeting its goal of increasing national market share by at least one percentage point each year. This figure represents approximately an 18 percent increase in revenues and a 20 percent increase in profits since the reorganization began. What is more, Barclays is beating the competition by spending less—£70 million, or the equivalent of about $123 million—to generate new customers; other industry leaders are spending significantly higher sums (£82–95 million, equivalent to some $143–166 million) to capture an equal share of the market. As for turn-around time on mortgage applications, Barclays HFD issues more than 95 percent of formal offers within 24 hours, and its current record for processing a mortgage application and delivering the money into the customer's hands is a mere *three days*. That speed, of course, helps relieve the customer's anxiety, which increases with every day he or she has to wait for a loan approval.

Barclays HFD has achieved many of these successes by initiating its restructuring along the horizontal lines shown in Fig. 7.1. Although it is still very much in the process of transformation, it is committed to completing the redesign ultimately to match the structure depicted here, and has already completed significant steps toward that end. Two key operations, sales marketing and service delivery, are being combined into a single end-to-end core process labeled as "Sales/Service Delivery." Empowered teams of employees are grouped according to the 12 geographical regions so as to provide the best understanding of the customers being served.

The teams' accountability for achieving end-to-end performance goals is illustrated in the chart by the lines that extend from the large circle to the ends of the process arrow. Selected from various areas of the Home Finance Division, the team members bring valuable skills and degrees of expertise to bear on the work of the process. What is more, the teams

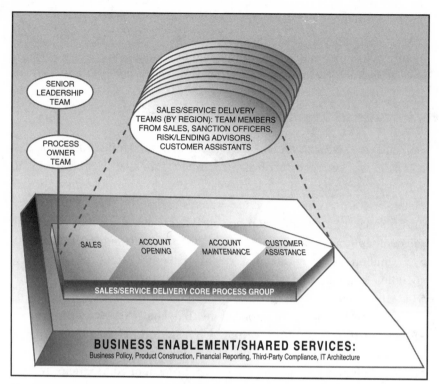

Fig. 7.1 Barclays Bank—Home Financial Division. The figure shows how the Home Financial Division intends ultimately to be organized.

already supporting areas as diverse as Manchester, Coventry, Leeds, and London take responsibility for their geographical regions by setting performance objectives and measuring the extent of successful compliance.

In complex processes such as sales and service delivery for home financing, these teams of ten or twelve people require the support of functions in order to perform its work efficiently. Thus, aspects of the vertical organization remain in place at Barclays HFD to support the horizontally organized teams in the performance of their work. Labeled in Fig. 7.1 as "Business Enablement/Shared Services," the block includes nonhorizontal services shared with other divisions of Barclays, such as third-party compliance, the finance area, and IT architecture. These business functions are to the sales/service delivery process what the stationary board is to the moving pieces in a game of Parcheesi or Monopoly.

A fourteen-member team of leaders "owns" the process in the sense that they take responsibility for keeping the various teams clearly focused on delivering the value proposition—which, of course, means making sure the teams provide the speedy, accurate, and financially viable sanction of mortgages to qualifying customers who will also receive the numerous added-value benefits described above. The process owners also make sure that—unlike the situation that existed in the vertical hierarchy, where multiple departments had multiple goals and multiple measures of success—the metrics are consistent across the units. The process owners determine whether the performance objectives of the two teams are in line with the overall strategy set by the senior leadership team, to whom they answer. This traditional line of reporting is represented by the placement of the senior management team above the process owners. The connecting line shows the hierarchical arrangement of authority implicit in the traditional vertical organizational chart.

Those top managers—Mike Ockenden plus the leaders of service delivery, sales and marketing, and business enablement—are responsible for overall business performance and for making sure that the HFD is delivering its value proposition. Ockenden also looks to his senior managers to develop an external focus that allows them to benchmark Barclays vis-à-vis the competition. These senior managers, however, are not faceless names on closed oak doors. In the Barclays corporate culture, nobody has a private office, nor are there executive parking spaces. Every employee sits in the same size chair behind the same size desk. Titles are forbidden, and people use first names when they address one another. In short, democratization at Barclays has a viable, tangible presence, which promotes a corporate culture that values everyone's contributions.

Corporate Culture . . .
It's trying to create a spirit that says we are all one group of people working towards the customer imperative.

Mike Ockenden, Barclays HFD managing director

An informally structured leadership team with representatives from all over the division acts as an interface with the rest of the Barclays organization and serves as HFD's agent of change. In the latter role, its members are expected to model desired behavior throughout the organization. Once or twice a year, all 50 or 60 members come together as a group, but much more frequently they network with one another when the need arises. All report into and are enabled by the senior management team.

A Flatter Hierarchy

Hierarchy has been flattened throughout the organization by redesigning and restructuring roles and eliminating much non-value-added work, by integrating work flows, and by vesting decision making in lower levels. In the service-delivery operation, for example, what were 45 different roles four years ago have been compressed to around ten roles today. Pat Flanagan, the director of service delivery, believes that broadening duties and responsibilities increases the teams' ownership of the end-to-end process, which, in turn, translates to greater flexibility.

Although bringing people together on teams establishes their real-world presence, merely situating them in one office or forcing everyone to sit around a single table does not make them function as a real team. The true cross-functionality of the team manifests itself in the effectiveness of collaboration, the common spirit of cooperation, and the regard for others that the members themselves develop as they learn how to relinquish their hold on proprietary issues and matters of personal "turf." Thus, a specialist in risk management, who might otherwise be restricted to evaluating a mortgage application according to strict numerical requirements, can gain a more complete understanding of the applicant with information provided by sales representatives, sanction officers, and customer assistants. Decision-making guidelines are still provided to the teams, of course, but the more complete picture and understanding of the applicant situation granted by the cross-functional approach enables the team to render decisions that more effectively optimize risk and revenue objectives, for example.

To instill the behaviors and values central to the horizontal organization, all 800 HFD employees go through a formal team learning process designed by Human Resources. The first stage involves basic training in how teams work together, personality profiling, and preferred learning styles. After mastering the theoretical principles of the team-oriented approach, people break into groups and spend three days off-site, exploring how the team dynamic works in practice. Further classroom work and a team project related to a business issue that cuts across the entire organization wrap up the first stage of training.

The second stage, aimed primarily at the senior leadership team, involves dilemma management techniques, cognitive mapping, and methods of stakeholder management.

We encourage people to develop themselves. We offer a series of support mechanisms to help people to learn.

Steve Morris, HFD resources manager

Skills training at Barclays HFD extends far beyond team-building specifics. A list of the courses, books, interactive videos, workshops, and one-on-one coaching available to employees runs to 50 entries and ranges from communication skills to leadership techniques to change management methodologies. Ockenden unequivocally supports providing training—be it development or skills—for anyone who wants it, so long as it helps that employee perform a job better: "If somebody comes to me and says that, for finger dexterity so that he or she can better operate a [computer] terminal, that person has to go to the local college and learn how to knit, then I will give them that training."

Ockenden points out that it is not unusual for the bank to invite 1,000 employees in the personal banking facility to attend a conference in Birmingham, where they study market trends and review quarterly financial statistics. He best captures the HFD attitude toward training when he notes that besides increasing job satisfaction, this cross-training has helped the team slice repossession losses in half. How? More efficient handling of customer problems for one thing, and avoiding the information loss that so often accompanies a handoff. Also peer competition naturally grows among team members and spurs them to better their performance.

The division is prepared to help people master the right skills in order to execute their responsibilities more effectively. For example, to enable empowered teams to make correct lending decisions, Barclays HFD provides a structured training course that involves basic lending principles. That is followed by what is known as "after care," in which team members sit with a lending manager for two or three weeks, talk through all their cases, and receive coaching on the spot. The aim is to develop analytical skills that will allow a team member to weigh pros and cons of cases and decide whether the divisions should approve a loan application.

Five years ago, the organization didn't just discourage people from thinking, it told them not to because there were lots of rules that did that for them and lots of managers to tell them what to do. Now, the organization says, "Don't come to work unless you're prepared to think."

Mike Ockenden, managing director of Barclays HFD

Basically, there are only two hard-and-fast policy rules in mortgage lending: (1) Can the customer afford the loan; and (2) has the customer demonstrated that he or she will repay the money. Team members learn to analyze a potential borrower's ability and character using the applicant's financial statement, credit report, and bank accounts. They can also access a help file that provides a set of guidelines to be used in specific cases, such as an applicant's looking to rent out the mortgaged property.

Bringing all the departments together and having an overall view of the whole process has allowed us to give each individual more responsibility for decision making because they are more aware of the full process, exactly what happens at every step.

Steve Wilson, HFD service delivery manager for customer assistance

---

An interesting result of this new empowered lending atmosphere—and indicative of how horizontal principles promote continuous improvement—is that team members who are handling the end-to-end process, from application stage to sending out the money, maintain their interest in and oversight of individual cases six, nine, and twelve months later. Gathering that information allows Barclays HFD to set up feedback loops so that front-end behavior can be adjusted if necessary.

In the area of customer assistance (also known as arrears), collections once comprised six different teams. As Steve Wilson, service delivery manager describes it, "What we tended to find was a lot of handoffs. Basically, if you answered a phone call and there was work to do afterward—you might find that a customer sent a piece of correspondence in—then the correspondence section would deal with it and not the telephone section. The responsibility belonged to someone else."

Today, multiskilling has reduced six teams involved in collections to just one. And quite often, the same person who takes the phone call will deal with a customer from the first unpaid pence all the way back to the customer's not being in arrears anymore; or, when that outcome fails to materialize, the process continues all the way to the point at which foreclosure—the least desirable solution, in Barclays' view as well as the customer's—seems to be the only way out. Before that alternative is taken, however, HFD representatives do everything they can to help customers meet obligations. For instance, a representative can identify customers who are paying more mortgage than necessary, then visit them in their homes to help them understand ways they can save money on payments. If a customer appears interested, the representative can say, "We've pre-approved you for the line of credit, and you can have the schedule in place for the next month's payment." In contrast to complex refinancing arrangements required by mortgage lenders in the United States and elsewhere, this service makes Barclays the envy of industry leaders.

A Partnership with Human Resources

In an unusual twist for a top executive, Mike Ockenden is also accountable for Human Resources, what he likes to call the "people initiative." He meets regularly with the director of Human Resources, reviews progress, discusses any problems on various projects, and works closely with this functional part of the division to make sure that it is a value-added part of the overall process. Human Resources has input on strategic decisions, offering its assessment of how they might affect its own policies and processes and how in turn they can help support the (division's) strategy.

A fine example of its integrated role within the organization is the performance management system that it devised at Ockenden's behest and in conjunction with representatives from every area of the business. In order to link performance management with the overall organization's strategic objectives, everyone (Ockenden included) comes up with a personal development plan that outlines what he or she will specifically do to make goals a reality. "Our senior managers say, 'This is where we're going, folks,' " explains Sarah Moody, Human Resources manager. "And our people say, 'Okay, this is how I think I can help us to get there.' "

Besides setting personal objectives, employees decide with Human Resources how their progress will be measured. Will it be through time, quality, quantity? Every quarter, employees sit down with a Human Resources representative to review objectives and make sure they are on track. Plans can be changed if they prove to be too easy or too hard. At the end of the year, employees are graded equally on what they achieved and the behaviors they exhibited along the way. The results of this assessment, in conjunction with a 360-degree appraisal comprising feedback from colleagues, supervisors, and customers, affect both regular pay and year-end bonuses.

This personal development system, then, not only solidifies the Human Resource function's role as a partner in the overall process, it also demonstrates how the horizontal organization holds employees accountable for achieving performance objectives. The new structure grants them more authority, but it links their evaluations and rewards to their achievements.

As a rather extraordinary aside to the new design, Ockenden not only develops his own personal plan, he also willingly shares his profile and evaluation with everyone in the organization. His behavior illustrates how a leader sets an example in order to promote corporate values of trust, openness, and cooperation.

Some of Ockenden's leadership roles are more traditional, of course. He makes strategic decisions as to where and how Barclays HFD will compete, coordinating the work of the sales and service process delivery teams. He also monitors the organization's performance, but he believes that the criteria for success in a horizontal organization are different than those in the traditional vertical hierarchy. He looks first at the customer imperative—what customers think about Barclays HFD, how it is performing, and whether added value is being delivered consistently. He also considers risk performance and financial returns to stakeholders, as one might expect, but a third, not-so-typical element of measurement has been added that involves regular "temperature-taking": How do *employees* feel about the organization? Do they feel they are making a significant contribution? Do they enjoy their work? Do they respect co-workers? "These are the cornerstones of the way we measure ourselves now," he says.

If the comments of Barclays HFD employees are any indication, most of them feel quite pleased to be working in an empowered, cross-functional, team-based horizontal organization.

I definitely like [the horizontal organization] better. I feel like it's a lot more fun now. It's a lot more open. I feel like I'm adding value now.
                    Sue Ward, HFD service delivery leader for the Southeast region

---

Echoing Sue Ward, the service delivery leader for Barclays' Southeast region, many employees described their work life as "a lot more fun" these days. And although Martin Johnson, service delivery leader for the Premier mortgage product, admitted to feeling less secure because his role is still evolving, he readily acknowledged that "it's much better than the old way and I wouldn't want to go back. I can see that the actions that I take and my team takes actually make a difference and increase the number of sales that we do. In the old way, I didn't feel as though that was even on my radar chart."

Ockenden works hard to let people know they make a difference. Sometimes that means just stopping by an employee's desk to offer a compliment on a job well done. But he also seeks to foster a culture of values and purpose that lets employees know that learning experiences are important and mistakes are okay, so long as they are not the result of negligence or repeated errors and are used as learning experiences. He tells a story about the time the computer system crashed at 3:30 on a Friday afternoon, one of the busiest periods for completing mortgages for customers wanting to move on the weekend. With concerned employees fluttering around his desk offering reassurances that things would be "fixed," Ockenden chose to confront the employee responsible for information technology. Shaking in his boots because he expected to be reprimanded, that employee must have been stunned when Ockenden asked him his name and then said, "John, I would like to thank you for pointing out the biggest single systems weakness we have in this business that could damage our relationship with our customers. Now that we know what it is, we can fix it and it will never happen again. Thanks very much, indeed."

This example could not have been lost on the many other employees who witnessed Ockenden's behavior. Without making a speech or circulating a directive, Ockenden let them know that, as he puts it, "if the wrong thing happens for the right reason, I don't mind as long as we make sure there's not a second time."

To me, the most reengineering you need to do is of mindsets. If you reengineer the mindsets, then people will change the process appropriately to meet the customer imperative, whether it's a big or a small change.

Mike Ockenden, HFD managing director

In today's technologically advanced but still imperfect world, where customer service sometimes takes on the elements of an absurdist drama (who has not tried to resolve a customer service issue by telephone, only to be shunted from operator to operator, perhaps being cut off in the midst of a transfer?), Barclays HFD has set its sights on a much higher level of performance. From its "touch and resolve" service, whereby a customer who calls with a question or complaint will receive an answer or a resolution in a single contact with a team member, to one-stop, no-hassle shopping for products ranging from homeowner's insurance, to utilities management, to property assessments, Barclays is singing a multitextured, polyphonic song that customers like to hear. It is determined to become the first choice in home finance, selecting the principles of horizontal organization as its means of transport to that ultimate destination. And the Barclays experience to date, though still in the early stages, indicates that success is well within its grasp. Horizontal design can deliver a winning value proposition on either side of the Atlantic.

As we will see in the next chapter, the Xerox Corporation has taken horizontal design to even more complex levels, expanding its reach practically company-wide. Although major portions of Xerox remain vertical and have their own internal functions, the corporation has developed what in effect is a "hybrid" organizational structure, part vertical and part horizontal, and integrated the new with the old so seamlessly that the new Xerox has given all stakeholders much to be excited about.

8 ORGANIZING AN ENTIRE COMPANY HORIZONTALLY
XEROX

Among our examples, Xerox stands apart because the initial moves in its transformation started in a series of changes that date back to 1982, when Xerox found itself in what Chairman and CEO Paul Allaire calls "deep trouble." Facing stiff opposition in the document and facsimile market for the first time—primarily from Japanese competitors—Xerox needed to undergo fundamental change in order to maintain its hold on the market. In one of the first well-documented examples of an American company applying total quality management to a large degree, Xerox began a quality initiative that focused, in part, on changing processes.

Allaire set an extraordinary goal for the new Xerox when he took over the reins of the company as CEO in 1990: to become the best company in its industry and one of the best companies in the world. In this phase of its journey, the company focused all its efforts on being world-class, emphasizing especially its productivity and the quality of its products and services. The key, as Allaire saw it, was to get all employees to utilize their capabilities. There would have to be a tremendous shift in the way the company defined its "business": Xerox would no longer view itself as only a "copier" company, but rather as a "document" company, so that it could meet the challenges of digital technology.

By 1992, Xerox found itself standing on the precipice of truly transformational change. Confronted with, in Allaire's words, a "crisis of opportunity," the company determined that it could not take advantage of new markets so long as it remained organized primarily around departmental functions and mired in a complex hierarchy with many handoffs and approval mechanisms. In short, its corporate structure had become an important impediment to its success. In order to grow, it determined that it had to change to a more horizontal, process-oriented company.

On the one hand, we see attractive markets, and we have superior technology. On the other hand, we won't be able to take advantage of this situation unless we can overcome cumbersome, functionally driven bureaucracy and use our quality process to become more productive.

Paul Allaire, chairman and CEO of Xerox Corporation

As Allaire explains, "We were a $10 billion-plus organization [now $18.2 billion], and we were functional in nature. So every function—sales, service, administrative, manufacturing, engineering, research and development—all came up the line and, in the end, reported to me. Short of ordering office supplies and conducting minor day-to-day activities, I was the only one responsible for anything in its entirety."

If a product went to market and did not succeed, there was no clear way to see what went wrong. Finger-pointing and shifting the blame were inevitable. People in the manufacturing division contended they had merely followed the orders of engineers, who, in turn, said they did only what those in product design and marketing had requested. Marketing blamed salespeople, who insisted they could not sell something the customer never wanted in the first place. "The only one responsible for the failure of that product, therefore, was me," Allaire says.

> The functional organization was not going to give us the new world that we had to get to.
>
> Hector J. Motroni, vice president of human relations at Xerox

The stage was set for the major transformation that would produce a more fully integrated, horizontal organization—a new Xerox. But first the company had to identify its value proposition and restate it in such a way that it would be clear to all stakeholders, as well as the public at large, and serve as the beacon marking the company's voyage to its destination. Recognized later for its achievements, Xerox received a Baldrige award in 1989 for having instituted company-wide management processes, extensive problem-solving capabilities, and quality management systems. In 1997 the company received a second Baldrige award in the services category.

The Value Proposition

As examples in previous chapters have demonstrated, a horizontal makeover is impossible without first formulating the unique set of benefits that will make customers choose one company over its competitors. What value could Xerox offer that would entice customers to come to it for their document solutions? The "Xerox 2005 Strategic Intent" statement expressed the company's mission this way: "Xerox, *The Document Company,* will be the leader in the global document market providing Document Solutions that enhance business productivity."[1] The company more specifically defined its objective as a promise to provide unique value by offering leading-edge products using privileged technology that are of the highest quality and deliver total document solutions quickly and reliably. Going several steps beyond its competition, the company also offered top-quality software, hardware, and service solutions backed by ongoing customer support and continuing business process improvements.

As Allaire accurately recognized, delivering the total solution described in that value proposition required that the business be reorganized into a number of horizontal, cross-functional groups organized around work flows. Theorists have identified the importance of companies understanding their "value chain"—the stream of activities a company performs in designing, producing, marketing, delivering, and supporting its products and services—and how the activities in the chain are performed and interact as sources of competitive advantage.[2] In the variation applied at Xerox, the company elected to focus on the activities it needed in order to design and deliver value to its customers. Rather than splitting up those activities into discrete functions and assigning each to a separate department, it chose to organize itself around the entire chain. In the variation applied at Xerox, the company organized these activities around sets of two linked teams—Business Group teams and Customer Operations Group teams—which together carry out the work of the value chain.

An Integrated Composite of Mini-Businesses

Fig. 8.1 depicts the new Xerox, an organization of four divisions: Corporate Finance, Business Operations, Customer Operations (now called a group), and Corporate Research and Technology. Insofar as each business division reports to an executive vice president who, in turn, reports to CEO Allaire and new president and COO Richard Thoman, Xerox 2005 is a vertical organization. But beneath the level of executive vice president, the organization takes on an entirely new face. After an initial transformation in the late 1980s, Xerox management sought to move decision making out of the corporate center and into Business Divisions and the Customer Operations Division, which could operate across the organization and accept end-to-end responsibility for supply management, products, and services. In order to inspire an entrepreneurial spirit among employees, increase customer responsiveness, decrease time to market, and thereby enhance its competitive advantage, Xerox empowered employees to break down the walls of the traditional vertical organization.

In 1996, the company made further refinements to this structure. Specifically, it streamlined Business Operations into the five Business Groups shown in the white boxes in the lower half of the chart in Fig. 8.1. In addition, the Customer Operations Division was renamed the Customer

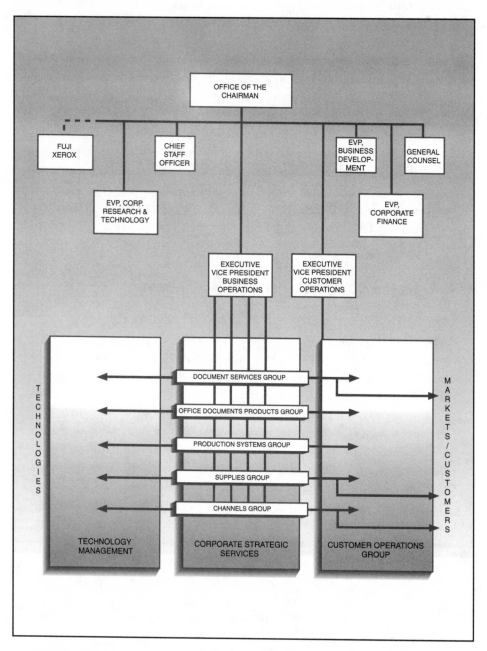

Fig. 8.1 Xerox 2005: The Hybrid Organization Chart

Operations Group and placed under an executive vice president with direct reporting to CEO Allaire.

The new Business Operations Groups constitute what Allaire calls "mini-businesses," which have been integrated into the Xerox 2005 design. A specialized arm of the Xerox Corporation, each mini-business devotes its attention to meeting its own objectives (formed in conjunction with those of the whole company), developing its special products and services, serving its customers, and exceeding financial expectations. Each mini-business is composed of a number of multiskilled, empowered teams or linked chains of teams focused on the value chain, including business planning, product design and development, manufacturing, marketing, sales, distribution, and customer service and support. And as a mini-business, each accounts for all of its own profits and losses, engages in contracts and agreements with third parties outside Xerox, and cooperates with other business groups within the company.

Business Operations Groups thus work in conjunction with the Customer Operations Group (each reports to an executive vice president as illustrated in Fig. 8.1). Supported by Corporate Strategic Services, for example, the five cross-disciplined business units form the vital organs of the new organization: the Document Services Group (DSG), the Office Document Products Groups (ODPG), the Production Systems Group (PSG), the Supplies Group, and the Channels Group.

These five groups are further subdivided into cross-disciplinary teams headed by general managers who act as core process owners and who take responsibility for seeing that performance objectives are met. The teams—individually or collectively, depending on the situation—have end-to-end accountability for taking an idea through all the stages necessary to produce a marketable product. That is, the teams have the information, training, and authority to undertake tasks that traditionally would have been divided among separate, multi-level functional departments. For example, some linked teams can themselves go directly to the market through their own sales forces or channel delivery units. This authority is pictorially represented in Fig. 8.1 by the lower branches of the bifurcated arrows that extend *across* the Customer Operations Group directly to markets and customers. The upper branch, extending into Customer Operations, indicates that the group in question can also work directly with the Customer Operations Group in delivering its own products and services.

Each business group depicted in Fig. 8.1 focuses on a different market or handles a special set of products and services. The Document Services Group (DSG), for example, takes responsibility for large accounts. It develops and delivers a number of services to big clients, such as document consulting, process reengineering, and the integration of document systems. The latter includes the design, installation, and support of local and wide-area networks (LANs and WANs, in the parlance of information technology).

Although Fig. 8.1 does not go into such detail, there exist four business units within the DSG itself, each of which is responsible for a product or service offering. These include Xerox Business Services, the Document Solutions Unit, the Software Solutions Unit, and the Network Services Unit. Because the business activities for each unit can change rapidly, the structure must remain flexible. Some units are large; others, small. Some units are self-contained; others invite experts to join the team as needed. And even the number of these business units can increase or decrease as markets and customers change.

The new Xerox, the organizational skeleton of which is depicted in Fig. 8.1, is a hybrid organization that takes advantage of both vertical and horizontal approaches. Although the top managerial layers remain vertical, responsibility for daily operations, productivity, marketing, customer relations, and other traditional functions now resides within horizontally aligned groups that have the support of the entire company behind them. This structure affords each group tremendous leverage in working with clients and suppliers, in reaching out to new markets, and in becoming more efficient and profitable.

The Horizontal Aspect of the New Xerox

Each of the five groups follows the same basic procedure in handling issues that fall within that group's province. After first identifying a customer's needs, team members determine what technologies exist both inside and outside of Xerox to help meet them. They consider competition and cost structure, as well as the feasibility of bringing out a new product or adding new features to an existing one in order to satisfy a customer's needs. Cross-functionality enables group members to ascertain how they can efficiently manufacture, advertise, and bring a product to market.

"They have total responsibility for a piece of Xerox in a worldwide sense," says Allaire. "The team's general manager has very much the same kind of responsibility I have. Basically, they make all the decisions from the beginning right to the end. They're close to their customers, and somebody can always be held accountable."

Accountability at Xerox means that people are assessed on both a results and a behavioral matrix. According to James Lesko, president of Xerox Supplies Group and a corporate vice president, Allaire devised the model and is quite adamant about the importance of the behavioral element. Low behavior and low performance means definite dismissal, as does poor behavior with medium performance. Interestingly enough, a poor performance if accompanied by medium-level behavior will not activate the hook. The employee so evaluated, however, will receive coaching and perhaps an opportunity to relocate to another group. Good performance plus good behavior, on the other hand, puts an employee in line for rewards and forms the basis of a compensation model aligned with and supported by the eight dimensions of the Xerox corporate culture (see sidebar).

The role of empowered workers on cross-functional teams is more demanding and obviously requires new skills and competencies. Jim Lesko says that the need for superior technical skills is much higher at Xerox since the transformation, just as there is increased need for general manager skills (particularly a strong financial understanding) for team leaders. Accordingly, the company has set up a process to assess which skills individuals lack and give them the training they need to meet those new challenges.

Skills training includes quarterly sessions for team managers in which speakers from outside Xerox talk about industry best practices or technological changes, or presidents of other horizontally oriented companies share their experiences. Key representatives from the various Xerox operating groups are selected by their peers to attend sessions at the corporate training center in Leesburg, Virginia.

Since the horizontal realignment, many more people at many more levels, down to and including secretaries, participate in sliding-scale in-

Xerox 2005: Cultural Dimensions

1. Market connected

2. Action oriented

3. Absolute results oriented

4. Line driven

5. Team oriented

6. Empowered people

7. Open, honest communications

8. Organization reflection and learning

---

centive bonus plans. The bonus is tied to the organization's goals as measured by both customer satisfaction surveys and financial results. Surveys conducted worldwide assess how satisfied Xerox customers are with products and how the company stacks up against the competition. The financial measure varies by position, but it is based on profit or revenue growth or on cash and asset management.

Customers don't care about your functional silos. Customers care about what you're giving them, how you're addressing their problems.

Norman E. Rickard, Jr., president, Xerox Document Services Group

Managers also receive evaluations reflecting, in part, how satisfied the people who work under them are. Each year employees report their levels of satisfaction in terms of four work parameters, listed here from largest to smallest: corporate, group, team, and individual. Managers meet with employees to address concerns and agree upon a plan for improving relationships and behavior. Each year both managers and frontline employees who meet objectives receive appropriate bonuses or other recognition. While such mechanisms allow for monetary rewards, an equally significant product is the increased sense of power and participation that employees feel in the horizontally oriented organization. No longer do they feel as if they have to avoid criticism of their supervisors or their peers and keep suggestions to themselves about how to improve operations.

Instead of handing out $25 checks, we have a dinner once every three months in order to recognize those people who have contributed significantly to solving a customer's problem or helping out a team. There's no limit to how much recognition we can give and the thanks we can show.

Norman E. Rickard, Jr., president, Xerox Document Services Group

---

Because the horizontal model empowers the workforce and fosters a culture of openness and cooperation, it promotes a greater sense of contentment among frontline workers. At Xerox the satisfaction scores for employees are at or near the top of the industry.

A New Role for Remaining Vertical Segments of the Organization

Extending throughout the hybridized structure, although not apparent in the organizational schematic, are many vertical enabling processes such as the time-to-market process, the integrated supply chain, the market-to-collection process, and customer service. People do not actually reside within these enabling processes, but there are process champions who are charged with making sure that they work effectively.

Time-to-market, for example, provides product development support by helping teams do a better job of taking an idea, evolving it, and bringing it to manufacturing. One of its responsibilities is to maintain engineering excellence. To this end, the champion developed a plan under which all engineers on Xerox's 40-plus teams follow a common process for designing products. This commonality ensures that each engineer has access to technical tools shared across the company and allows for easier movement of engineers between different teams as customer demands require.

In an Asian joint venture called "Japan 50/50," for instance, Xerox and a Japanese company work in similar engineering environments that allow Xerox to take designs from the partner company and manufacture those products in Xerox factories.

As is true at other organizations discussed in this book, Xerox engages in activities—specifically, research and product delivery (which encompasses sales)—that continue to be functionally organized. These remain as functions because of the nature of the work and also because they must maintain needed economies of scale in skills to sustain leading-edge expertise and technical knowledge.

The research function's primary responsibility (Xerox makes a distinction between "pure" research and product development), for example, is to develop new technologies that are restricted neither to a single market nor to a specific time frame. Xerox does not want its PhDs hemmed in by next year's market demands. The technological options must be flexible and numerous enough to allow each of the business teams to draw from them. The innovations might be in computer science or color technology, but the options will be such that various teams can find ways to use them in their products. To maintain and replenish technical expertise, Xerox also supports special interest groups and makes both best-practices information and extensive course work available on its IT network comprising six intranets. Planning for this internal communications network took seven months (April-October 1996) as the company surveyed each business unit on such matters as its expected returns on investment, the products and services it would make available on the website, its security requirements, and its measures for tracking usage by and applications to both employees and customers.

Since October 1995, the Field Information Research Systems Team (FIRST), located in Lewisville, Texas, has managed one intranet site for Xerox. That site logged approximately 75,000 hits a month, enabling over 25,000 field representatives, salespeople, and other Xerox employees to find and retrieve the kinds of information they need to solve customers' problems and increase sales by means of sharing best-practices information. According to one count, during the Memorial Day weekend of 1997,

Xerox employees and managers downloaded files from a FIRST site near-ly 4,500 times.[3]

The reasoning behind leaving product delivery as a function stems from Xerox's desire to present one face to the customer. If a customer has a need for ten different office products that come from ten different business groups, that customer does not want ten different Xerox technical representatives coming around to handle the business, Allaire says. Or, if products break down, one technician should have the expertise to fix whatever needs fixing. Similarly, when a sales representative makes a call on a customer, the customer often does not know exactly which product he or she needs. Both efficiency and the customer relationship suffer if the salesperson has to say, "I'm sorry, I'm from Business X, and it turns out you need Product Y. I can't sell you that so you'll have to wait until my colleague can stop in."

Before our transformation, many of our functional units had the attitude of "not invented here." Our Palo Alto Research Center (PARC) pushed hard for us to move into new PC icon applications, but much of this never made it out to the customer because no one along the value chain thought it was important. That would eventually prove very profitable for Microsoft, Apple, and IBM.

Hector J. Motroni, vice president of human relations and corporate vice president of Xerox

---

Xerox does recognize, however, that differentiation by expertise is sometimes necessary. Thus, on the sales side, there are broad distinctions between printing system, production system, and copy duplicator sales representatives, and they are supported by color specialists, systems specialists, and so forth. Reporting lines, however, do connect up through the same leaders.

In the case of the research function, Xerox has implemented various mechanisms to make sure that new ideas do not lead to "an output looking for a customer," as Jim Lesko calls it. The technology decision-making board is the prime vehicle for bringing new opportunities into the business groups, but Xerox also makes use of a business development forum, comprising the group presidents, the heads of corporate research and of strategy, and some leading technical experts, as well as a team to assess industry trends and help determine where future investment dollars should be directed so as to align pure research profitably with the needs of business.

Xerox also has worked to make the research arm much more customer-oriented. Whereas the technical wizards once viewed their job as just developing interesting technology, now they interact with internal customers in the business groups as well as with external customers so that they can better understand what the needs are. This newfound connection means that technologists, spotting areas of opportunity among certain customers, might now suggest that a business group move a product to market more quickly or use their understanding to redirect a line of research.

Both of the remaining functions, in fact, well understand that they must work as effective partners in process performance. As Lesko says, "The functional parts recognize that their survival depends on providing value to the organization at this horizontal team level. They now have to ask themselves, 'How do I become a world-class supplier of my functional expertise to these teams?' " And if they don't? The teams will look outside to find what they need.

There's a tension between a totally separate [horizontal] business team and a group that is more functionally oriented with expertise in a particular area. The right mix of the horizontal and the vertical is something you struggle with.

Paul Allaire, CEO, Xerox Corporation

Impressive Results at the New Xerox

Allaire thought at the outset of the restructuring that these mini-businesses might be able to respond faster and more effectively to customer needs. He was right: Since 1992, not only has Xerox increased its presence in markets where it had formerly had little or no visibility (for example, personal products and color copiers), but the company has also launched an impressive array of some 170 new products in six years. That increased market presence has been visible on the bottom line, too: Between 1991 and 1996, earnings per share shot up almost threefold, while revenues per employee increased one and a half times.

Results are not always measured in dollars and new products, however. More subtle changes have taken root in the fertile soil of the new Xerox's corporate culture. Employees report a much higher sense of satisfaction with their work, their greater responsibility, and the more immediate response from customers whose problems they solve. Moreover, these employees find that with the new skills Xerox helps them acquire, they can have an even greater impact on the company's ability to develop new products, reach out to new markets, and attain stretch goals.

In addition to new skill sets, working in an empowered environment requires a certain mind-set. Managers must learn to look not just at functional responsibilities; instead, they must take a holistic view of the business. Lesko notes that Xerox encourages both managers and team members to work and think proactively in an open, cooperative, and collaborative environment. They have to leave behind the mindset that an employee first seeks permission to work on an idea or problem.

The Personal Copier Success Story

Indicative of how the 12 principles for designing and institutionalizing the horizontal organization work in a mutually supportive way to improve speed, flexibility, and quality is the story of Xerox's personal copier product. Prior to 1992, when Xerox created its personal document products division, the company was a distant player in a market dominated by foreign companies and a handful of domestic ones. But by 1996, it had emerged as number one in market share of personal copiers sold through retail outlets in the United States. (In 1997, the personal document products division became part of the Channels Group, shown in Fig. 8.1, which now comprises three business units: Channel Operations, the Networked Products Unit, and the Personal Products Unit. The latter business unit has responsibility for personal copiers and several other products designed for individuals and small businesses.)

When Xerox began its personal copier initiative, its experience in that marketplace per se was limited, but through careful research and customer surveys it achieved a keen understanding of what customers wanted and what kinds of product could be made to work. Based on this analysis,

Xerox determined that it would be important to offer customers the choice of multiple service options, including self-service repair whereby customers, armed with 24-hour telephone support and a Xerox repair kit, can fix the most common problems whenever they occur, even late on Saturday night when repair shops are typically closed or an hour before a big presentation when there is not enough time to ask a repair technician to make a house call.

As for the 24-hour, do-it-yourself repair hot line, callers to the 800 number are guaranteed a human voice in 15 seconds or less—and not just any voice, but the voice of a knowledgeable helper with creative solutions that will get a customer's copier up and running again. Lesko, who had significant experience in the personal documents business before moving to the supplies group, tells of a letter from a 71-year-old woman who had never fixed anything in her life until she repaired her copier in 10 minutes using a telephone helper and parts that Xerox shipped overnight.

In order to bring such a service into reality, Xerox approached potential suppliers with specifications for a new modular product with multiple service options. Besides working closely with third-party suppliers and utilizing its extensive customer knowledge to design the personal copier product, Xerox also began to develop the channel infrastructure needed to sell to small-business or home-use customers. Previously, the company had sold only on a business-to-business basis, so the switch to retail sales required a new structure. The company developed a cross-functional approach that made linked teams jointly responsible for the end-to-end chain of activities from setting strategy to selling products and delivering service. The "upstream" team focused on the general management of the business, including developmental strategy and planning, vendor selection, manufacturing, and product price positioning. Meanwhile, a "downstream" team had go-to-market responsibility, which included retail selling strategy, customer service, logistics, shipping, and certain administrative functions.

To marry these teams in an effective, collaborative partnership, Xerox gave overall end-to-end responsibility to one business manager. In addition to being a part of the day-to-day workings of the teams, this manager had responsibility for bringing the new copier to market worldwide, as well as full profit-and-loss accountability. He was empowered with the necessary information and authority to make tactical decisions and trade-offs quickly that allowed Xerox to jump-start this mini-business everywhere around the world. What is more, the manager shared a staff and reporting relationship with the team members as well as a compensation plan linked to the project's success.

Both teams were held accountable for common end-of-process objectives such as customer satisfaction, product profitability, and market share. To track customer satisfaction, the company monitored call acceptance according to the percentage of customers who hung up before their calls were answered and the length of time before they received answers to their questions. A formal survey process checked to see how satisfied customers were with the eventual service response and with the overall Xerox experience. Xerox took stock of those results and completed follow-up studies to make sure improvements materialized and satisfaction increased.

The close proximity of the teams to each other and to their manager (there were no hierarchical layers separating the work of the processes from the authorizing agent) meant that critical information was quickly shared and acted upon. Gathered around one table, manufacturing representatives met with vendors, logistics experts, sales and service personnel, and others to determine what features actual customers had requested. Feedback as to product acceptance and competitive challenges rapidly translated into retooled product on retailers' shelves.

In one such example, a retail field operations person in Canada went to the team's general manager when she spotted a competitor test-marketing a copier bundled with a free cartridge. She feared that the competitor's strategy, if it were rolled out on a broader basis, would hurt Xerox sales. The business team agreed and on its own decided to launch the same strategy across the United States in a preemptive strike designed to protect Xerox's competitive position.

"That was one of the catalysts that got us to the number one market share position in 1996," Lesko says with admiration. "A customer operations unit talked to the retail channel operations unit, which, in turn, talked to the business operations unit. They all recognized the problem and collaborated to come up with a solution very quickly."

The same customer research and analysis that determined the benefit and value to customers in relation to the self-service idea prompted the empowered personal copier teams to offer other distinctive value-added features, too. Betting that its customer-care initiative would cover most repair eventualities, Xerox stepped out to become the only personal copier maker to offer a three-year service and replacement guarantee. Xerox is still the only copier maker to offer this long a guarantee. It pledged to provide easy, flexible service options—such as overnight exchange of a defective product or depot repair—for any problem that could not be handled over the phone.

Looking down the road, Xerox expects soon to use new information technology to enable personal copiers to diagnose themselves and begin self-repair over the phone. What might have been material for a futuristic novel some years back is already a reality for some of Xerox's larger business customers. The Channels Group has developed sophisticated remote diagnostic capabilities that travel through modems to track down existing problems or find and prevent problems before they occur. Similar to computer programs that can spot a potential failure of a car's brakes, the Xerox software provides immediate solutions so that a personal copier, for example, can be repaired in minutes—sometimes before the customer even suspects a problem exists.

Information technology continues to prove invaluable to the personal-copier teams just as it does daily to everyone across the organization. "The ability to have a PC/client server platform is a tremendous collaborative tool," Lesko says. E-mail allows empowered employees in remote locations to share information, tap into data related to the status of programs, business results, and supply and demand. As with the field operations person in Canada who spotted the copier marketing threat, it is not always feasible to meet face-to-face; yet quick action can mean the difference between disappointment and success.

The Xerox phenomenon, of course, is not limited to personal copiers. Its growth across the whole business spectrum is directly attributable to its application of horizontal principles across a broader area of its operation. "We used to have one large funnel in the corporation and you could grow as fast as you could move things through that one funnel," says Lesko, echoing Allaire's observation about Xerox's inefficient structure before the makeover to the horizontal. "Now, you may have ten or

20 paths, along which move product ideas, creative solutions, timely responses to the marketplace.''

Lessons from the Horizontal

As the accounts of Motorola's Space and Systems Technology Group, the General Electric production plant in Salisbury, North Carolina, the Barclays Bank Home Finance Division, and the new Xerox Corporation suggest, the shift to the horizontal organization is far less a matter of organization size or type than it is a question of organization will. Whether it is a single operating unit within a company, an entire division, a whole company, or even, as in the case of the Occupational Safety and Health Administration, a government bureaucracy that is being transformed, whether the enterprise is product-focused or service-oriented, the horizontal structure introduces fresh, value-added approaches to solving problems great and small. It can help turn stale, unprofitable organizations into dynamic enterprises.

The final four chapters address the means for dramatically improving performance at your company by taking it along a transformation to the horizontal organization similar to what we have witnessed in these examples. Leading that makeover entails a three-phase process that focuses attention on setting a clear direction, formulates the right organizational design to meet the desired objectives, and institutionalizes the changes by building in the required skills and behaviors. The initial direction-setting phases will be the subject of chapter 10. The subsequent two chapters outline the 12 principles for designing and institutionalizing horizontal organizations.

Although painstaking and sometimes initially uncomfortable for managers and frontline workers, the organization-wide redesign holds great promise for each. It is not to be undertaken lightly, nor should it be seen as a stop-gap measure. If begun half-heartedly, allowed to languish, undertaken without adequate planning, discipline, or refinement, the makeover is likely to have disastrous results. But if undertaken with enthusiasm and care, and presented in a way that inspires the people of the organization to support the effort, the transformation can achieve its primary purpose of restructuring the work that people do, the way they do it, and how they feel about it. Rather than treating people as mere functionaries with narrow departmental quotas, the horizontal organization invites them to become empowered team members with far-reaching responsibilities—or, in some cases, to become process owners themselves—people who are ready to collaborate with others to design, make, and sell the products that win customers and ensure success for your company.

Part THREE
HOW TO BUILD A HORIZONTAL ORGANIZATION

9 THREE PHASES TO MASTER

SET DIRECTION, FORMULATE DESIGN,
INSTITUTIONALIZE THE APPROACH

Several years ago, a major European natural resources company decided to undertake a transformational change that managers hoped would significantly improve performance and present a flexible alternative to a strict command-and-control pattern of behavior. Management also hoped to improve the company's position vis-à-vis competitors in the oil and gas markets, then as uncertain as the earthquake-prone landscape over which some of its pipes were laid or its tankers sailed. No one could predict which suppliers would be around in a year or what the next unforeseen setback in the Middle East would mean for industry survivors.

Although this European resources company concocted its transformation in the midst of uncertainty, it was not the unpredictable nature of the external environment that led to the company's problems. The chief culprit was a lapse of leadership within the corporate domain. True, management had inherited high debts from questionable acquisitions, but the CEO's management style—described as abrasive and dictatorial—was often singled out as a leading cause of the troubles. While frontline employees watched the sparks fly as top managers cut and welded the company's structure, no executive ever bothered to ask them for their ideas or how they felt about the reorganization, let alone explain why it was necessary and what roles those employees might have in the new company. In short, the reorganization effort had commenced without a thorough understanding from everyone, particularly frontline workers. In other words, new behaviors and skills were required if the new company were to be successful, but the effort to develop these skills took place only at the time. Frontline workers weren't directly involved in developing the new behaviors and skills that would lead to the creation of a new organization and improved performance.

Feeling excluded and disenfranchised, the company's employees reacted in a predictably human way: They resisted *all* change. As the company's transformation unraveled, its main stakeholders pulled even harder at the frayed ends. Stockholders protested the news of a cut in the dividend. The chairman left the company. Frontline people became increasingly confused about where the company was going and whether they either wanted to go with it or would be asked to continue in their work. What new skills might be needed? Would the company even remain viable long enough to make attaining new skills worth the effort? With the company in the throes of major leadership changes, no one could provide answers, easy or otherwise, to such pressing questions.

Why did this European company fail so miserably in its attempt to change? (Incidentally, this particular company is not an anomaly: Many efforts end up on the scrap heap of defeat, and the sources of disaster often run deep.[1]) Even the casual observer could spot the error here: Management neglected to win support from frontline workers and other stakeholders and actively engage them in the transformation.

Organizations contemplating a realignment need not despair at the odds against success, however. Although each situation is different—after all, each organization starts from a different place and faces different challenges depending on its readiness for change—there are guidelines for increasing the chances for success and decreasing the likelihood that an organization will stumble on a land mine. This chapter discusses those guidelines and introduces the three sequential phases that are key to pulling off a successful transformational change. Managers must always bear in mind, however, that the details have to be tailored to their individual circumstances.

Getting from Here to There

As should be clear by now, horizontal reorganization cannot be undertaken half-heartedly or as if it were merely a cosmetic makeover. It usually involves a major performance-based "transformation" encompassing all that the word implies—that is, dramatic and ongoing change that cuts a broad swath across an organization, affecting the broad expanse of employees, how they conduct their jobs, what responsibilities they take, and what behaviors and values they demonstrate. The goal of this transformation is to achieve a dramatic and on-going improvement in performance. An overhaul of this magnitude, needless to say, requires total commitment from everyone: top executives, middle managers, front-line workers.

But how can leaders determine whether a horizontal structure is the best way of meeting the challenges of the future? Perhaps they should opt for a hybrid structure, combining the best features of both the vertical and the pure horizontal design? Or maybe they should concentrate their improvements in areas that do not require such a major restructuring?

Deciding what road to take requires that leaders first conduct a strategic analysis to determine what the company's winning value proposition is. Once that value proposition is clearly identified and articulated, they can then decide if developing a horizontal organization in part or all of their enterprise is appropriate.

Questions to be answered to determine if a horizontal organization is appropriate include:

■ Is dramatic, ongoing performance improvement really necessary? For example, some situations may simply require a company to fine-tune its strategy. This is important to answer since developing a horizontal organization may require significant change.

■ Are meeting cross-functional challenges (for example, improving speed, providing "total solutions," or improving customer service) a critical part of delivering the winning value proposition and improving the company's performance?

If leaders answer yes to these questions, then they need to focus on issues that will lead them to possible solutions. For example:

- To what extent will the makeover require changes in the multiple levers of organization performance—i.e., strategy, structure, systems, skills, shared values, staff, and style? Will skills and behavior changes be required of a significant portion of the organization's members? The results of the strategic analysis, as well as the 12 principles of the horizontal organization, can be compared with the present strategy and organization to help determine the extent of the changes required.

To be sure, the horizontal organization is not an all-purpose panacea for whatever ails an organization, but affirmative answers to the above questions indicate that it can profit from a horizontal realignment. Before leaders can begin any transformation, however, they must consider yet a second set of questions:

- Does the organization have significant problems that need to be dealt with first? For example, is it burdened by a desperate financial situation that requires immediate first aid? Remember that resources and energy are finite. The horizontal makeover may have to take a back seat while leaders focus on other, more pressing needs.

- Are the fundamentals of high performance in place? In other words, does the organization have leaders with a clear understanding of the company's core markets, a strong, company-wide performance ethic, world-class skills (in at least one dimension critical to competitive advantage), adequate investment in new products and services, and an appropriate capital structure? These are some of the fundamentals that are applicable to every organization, whether vertical, horizontal, or hybrid. Without them, no method or magnitude of redesign will help.[2]

- Do company leaders understand what adopting the horizontal organization will entail? Leaders must recognize that the changes will be significant and multidimensional, touching the entire organization. Are company leaders prepared to address the personal changes and actions required of them? Leaders, in other words, must have the personal courage and long-term commitment to drive and support a change of this magnitude.

Assuming that all systems are go, there are three sequential phases that require attention: Management must (1) set a direction, (2) design the appropriate organizational structure, and (3) take steps to institutionalize the changes. Each of these phases will be addressed in detail in the following three chapters, but it is important to gain some sense of what lies in store for a management team that undertakes major transformational change.

The poet Robert Browning perhaps stated it best: "A man's reach must exceed his grasp, or what's a heaven for?" That sentiment informs what many a manager must learn in setting a direction, namely the importance of establishing an aspirational goal. Although often overlooked in the tool kit of design, aspirational thinking is a useful instrument of change because it builds a healthy tension and establishes the proper atmosphere for change. For example, aspiration-based planning inspires people in an organization to stretch beyond what they think they can achieve. It encourages out-of-the-box thinking and the setting of performance targets high enough to foster innovation. It motivates members to invest the time and energy required to make significant changes in their behaviors and skills, which is, of course, crucial to implementing a horizontal organization.

What is more, after reviewing the competitive and dynamic environment, management is challenged to articulate transcendent goals for the organization and to project where it should be in, say, eight to ten years if all goes as planned. OSHA, for example, admirably aspired to the impossible: "to eliminate all preventable injuries, illnesses, and deaths from the American workplace in ten years." Xerox aimed to become a "world-class" document provider, indeed the world's leader in document solutions. By making future achievement important in the present, managers headed off the kind of incremental thinking that often mires an organization in a swamp of mediocrity and underperformance. These long-term aspirations also shaped the multilevel design changes that OSHA and Xerox were implementing, assuring that they would become platforms for growth.

As we have seen in previous chapters, high-performance companies as disparate as Motorola, Ford, and Barclays Bank have achieved remarkable results by asking all employees to stretch beyond what they thought themselves capable of achieving. Although initially pressed from outside, employees eventually internalize these stretch targets and come to feel a greater sense of both pride and accomplishment in their work.

Before moving on to the second phase of designing the appropriate organizational structure, leaders cannot bypass the strategic analysis that will help them better understand their environments and potential outcomes. (Rigorous and disciplined analysis, of course, is required at every stage of horizontal design, implementation, and operation.) In this initial direction-setting phase, strategic analysis ensures that the changes introduced as part of the redesign and transformation effort will contribute to competitive success and overall strategic goals. Standard tools such as market/customer research, analyses of competitors' costs and capacities, Michael Porter's five-forces framework,[3] scenario planning, game theory, economic modeling, and so forth enable an organization to make choices that create differential value to customers and competitive advantage while delivering this value at a price and within a cost structure that provides desired financial returns. With its value proposition thus identified, the organization is now ready to determine if a horizontal structure, or some hybrid approach, is appropriate, either for certain parts or throughout the entire organization.

Formulating Design: Performance Is the Raison d'être

As leaders begin the process of actually designing the organizational structure, it is essential to remember that improved *performance* is the overriding objective: The horizontal organization is simply the means to that end. And strategic analysis, once again, is the tool that will help leaders to articulate design criteria and performance targets, thus providing the linkage between organizational design and the end results, which are most critical to customers and stakeholders.

For each of the organizations highlighted in Part II, a value proposition and the elements required to achieve the desired performance served as the embarkation point for the redesign and change effort. Leaders helped articulate the aspirational goals and identify the value propositions to pinpoint which competencies and processes were needed to execute strategy and thus deliver superior value to customers and win competitive advantage. The Home Finance Division of Barclays Bank, for example, aspired to become the preferred place for home financing. To achieve that lofty goal, it sought to design "a total solution that de-stresses the home ownership process." Having articulated that value proposition, Barclays HFD was then able to identify the core process critical to deliver it, determine which competencies were needed, and plan how to design and implement the other principles of horizontal organization. In short, its structure evolved from the demands of its strategy to produce its desired performance goals.

Logically speaking, how could it be otherwise? How could Barclays even know what constitutes success if its performance targets were not derived from a value proposition that would win desired customers? How could it choose the correct core processes or determine that its structural design would fit its needs without first laying out what it wanted to achieve and the value proposition required to achieve it?

When it is feasible to set them, hard measures provide the best performance targets. Quantifying potential benefits allows senior executives to make informed decisions about investment in the transformation process and its priority in their overall management agenda. Precise measures also can bring focus and clarity of direction to the front lines, as exemplified by the experience of GE Salisbury.

Institutionalizing Change

The third stage of transformation, in which management seeks to institutionalize the changes it has made by building a companywide commitment, as well as "locking in" the required new behaviors, skills, and values, depends on a combination of strong leadership and performance. It is crucial that the organization have leaders who can inspire employees and persuade them that the changes are required by market forces rather than by personal whim, that they are designed to achieve positive benefits for everyone and not just a few top executives, and that they are designed according to sound business practices to empower workers in a way that will improve both the company's performance and that of individual workers while at the same time enhancing the quality of life in the workplace.

Change of any sort, but particularly one so fundamental as a shift to the horizontal organization, requires the creation of a sense of urgency. Typically, managers lay out a business case for the transformation by detailing for workers and shareholders the challenges and opportunities that exist. These might include current or anticipated disruptions in the supply chain, threats posed by competitors, superior products or services of competitors, real or anticipated threats of customer defections, or untapped opportunities for growth.

In their article "Memo to a CEO: Leading Organizational Transformations," Dichter, Gagnon, and Alexander recommend creating a special group (e.g., a steering committee) of senior stakeholders to take the lead in managing the change effort.[4] Comprising those line and staff executives whose support is critical and who are willing to put their careers at risk to help assure success, this group can also coordinate the efforts of what in effect becomes two organizations existing side by side: the organization that was and the one that is being created. The old-style organization must continue to exist, produce, and function even as the new one is being created. As in succession myths found in practically all cultures, however, the old grows more feeble and outmoded as the young takes on new and vibrant life. For the interim in which the old-style bureaucracy exists side by side with the horizontal organization, the committee of senior stakeholders can provide the bridge from one to the other.

It is also important to understand that fundamental transformations emphasize leadership rather than just management. As John Kotter points out in a recent book on leadership, the two activities are vastly different: Whereas managers engage primarily in planning, budgeting, staffing, and solving problems, leaders (whether in politics, business, the military, or any other area) focus on setting direction, persuading others to accept the change, and motivating them to overcome barriers, potential and real, to the change effort.[5] Of course, this is not to say that great leaders cannot also be great managers, but leadership makes itself felt when a clear direction is married to a forceful strategy, backed up by adequate resources in time, funding, and training. Managers who would also be leaders must inspire people to work constructively as team members, in part by building commitment to the change effort and entrusting those teams to take responsibility for a core process.

Marmol and Murray reiterate the need for demanding leaders who may appear, particularly to an outsider, excessive and driven. At the top of high-performance companies, one is likely to find single-minded individuals committed to directing the transformation. Those leaders are perhaps "unreasonable," as Murray puts it, when judged according to standards set outside their companies, but not when judged by internal measures.[6] As a general rule of thumb, they spend 20 percent of their time or more leading the change effort—motivating people and garnering support from all areas of the organization, shaping and establishing performance goals and actions required, holding people accountable for meeting their commitments, setting examples to help communicate the values of the new organization, providing resources, reshaping attitudes, solving problems, and breaking down the barriers of old standards and entrenched practices.

No matter how strong the leadership, however, any change effort inevitably will encounter resistance, cynicism, and resentment over the investment of time, energy, and required changes in skills and behaviors. That is where performance comes into play. Positive results overcome nay-saying, or as I like to put it, "performance trumps ideology." When customers are being won and stakeholders are reaping the benefits, who can argue with the horizontal engine of success?

The achievement of performance objectives also confirms that the principles of horizontal organization are much more than just a nice idea. They are a consistent set of aligned, mutually supportive elements that work together to achieve both a dramatic step-up in performance and on-going, continuous improvement in performance. For example, when members of cross-functional, empowered teams who have developed new skills and received new tools for meeting an important performance challenge achieve their goals, they recognize the connection between those new enablers and success. Inevitably they want more. Thus begins a positive, self-reinforcing circle of progress, productivity, and performance that reinforces new behaviors and attitudes, which, in turn, strengthen the new structure and generate ever increasing levels of performance.

Balancing the Effort

It bears repeating that disciplined analysis is necessary throughout the change effort. Leaders must think carefully about the specific challenges

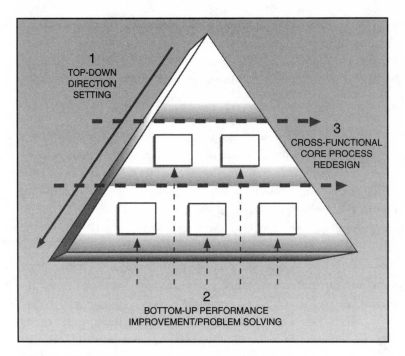

Fig. 9.1 The Transformation Triangle

Source: Steven F. Dichter, Chris Gagnon, and Ashok Alexander, "Memo to a CEO: Leading Organizational Transformations," *McKinsey Quarterly*, no. 1 (1993): 91.

their organizations face and how best to meet these challenges, how to redesign processes for maximum impact, how to identify and fill skill "gaps," how to manage the change effort that will lead to a successful transformation. A change effort of this magnitude cannot be accomplished unless leaders recognize at the outset that change initiatives must flow in all directions—up, down, and across the organization—in a single, fully integrated, and supportive effort.

The story of the European resources company that opens this chapter shows that the top-down approach almost invariably spells disaster when applied by itself. But that describes only one panel of the triptych. Dichter, Gagnon, and Alexander note that transformation often falls apart because of a breakdown along one or more of the three axes of change:

top-down, bottom-up, and across core processes.[7] Together, the three form a "transformation triangle" (see Fig. 9.1) that the authors define as a "balanced, integrated framework for combining separate initiatives into a coherent overall program."[8]

To prevent the change effort from wrecking the company, managers and visionaries (preferably the same people) have to spread the transformation throughout the organization. And they must begin with themselves because the first place the change effort will run into problems is in the boardroom or the CEO's suite, wherever the strategic planning takes place. (Incidentally, the misconception that all top managers have the same assumptions about the business's current state or its future is a portent of impending doom. It is a distinct likelihood that managers of individual functional units or divisions will be concerned about protecting their own turf.) When conflict among managers occurs, the CEO, or a group of managers empowered by the CEO, must be prepared to step in, set priorities, and coordinate objectives.

The outcome of a major transformation also depends on establishing a "language of change," one that all stakeholders can speak and understand. It is important for leaders to develop a set of consistent initiatives, to refine the change processes as they require, to determine at frequent intervals what is and is not working, and to make sure that needed improvements/refinements are put in place. To be sure, change efforts succeed when critical stakeholders fundamentally agree on the major assumptions relevant to business conditions and future market realities, share values such as mutual trust and responsibility, and believe in the power of people working collectively to solve problems and discover a better way of producing value-added products for their customers (see sidebar 1).

If top-down failures commonly result when managers have not devoted a minimum of 20 percent of their attention and time to leading the change effort, bottom-up disaster is virtually assured when large numbers of people throughout the organization are not actively engaged in the effort to improve performance and cannot agree on performance objectives or understand how these efforts support the long-range goals of the organization (see sidebar 2). Too often, bottom-up initiatives focus only on immediate desires—improved production levels, better quality control, greater autonomy for workers, higher salaries and benefits—that

1
Top-down change initiatives to be undertaken by management:

❏ Establish a rationale for the change.

❏ Set performance goals that are aspirational and quantifiable targets with clear milestones firmly linked to the value proposition.

❏ Form a cohesive, high-performance steering group.

❏ Design a disciplined, integrated change process.

❏ Oversee the quality of progress in the change effort.

❏ Open up bottlenecks to change wherever they appear.

❏ Take symbolic and visible action (say, in hiring and promotions) to demonstrate the required new behaviors and skills.

❏ Establish a well-honed communication and integrated measurement system that includes feedback loops and that cascades throughout the organization.

❏ Draw up tough but doable performance goals and hold people accountable for meeting them, and also for meeting change commitments (for example, managers might be measured on whether they have devoted sufficient time to skill and behavior training and on how well they have exhibited new values).

❏ Foster continuous improvement by raising performance objectives.

❏ Maintain the focus on performance.

may not directly link or support the organization's strategic needs. Sad to report, many frontline employees have no clue about long-term strategies because management has kept them in the dark. And while change efforts driven from the top must also engage "bottom-up support," bottom-up efforts require top-down support as well. Change efforts that

2
Bottom-up change initiatives to be undertaken by lower-level organization members:

☐ Establish individual and team performance targets that support overall objectives.

☐ Introduce a wide array of tools to enable frontline problem solving and effective empowerment.

☐ Actively engage in problem solving focused on improving performance.

☐ Redesign work units and levels to operate in an integrated fashion.

☐ Build new skills through real work and just-in-time training.

are exclusively or primarily bottom-up lack the top-down support needed to be "rolled-out" across the organization. They tend to exist in isolated pockets of the organization where the effort meets with inbred resistance in other parts of the organization. Little wonder, then, that so many bottom-up change efforts fizzle out before they have any significant impact on company structure or performance.

The third axis (see Fig. 9.1 and sidebar 3) represents those linkages across functions directed by people who take responsibility for a relatively small number of core processes.[9] As discussed in previous chapters, these cross-functional core processes are at the heart of a company's effort to deliver its value proposition. They are the means by which it fulfills its promise to design and produce a value-added product or service that will win customers. Even large organizations such as Ford have only a handful of core processes, usually no more than four or five, around which their overall goals and business efforts revolve. But if those core processes are not firmly linked to company objectives, any attempt at transformation is likely to end in disaster.

Each leg of the triangle bears its own portion of responsibility for the success of the change effort. For example, top-down direction setting

3
Change initiatives to be undertaken across the functions:

❏ Redesign core processes.

❏ Set up "diagonal-slice" redesign teams comprising multiple skills and functions.

❏ Provide team training.

❏ Promote a cooperative, collaborative culture.

❏ Establish organization-wide best-practice workshops.

❏ Establish cross-functional performance objectives.

❏ Evaluate and reward cooperative, cross-functional behaviors.

❏ Design cross-organizational communication sessions or town halls.

❏ Rotate jobs.

❏ Develop whole-job understanding through multidisciplinary training.

creates focus and accountability throughout a company and helps to ensure that newly acquired knowledge, skills, and behaviors will not remain isolated in the pilot area but will be spread throughout the organization. Encouragement from the top does not, by itself, guarantee success, however. To buy in to and support the change, people at all levels of the organization must witness new behavior, inspired by the principles of horizontal organization, that the leaders of the organization themselves exhibit. Above all, everyone must be allowed to become an active participant in the change effort. Broad-based, bottom-up involvement is necessary to get people at all levels to engage in and learn a fresh approach to solving problems and improving performance. Otherwise, organization members may begin to feel as if the change is being forced down their throats, and they will resist the initiative as surely as did the rank-and-file employees at the European resources company.

The importance of this cross-functional emphasis is apparent both in the initial redesign stage and in the ongoing change effort. Linking activities and information in new ways as part of the redesign can bring about breakthrough improvements in quality, timeliness, and customer satisfaction. And as the change effort proceeds, cross-functionality provides people with new ways to communicate, learn from one another, and work cooperatively to solve problems.

Drawing the Road Map

Although transformational change is iterative and marked by continuous learning, improvement, refinement, and adjustment, the sequence for getting from here to there does matter. In the next three chapters, I discuss the sequential phases as they relate to the experience of the path-breaking companies cited throughout this book. These phases can be seen as a road map that will lead organizations on their journey.

While the exact flow of activities will vary with the specific challenges facing an individual organization and its degree of readiness for change, leaders must proceed as with any other mission-critical endeavor: They must determine and identify adequate resources for the change effort (training of employees is typically given short shrift) and establish milestones, accountabilities, responsibilities, and quality-control checkpoints. The best leaders want to know at all times how people throughout the organization are responding to the changes; thus, they insist on establishing a communication system that includes "feedback loops," a mechanism that allows employees, customers, suppliers, and other stakeholders to point out what is working and what is not.

Such feedback loops serve to empower people by increasing their sense that they are making important contributions to the transformation itself as well as to the products and services the organization produces. Whatever communication channels are put into place, they absolutely have to run in multiple directions, not only within the organization itself, but out to people in the organization's supply chain and its customer base. No change leader can afford to alienate or exclude any of the company's stakeholders.

In addition, disciplined thinking must be applied to designing the specific change activities and the enabling structures—such as mapping required skills, developing and refining pedagogical approaches, planning the migration path to the new organization, designing in details the new jobs required, and so forth.

Chapter 10 takes up the initial stage of establishing direction for the change effort, beginning with a thorough assessment of your business's current markets, customers, and core processes. Chapters 11 and 12 focus in greater detail on the 12 principles that underlie the transformation to a horizontal organization: Chapter 11 develops five of the 12 principles which are concerned primarily with the design of the new structure; chapter 12 takes up the subsequent seven principles, which address the behaviors and skills necessary for a horizontal organization to be successfully institutionalized. Whether the principles are applied to an operating unit such as GE Salisbury's build-to-order process, to a single division as at Ford Customer Service, or to an entire company as in the case of Xerox, horizontal approaches are working effectively to solve business problems from the top floor to the shop floor.

10 PHASE ONE—SET DIRECTION

WHERE AND HOW WILL YOU COMPETE?

As any seasoned traveler knows, getting the most out of a trip to a far-off destination never visited before requires a bit of work prior to boarding the plane and preparing for takeoff. It helps to devise an itinerary and to bone up on the climate, the culture, and the people who inhabit the place. Otherwise, how will you know what kind of clothing to pack, how much money to take along, or what kind of opportunities and activities will be available once you get there? Without some pre-trip effort, you are liable to waste valuable time and energy upon arrival just getting the lay of the land, instead of taking advantage of all the place has to offer.

In much the same way, an organization preparing to undertake transformational change must use the analytical tools mentioned in chapter 9 (scenario planning, five-forces modeling, market/customer research, and so on), or some reasonable alternatives, to chart its itinerary for the journey ahead. This assumes, of course, that you know first where it is you want to go, and as discussed in chapter 9, the preliminary work on setting direction—that is, identifying the value proposition and defining your aspirations for your organization—needs to have your full attention. *Only then* can you determine if "going horizontal" is the most appropriate decision. After making this determination, you can then survey the territory and begin to evaluate what you need to do next to determine the nature of the performance challenges you face if you are to deliver a winning value proposition.

This up-front strategic planning process focuses organizational design on those things that are critical to achieving competitive advantage. By providing a distinct linkage between strategy and design, it ensures that the entire enterprise will be marching in the same direction and that the targeted performance gains will be achieved. The process involves two intertwined activities: understanding the competitive environment and articulating the organization's long-range aspirations. This chapter discusses how an organization should proceed on these two fronts and considers specific examples from the six major case studies.

Understanding the Environment

The environment in this case has two components, external and internal. The "external" part comprises the fundamental forces at work in the industry—that is, competitors, suppliers, technology, the society at large—whereas the "internal" environment focuses directly on the organization itself in terms of its structure, culture, resources, and people. By taking a broad view of where it competes and how well equipped it is to meet the challenges of the future, an enterprise must seek to assess realistically its strengths, weaknesses, opportunities, and threats.

Assessment begins with management's asking what industry the company wants to compete in. Which customers does it want to attract? What value proposition can it offer those customers that would cause them to want to do business with the company rather than a competitor? At the same time, how can the company capture attractive returns for itself? What core processes are critical to the delivery of that value proposition? Is the organization properly designed and resourced to deliver the winning value proposition? If not, how can it get that way?

Although some of these questions may seem simplistic and straightforward, further examination reveals their complexity. Take the question of customers, for example. As Mark H. Moore, a professor at Harvard's John F. Kennedy School of Government, points out in his book *Creating Public Value,* customers are important for an obvious reason: An enterprise's ultimate success depends on its producing something that customers want.[1] Marketing and customer research will help an organization discern current customer wants and needs. But what is not so easily discerned is what those wants and needs will be next month, next year, or several years into the future. For any number of reasons customers may change their minds about what they consider to be valuable: Situations, lifestyles, expectations, and experiences vary over the longer term, yet being able to make reasonable, long-term predictions while remaining flexible enough to accommodate new insights into customers' ever-changing needs and wants is crucial to an organization's success.

To accomplish these feats, the company must build ongoing relationships with its customers. In a horizontal organization, where all energies are channeled toward satisfying the customer, ongoing relationships are second nature and bear fruit in a variety of ways. At the Ford Customer Service Division (FCSD), for example, information uncovered through multiple customer contacts is continuously fed back into an activity called "Upstream Customer Service," which works closely with product development. As they develop new models, designers address customer reactions and complaints to earlier products and their suggestions for improving them. If customers stipulate an upper-limit price for a particular repair, for instance, FCSD can work with suppliers, designers, technicians, and others to factor in all costs so that it can meet its customers' requests.

At the GE Salisbury plant, feedback from customers comes not only through traditional avenues, such as focus groups, but also through conference calls and meetings with team members. Former plant manager Jeff Traver described it as an "in-your-face" relationship: GE Salisbury customers often interact directly with production teams on the plant floor or work with them at their own facilities. The plant has such close contact with its customers that any relevant change in their outlook or experience is communicated in short order.

This direct, personal relationship with customers is a hallmark of the successful horizontal organization. Xerox, for instance, maintains close, ongoing customer contacts, including even sending its research PhDs out into the field to visit with customers in order to get a better understanding of who they are and what their future needs are likely to be. Jim Lesko, corporate vice president, describes the new horizontal Xerox as a system of multiple "funnels" directing the flow of new ideas, creative solutions, innovative products, and timely responses to marketplace changes. "It is practically impossible," he explains, "for one person to keep track of all that activity. The amount of energy, scrutiny, and focus is ten times what might have passed through a single funnel in the pre-1990 command-and-control approach to managing the organization."

The need to gain an understanding of competitors is important for an obvious reason, too: Having a desirable product or service is of little use, as Moore observes, if someone else has a better one.[2] And even a breakthrough product that soundly beats the competition today may be matched by another producer tomorrow.

So what is a company to do? Managers and planners not only have to identify a competitive advantage, they also have to monitor regularly the products and services of competitors and do their best to understand where competitors are likely to head in the future. In order to make proper use of that understanding, of course, your organization needs to be so well integrated internally that it can innovate in order to stay ahead of the competition, not just react to it.

A valuable reminder for management, then, as it attempts to understand its competitive environment, is that change and uncertainty are a critical part of the equation. "Observe constantly that all things take place by change. . . . [T]he nature of the Universe loves nothing so much as to change the things which are and to make new things like them," advised Marcus Aurelius, Roman emperor and philosopher of the second century.[3] To be sure, leaders who have opted to reorganize horizontally already understand that *nothing* remains static—neither customers, nor competitors, nor technology, nor resources. That recognition is, in fact, one of the very reasons they have chosen to abandon their inefficient vertical structures. But as they prepare the way for transformation, these leaders must constantly remain focused on the future and think in terms of positioning their organizations both to recognize and to create opportunities as well as being able to respond speedily and efficiently to threats.

The Xerox Corporation did just that in 1990 when it began planning for its major transformation. CEO Paul Allaire and a team of top managers undertook a thorough assessment of the company's condition, including its financial state, industry position, and production capabilities. They considered projected developments in technology and imaging, color and photographic reproduction, new standards in quality, digital compatibility, and many other changes in the business environment. Team members spent hours hammering out a collective "View of the World," reconciling economic forecasts and contradictory assumptions about market trends. In groups and in one-on-one sessions, they met with Xerox employees, suppliers, and customers to uncover widely disparate assessments about those trends and to incorporate as many viewpoints as possible into the overall company strategy.

In its "Xerox 2000" document, managers formulated a statement of clear forward direction and strategic intent. Although it appeared in various forms—print, audio, film, and electronic—the document itself conveyed a single, consistent message about the direction the Xerox Corporation had set for itself. Reproduced in Fig. 10.1, the "Xerox 2000" strategic intent guided the company for approximately five years as it constructed a mosaic of businesses, competencies, and infrastructure.

But what took place next underscores the fact that things change and transformations must be ongoing. To fix objectives in stone is to build a monument to the past. Instead, managers must constantly work at the business of refining objectives, searching for new sources of value, anticipating change, and responding appropriately in the marketplace. The transformation must be flexible and subject to redirection as opportunities and economic conditions warrant.

This is not to imply that Xerox zigzagged across the business landscape. On the contrary, the strategic intent stated in Xerox 2000 (Fig. 10.1) remained largely unchanged as the company developed and refined its structure. Based on changes the company observed in customers, competitors, and technology, it revised its initiatives to reach those goals more efficiently. But because markets can change in the twinkle of an eye, Xerox recognized that a shift to a strategy emphasizing global business solutions had become increasingly important. Thus, company managers undertook a major restructuring of business divisions, transforming traditionally vertical functions into horizontally oriented business divisions in 1992. Then, in 1996, the company refined its strategy and direction in a document entitled "Xerox 2005" (see Fig. 10.2).

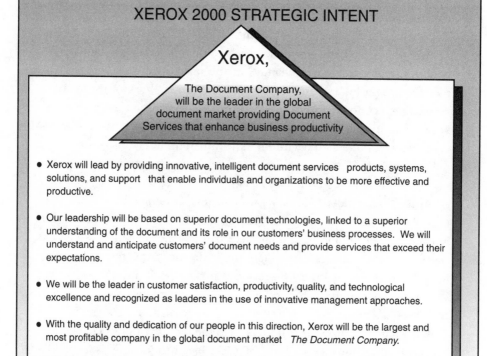

Fig. 10.1 Xerox 2000 Strategic Intent

The two documents offer contrasts in content, presentation, and business philosophy. When a company as large and complex as Xerox refines its strategic intent, it faces the task of creating something that at once conveys the company's message to thousands of employees and presents a persuasive argument to suppliers and customers worldwide.

Xerox changed the "document services" wording of its 2000 mission statement to "document solutions" in the 2005 statement of intent, a subtle but powerful evolution designed to appeal to the business sector, which had need of Xerox's hardware and software products. Whereas the earlier document distinguished between "individuals" and "organiza-

Xerox,
The Document Company,
will be the leader in the
global document market providing
Document Solutions that enhance
business productivity

- Xerox, with Fuji Xerox, will distinguish itself by providing coherent enterprise document solutions — hardware and software product, services, and supplies — that meet the needs of customers worldwide.

- In a world of intense global competition, rapid technological change toward document products that are all connected, digital, and color-capable with substantial value-added, and the widespread deployment of document solutions, Xerox's success will rest on three pillars:
    - Our superior understanding of the document and its role in our customers' information- and knowledge-based processes
    - Our innovative products and services, incorporating advantaged technology
    - Our dedicated people and productive business processes

- Xerox, with Fuji Xerox, will distinguish itself by providing coherent enterprise document solutions — hardware and software product, services, and suppliers – that meet the needs of customers worldwide.

Fig. 10.2 Xerox 2005 Strategic Intent

tions" in the first bulleted item, the latter document refers simply and universally to "customers." Moreover, the more recent statement pairs Xerox with Fuji Xerox to point up the new emphasis on global stretch and expertise. Indeed, each sentence in the 2005 statement contains either the word "global" or "worldwide." Contrast this to the 2000 statement where the term "global" appeared only once in the four bulleted items. By taking the strategic intent statement out of the upward-pointing wedge in Fig. 10.1 and placing it alongside the box with rounded corners and a "horizon" design through the year 2005 (Fig. 10.2), the designers of the second Xerox document convey a sense of balance, depth, and reach across time. Taken out of the "attic" in the 2000 design, the statement of strategic intent is presented as a "window" to the future in the 2005 design.

Both substantive and symbolic, the Xerox 2005 strategic intent provides a clear example of a powerful statement that sets a direction for an entire organization.

Articulating Aspirations

A favorite tactic of many therapists is to ask clients to describe themselves, say, ten years down the road: What do you want to be doing? What do you want your life to look like? Where will you be? If you were to be very happy with your life, what would you need to be doing, or what would need to happen? And then comes the kicker: The therapist always says, "Okay, so what do you do now to get yourself to that ideal?"

A similar question is a key component to the aspirations-based planning that is critical in setting direction for a performance-based transformation. Having gained some understanding of the competitive environment, leaders now set about envisioning the future they desire for their organization and identifying its core ideology, which will allow them to answer their own version of the therapist's critical question: "Okay, so what do you do now to get the organization to that ideal?"

To envision the organization's future, management must identify bold stretch goals, then articulate vivid descriptions of what achieving them will mean.[4] Articulating a vision provides a centerpiece around which an organization can marshal all of its resources. As the word "vision" implies, there are no artificial boundaries, but rather an effort to embrace the future in all its wondrous possibilities. This kind of out-of-the-box thinking gives an organization a needed sense of purpose and allows it to make the most of its opportunities.

Some CEOs describe their role, at least in part, as resembling that of the therapist who engages people in the kind of visioning exercises described above. The CEO gives people the luxury and freedom to imagine what ideal state they would like to reach by some specified date. Prepared in 1996, the Xerox 2005 statement, for example, presents a vision for the company ten years into the future. After projecting ten years out, an organization works backward to determine what it has to do to make the stretch goal a reality. If XYZ Company, currently a $1 billion operation, is going to be a $10 billion operation by 2008, what does it have to achieve by 2003? By 2000? "The conventional approach of starting from the present may move a company toward its intent," say Gouillart and Kelly, "but usually too slowly. The tendency is to sketch out incremental moves that preserve too much and alter too little."[5]

As Collins and Porras discuss and describe it, core ideology is that set of implicit and explicit values and beliefs that are the essence of an organization's culture.[6] That ideology comes into play as the omnipresent navigational force in the transformation to a horizontal organization. It is the North Star of dos and don'ts that guide the organization's decision making and help to determine how the new strategic direction will affect specific constituencies. It is the leader's job to translate the aspirational goals into actions that are consistent with the core values. And just as in the home or the schoolroom, communicating values in the workplace is best achieved by living them, day in and day out.

Nowhere is this philosophy more apparent than at the Barclays Home Finance Division. As you will recall from chapter 7, the Barclays HFD managers hold very distinct values relating to status and privilege, and starting at the top with managing director Mike Ockenden, they readily exhibit them in their day-to-day dealings. They no longer conduct business behind closed office doors; each has a desk no larger, no smaller than any other employee's; and everyone's job title has been replaced by a first name.

Moreover, values and behaviors carry equal weight with performance results when employees are evaluated on how well they have met the goals set forth in their personal development plans. Ockenden is so vested in promoting a democratic culture that promotes trust, openness, and cooperation that he willingly shares both his personal profile and his evaluation with the entire organization.

Barclays HFD aspires to be the United Kingdom's preferred home mortgage lender, and it believes—according to its official statement of strategic intent—that its most important resource for achieving that goal is its people. Because Ockenden wants his employees to know just how important they are to the company's strategy, he goes out of his way, in his own words, to "create a spirit that says we are all one group of people working towards the customer imperative." As empowered frontline workers at Barclays (and at other horizontal companies where core values are embedded in the quest to achieve aspirational goals) take responsibility for the end-to-end processes that produce their value-added products and services, they are increasing their personal investment in the organization's mission and strategic intent. That investment, in turn, pays off in greater commitment by the employees to the values the company wishes to promote.

Staking a Claim

As in an interlocking puzzle, the pieces must come together to help you identify your organization's central strength, the sources of its competitive advantage, apart from all others in the field. A rigorous analysis of the environment has helped you decide where you want to compete and what your strengths and weaknesses are. You have also assessed the "critical buying factors" or "customer breakpoints," those dimensions of value that really make a difference to customers (and will attract those customers to you rather than someone else), as well as what your potential competitors will offer to customers. You know what you aspire to achieve if everything "goes right." The time has now come to stake out a competitive territory and to state your differentiable value in terms of a specific value proposition.

As we have seen, the value proposition is a clear, simple statement of the benefits a particular organization will provide to a target group of customers. In order to maintain its competitive edge, the organization must set a price attractive to those customers and consistent with its financial goals. The value proposition is based on exhaustive research into customer wants, needs, and price requirements, as well as the organization's capabilities for meeting those wants and needs. Managers need to complete an economic analysis of the potential returns from specific business lines and market segments as well as an assessment of the likely challenges they will face from competitors and how the industry might evolve. Performing the necessary analysis on a continuing basis helps ensure that the organization maintains a crisp definition of its value proposition and understands the key benefits that targeted customers want.

The value proposition is also important because it:

- Gives direction and purpose to the organization's activities

- Focuses the organization's work directly onto the customer

- Articulates the nature of the performance challenges inherent in winning customers, thereby allowing you to determine if and where in your organization a horizontal, vertical, or some other approach is appropriate

- Identifies the critical core processes of an organization and what they are designed to achieve

- Shapes the design of all elements of organization performance, such as structure, skills, and systems

- Serves as a goal against which the organization measures its success

- Redirects the organization's activities if the need arises

As I mentioned in chapter 1, this method of organization ensures that every step and element is purpose-built in carrying out a winning strategy. And at this point, strategy can be seen as a set of actions that deliver superior value to desired customers at a cost that provides desired returns.

Although the term "value" is usually associated with the world of private business, the concept of a value proposition is applicable to the public sector as well. In *Creating Public Value*, Moore argues that one of the three critical tests in developing strategy for a public sector organization is that it be "*substantively valuable* in the sense that the organization produces things of value to overseers, clients, and beneficiaries at low cost in terms of money and authority."[7] Clearly, public sector agencies do bring things of value to society. OSHA, for example, protects human life, which is valuable in terms of both the lives themselves and of the savings to the general economy from averting lost work time, medical expenses, workers' compensation costs, and so forth. As noted in chapter 2, besides 6,200 deaths, a reported 6.2 million workplace injuries occurred in 1996 (albeit the lowest rate since the Bureau of Labor Statistics began tracking such statistics).[8] These injuries directly cost some $60 billion annually in workers' compensation and indirectly another $50 billion or so in expenses such as those tied to loss of productivity. Program evaluation, benefit-cost analysis, and similar tools can help identify the net value that an agency such as OSHA offers.

Public agencies such as OSHA are compelled to offer a strong value proposition because they, too, face "competitive threats." For example, Congress can discontinue an agency's funding (and has made such threats to OSHA in the past) if other alternatives offer what the legislators perceive to be a superior value proposition. Additionally, the value proposition identifies the goals against which the organization measures its success and redirects its particular strategic approach if conditions warrant: For example, if the agency fails to achieve its value proposition of significantly reducing injuries, illnesses, and deaths, or if the costs of doing so exceed the benefits, the organization can and should redirect its activities.

A pertinent example occurred early in the OSHA redesign effort when an attempt to use a partnership with poultry companies to drive needed safety changes in the poultry industry itself caused an uproar in organized labor. As Joel Sacks, former acting director of reinvention at OSHA, describes it, labor had valid reasons for its opposition. First, unions developed the perception that inspections of the poultry companies were to be relaxed in return for their participation in the program, which labor viewed as an infringement of workers' rights. Second, poultry was targeted by OSHA because it was considered to be particularly dangerous. Labor countered with the argument that the high level of danger was precisely the reason why poultry inspections should not be discontinued.

Rather than allowing labor's objections to sink the whole initiative, OSHA head Joe Dear acted quickly to adjust the strategic approach and keep the program moving forward. He called together all the stakeholders and engaged them in working toward a common goal consistent with OSHA's aspirations. As Sacks points out, "The upside of the story is that by sitting with these stakeholders, getting them involved, and helping them recreate the program, we now have a [poultry] program in Atlanta that organized labor is using as a model of what we need to be doing in other parts of the country."

Laying the Groundwork for Change

You are now prepared to undertake the second phase of building the horizontal organization, that of actual design. Before beginning to design the appropriate organization to meet your particular needs, however, it will serve you well in the future if you start laying the groundwork for the behavior and skill changes that must accompany any performance-based transformation. Most of the specific skills will not become clear until after you have identified and redesigned the core processes. Nevertheless, now is the time to begin building the case for major change. Leaders must:

- Create a sense of urgency

- Line up broad-based support

- Set up a means of quality control

- Create enabling structures

In creating a sense of urgency, it is important to stress that implementing a horizontal organization, either by itself or in any hybridized combination, is *not* the main objective. Improved performance, as I noted earlier, is the overriding goal, and stakeholders must understand up front exactly why you are undertaking transformational change and what you are aiming to achieve. It is important to draw on the results of the disciplined analysis done in the initial stages of direction setting to illustrate the solid link between desired performance gains and the benefits of horizontal organization.

At Xerox, for example, extensive analysis of customer requirements, new technology, the economic environment, and competitors provided a clear understanding that the company could not achieve its desired level of success as it was structured in 1992. Functional roadblocks were impediments to achieving strategic goals. "A very centralized decision-making organization," as corporate vice president Jim Lesko describes it, prevented the company from competing effectively in the face of new industries, new competitors, and changing customer requirements. With every decision ultimately funneling through a very narrow channel at the top, the company essentially had reached the limits of growth. Although financial returns were adequate, the company was not up to the challenges posed by new technology and new markets.

Communicating the case for change is primarily the job of top leaders. At Xerox, CEO Allaire was "all over this," Lesko says. People understood that Allaire was behind the organizational changes, that he had been closely involved in every detail.

So, too, at the Ford Customer Service Division, where vice president and FCSD general manager Ron Goldsberry decided that transformational change was needed in order to shore up badly sagging customer satisfaction rates. As related in chapter 2, the problem became so severe as to undermine customer loyalty, which, in turn, began to threaten overall Ford Motor Company sales. Calling FCSD diverse, fragmented, and "very chimney-oriented," Goldsberry saw that a horizontal organization offered him the best opportunity to align processes, goals, and objectives.

Goldsberry has traveled around the world communicating the need for the change and enlightening stakeholders as to the benefits of horizontal organization. In fact, he lists "teacher" as one of his main roles these days. And one of his greatest accomplishments as a teacher is helping FCSD employees come to understand just how serious the threat was to the company, to help build the commitment from them to accomplish the structural and behavioral changes required at the division. Tony Kaduk, manager of FCSD's vehicle service program, says that Goldsberry has "delivered a very consistent message" in person and through memos about the need to focus on customer satisfaction.

At each of the organizations examined in this book, performance problems were defined after exhaustive analysis of the external and internal environment, and then the case for major change was communicated by the top and throughout the organization from the top down. A pro-active communication strategy, like that used by Joe Dear at OSHA, is critical for addressing the diverse points of view of key stakeholders and for enlisting broad-based support for the change effort.

With the first set of plans and objectives that Dear drew up for OSHA, he clearly spelled out the threat the agency faced from loss of political support as a result of its failure to fulfill its mission. He then laid out the specifics of needed performance improvements and targeted certain programs for change. Traveling around to the various OSHA field offices, Dear sat down with staff members and talked one-on-one about the need for change and invited their suggestions. He also communicated with OSHA staffers through speeches and memos.

First, Dear made it clear that if OSHA managers did not change the organization themselves, then somebody—perhaps one or another member of Congress—was likely to do it for them. But after laying out the threat, he then quickly moved to provide a meaningful vision. "Joe could paint an inspiring picture of where OSHA needed to be in the future," Joel Sacks recalls with obvious admiration. "He got people excited and interested in working to make the redesign a reality. Dear also formed a cohesive, high-performance design team and 'gave them a clear charter' to do three things: Create a redesign model, test it, and start implementing it nationwide, all of which was critical to the success of the effort," Sacks adds.

Dear obviously had more than one group of stakeholders that he needed to convince, and his efforts reflected that. He gave speeches to outside labor and employer groups, where he emphasized both the need for major change and the benefits that would accrue to the various stakeholders. But perhaps the most crucial selling effort was the one Dear conducted for Congress because he recognized that he had to buy sufficient time to keep the agency operating until positive results could begin to appear.

For his part, Dear believes that the key to selling a change effort is the leader's level of personal commitment. "Leaders have to expose themselves to incredible personal and professional risk. People need to know that every leader is at least as far out on the limb as they are in terms of having to make the change work. If people see genuine commitment, your change-ready folks will come forward. They will commit."

Controlling the quality of the change effort depends not only on establishing checkpoints and design parameters for the changes to be implemented but also on establishing quantifiable measures and targets wherever feasible, and making sure that stakeholders understand how these measures and targets support the objectives of the company's overall change effort.

Motorola developed its famed Six Sigma quality control measures, representing a near infinitesimal ratio of defective parts per million parts produced. To measure customer satisfaction and its own productivity, and as part of its drive to achieve its value proposition, GE Salisbury adopted this performance measure, seeking to hold complaints to an equally small percentage of all its transactions with customers. What distinguishes these companies' direction setting is the specificity of their quantifiable outcomes.

4
Successful communication requires a strong senior management role to:

☐ Develop a communications plan and make sure that plan is faithfully executed

☐ Communicate openly; tell the truth

☐ Listen to and take advantage of feedback

☐ Use clear, direct language

☐ Dedicate sufficient support resources, both people (an internal champion and a multifunctional task force) and money

☐ Devote personal time and attention

☐ Make important decisions that visibly reinforce message (e.g., people, resources)

Likewise, as part of the 2005 initiative, Xerox established a "management model" to embed and measure quality—a critical element of its value proposition—throughout its organization. That model comprises six categories: leadership, human resources management, business process management, customer and market focus, information and quality tools, and results. In the area of results, Xerox collects empirical data to measure customer satisfaction and loyalty, employee motivation and satisfaction, market share, financial results, productivity, and profitable revenue growth. Consistent with the Xerox 2005 strategic intent and value proposition, these areas present quantifiable and ambitious objectives for the company which are nonetheless achievable.

Such performance objectives serve as a measure of progress toward your goals. They are not the *only* measure, of course, but they represent powerful arguments as to whether the direction you have set for your company is the right one. It is important to note, however, that although the steps outlined in this chapter are designed to help you formulate the correct strategy, there are no guarantees. Setting the correct course is complex and difficult, but *even a course that is correct for today must be constantly revisited to make sure that it is still correct for tomorrow.*

You are now ready to begin designing a horizontal structure to reach your performance targets, a challenge that will occupy us in the final two chapters of this book. Some departments in your organization, of course, can—and in many cases should—remain functional, but the primary objective in transforming your company to a horizontal organization will be to build cross-functionality in order to improve performance. The checklist that ends this chapter summarizes the main steps you should take in setting the future direction of your organization. The journey can be arduous, but like the seasoned traveler mentioned at the beginning of this chapter, you can prepare yourself and your fellow travelers so that you do not arrive at a place that is totally unfamiliar.

A Checklist for Setting Direction

- Use rigorous, disciplined analysis to understand your competitive environment.

- Articulate aspirational goals and identify core values.

- Define your value proposition for those markets or customers you want to win.

- Use the value proposition to determine the critical processes that need to be in place. This is the initial point where strategy actually starts to drive organization design.

- Create a sense of urgency and inject passion to rally your people behind the transformation to a horizontal organization.

- Build a strong line of communication to all stakeholders so that everyone is aware of objectives, overall progress, and tangible successes.

- Establish a limited set of quantifiable performance targets.

- Establish a steering committee of senior stakeholders to hold people accountable, secure resources, identify problems, and provide buffers.

- Evaluate and refine your organization's strategic intent as market conditions and company results warrant.

11 PHASE TWO—FORMULATE DESIGN

HOW WILL YOU DO WHAT YOU DO?

Even a cursory glance at the organizational charts in chapters 2 and 5-8 reveals that no two are exactly alike. What works well for OSHA or Xerox should not, indeed cannot, be adopted wholesale by the likes of a GE Salisbury plant or the Supply Management organization within Motorola's Space and Systems Technology Group (SSTG). After all, each organization must devise its own horizontal structure according to the core processes it designs to create and deliver its value proposition. No two organizations will have the core processes designed the same way (despite surface similarities), just as no two individuals have the same personality, history, and purposes (even though they may share the same name). And since organizations will not have the same core processes designed in the same way, their horizontal organizational charts will accordingly differ in often subtle, but nonetheless distinct, ways.

Also affecting the composition of each core process group is the specific combination of skills and experiences needed to deliver the value proposition. No two organizations, however similar they may appear, will need exactly the same set of skills and expertise. Thus each structure will reflect the organization's strategy by grouping together certain employees and teams, manipulating the value chain to help them perform at the highest level possible, and constantly improving their performance. A cheerful, patient, and knowledgeable customer service representative, for instance, can play an important part in winning customers for the company, just as the best designed value-added product or service can. Multidisciplinary teams at Motorola, for example, possess the integrated set of skills required to execute the work of the supply management core process, thereby improving quality and reducing cycle time. Both of these objectives are central to Motorola's value proposition.

Individual differences aside, all horizontal organizational charts have in common several important features, some of which are carried over from the traditional hierarchy or bureaucracy. For instance, in each chart a general manager or senior executive retains oversight responsibilities. Authority stems from that executive and extends down throughout various organization areas or sometimes, indeed, through the entire organization. In the horizontal organization, that executive continues to exercise traditional responsibilities including setting strategy, allocating resources and control, even while spending new or additional time in tasks such as coaching, leading change, and building consensus.

In the case of Ford's Customer Service Division (FCSD), the line of authority and responsibility runs from Ron Goldsberry, vice president and general manager, to the four process owners, thence to the core process groups comprising literally thousands of frontline Ford workers who take responsibility for the end-to-end process and achieving its performance goals (see Fig. 11.1). Those four core process groups, comprised of multiple cross-functional teams, work side by side with people in various vertical or functional areas and departments, who are responsible for vertical activities. Areas such as finance, strategy and communications, and human resources remain "outside" the main core process groups, although all three contribute analytical data, planning, and other supporting information essential to the process group's performance. They become, in short, "partners in process performance."

Another feature common to horizontal organizations and visible from

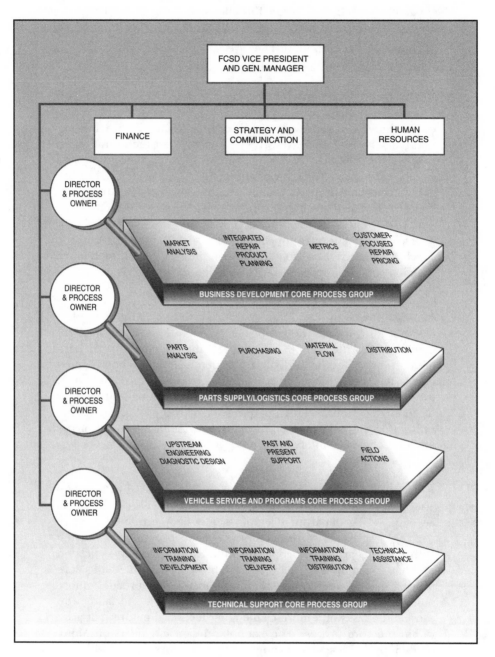

Fig. 11.1 Ford Customer Service Division

the organization chart is being formally structured around a process. Core process groups (CPGs) are the formal organizational departments of the horizontal organization. They are *not* functions. Indeed, they differ from traditional vertical silos in three important ways:

■ The core process group is designed to deliver external, end-of-process performance objectives, which are themselves part and parcel of the value proposition. CPGs are not focused on delivering internal *functional* objectives. In order to support the overall value proposition of FCSD (fix it right the first time, on time), the parts supply and logistics CPG, for example, needs to have the right parts available so that properly trained frontline workers can repair vehicles right the first time and on time. Integral to the efficiency and effectiveness of the four core process groups of FCSD, of course, are the efforts of functional units such as human resources, which finds the right people to work on the teams, and the finance function, which supplies resources needed for the CPGs to achieve their process-based performance objectives.

■ As a result of process redesign and the vesting of more employees (not just those at the senior management level) with decision-making authority, the CPG is "flatter" than a functional department. It integrates the work of various people in highly coordinated efforts to meet performance objectives. In a core process group, team members are peers working either in individualized tasks or in concert. Emphasis falls on the work of the group as a whole rather than on individual performance, although the group or the process owner will intervene when performance, for whatever reason, goes off track.

■ The traditional functional department is composed of individuals with a relatively narrow, homogeneous set of skills (for instance, an engineering department employs only people trained in engineering) regardless of the company's value proposition. But the CPG typically arranges people in multidisciplinary ways—dictated by what is required to deliver the value proposition. While core process groups prefer that their members have broader, more multidisciplinary skills, they can also include those specialists who can handle tasks of a more challenging technical nature that arise within the core process. For example, design engineers on Motorola's Supply Management commodity teams work directly with suppliers. They are thus in a better position to ensure that parts will meet quality specifications and Motorola's "ease of manufacturing" requirements, and that the teams continue to perform at the highest level as they work with the other links in the value chain.

These distinctions between core process groups and traditional functional departments are crucial to understanding how to transform your company into a horizontal organization. It is not enough merely to move one structural "box" to another place in the organizational chart; essential to the horizontal organization is the creation of key process-based groups. As discussed in chapter 10, you must first create the vision and establish the strategy you think will get you to where you want to go. Obviously there are no guarantees that this strategy will work, but without it no amount of horizontal design will help you.

Nor will the simplistic exercise of "moving boxes" around in the organizational chart answer the question of which employees and teams work best in which situations or at which tasks. In addition, organizing horizontally requires that you consider the specific skills and behaviors necessary—as well as how to develop these skills and behaviors—to achieve the highest level of productivity and continuous improvement in the delivery of your value proposition. It is both inadequate and infeasible to substitute a movement of desks and offices for purposeful development of a successful organization.

Once you see how the value proposition determines which processes are critical to the new organizational structure—what those processes are designed to achieve and which combinations of skills and experiences are important—you can see explicitly how in the horizontal organization strategy directly drives the design of the whole.

This chapter presents the initial design and change management steps that will help you create a horizontal structure that is perfect for your organization. Unlike many recent and fashionable imperatives to alter radically both what you do and how you do it, this chapter presents an approach that you can use or adapt to your special circumstances. Underpinning that design are twelve principles,[1] five of which we discuss in this chapter:

- Organize around cross-functional core processes, not tasks or functions.

- Install process owners or managers who will take responsibility for the core process in its entirety.

- Make teams, not individuals, the cornerstone of organizational design and performance.

- Decrease hierarchy by eliminating non-value-added work and by giving team members who are not necessarily senior managers the authority to make decisions directly related to their activities within the process flow.

- Integrate with customers and suppliers.

Using these five principles (plus the seven discussed in chapter 12), you can develop an organization structure to bring together the right people to perform the right processes and deliver the value proposition to your customers. The five principles taken up in the present chapter constitute the "design" phase of the transformation, whereas the seven principles discussed in chapter 12 speak to the issue of how best to develop those behaviors and skills necessary to institutionalize the change and help assure the success of your horizontal organization. Informing these twelve principles must be a plan for managing the large-scale change that moving to a horizontal structure entails. To achieve success in this effort, business leaders must do more than make pronouncements and issue orders from atop the organizational pyramid; they must be willing to be personally involved in leading the change and enlisting the support and involvement of all key stakeholders in the transformation.

Organize around Processes

While undertaking a change of this magnitude can be both risky and intimidating, doing nothing can be worse. The first step, therefore, in deciding whether and how you should begin a major transformation is to study carefully what your company does best and compare that with what you *want* it to do. In most cases, the end-to-end core processes fundamental to your business can be enumerated on the fingers of one hand: Whether you lead a global telecommunications company or operate a small family-owned business, you will find no more than five, more likely two or three (and occasionally one, as in the case of Barclays), core processes that form the essence of your business (see sidebar 5).[2]

5
A Test for Core Processes

1. Does each process or interdependent set of activities, information, decisions, and material flows, significantly impact the delivery of value?

2. Has the entire chain of related activities, information, decisions, and material flows extending even across functional, geographic, business unit, and company boundaries been included? Note: This means that all upstream— those close to suppliers—as well as those downstream— those close to your customers—have been integrated into the core process.

3. Does the core process account for a significant portion of the company's costs or revenues?

4. When fully optimized, does the core process exist independently of other core processes you have identified?

5. Does the process have measurable outcomes?

Some organizations have relatively simple core processes; others are extremely complex. Some produce tangible products that can be immediately shipped to customers; others perform tasks in a service. Some processes, when redesigned for maximum efficiency, can be performed by one team or occasionally even by a single individual.[3] In other cases such as Ford's Customer Service Division, the complexity and length of the core processes requires multiple teams comprising thousands of employees and many process owners.

The activities and skill sets required by the core processes dictate how many and what types of teams you should establish. If the processes are relatively simple, with fewer steps, one set of teams may be all that you need. If the processes remain relatively consistent, but their products change—say, you make the same product with specific refinements for different customers or different geographical regions—you may decide to install *parallel teams* to handle the work. As we have seen in the example of Motorola's Space and Systems Technology Group (SSTG), different commodity teams manage the entire supply process, each taking responsibility for a particular commodity.

If your organization has a core process that is too long or complex for a single team to handle, you can use *linked teams* to carry out the process sequentially. Ford Customer Service Division (FCSD) provides an excellent example of such linkage, whereby teams of experts in parts supply and logistics, for instance, engage in analyzing the parts supply network, purchasing, directing the flow of materials, and distributing parts to dealerships worldwide. Meanwhile, these teams work directly with teams in business development and technical service to build the right capability in all dealerships that encourages problem solving, process mapping, and other activities designed to fulfill Ford's promise to fix the problem right the first time on time.

A third possibility is the *adjunct team,* which is illustrated by the Xerox product development team. This group has end-to-end responsibility for each new product's evolution, but the team often borrows people from other teams whenever it needs their special skills and expertise. Although the core membership of the team remains stable, the number of team members can fluctuate whenever new skills are required.

As illustrated in chapters 2 and 5-8, process teams[4] may exist at practically any level within the organization and may integrate technical expertise and multidisciplinary skills. At the simplest level (*not* to be confused with a "simple" process!) is the team focused on a single set of activities comprising a process within a larger core process. The GE Salisbury plant, for instance, is organized around the build-to-order process that can be viewed as a critical part of a more extensive, "end to end," "order generation through fulfillment" core process. Building over 70,000 variations of one product, teams within the build-to-order process bring their efforts and expertise to bear on creating and delivering the company's value proposition. But their work also cuts across functions and company boundaries to include engineers, suppliers, and customers.

Companies such as Motorola and Barclays Bank must decide whether to establish separate business units for each line of business and whether to focus these business units along dimensions such as geography, products, or customers. Once the decision has been reached, however, leaders are still left with the question of whether to "go horizontal" or remain vertical in some part of all of the business units that are established. Some units of Ford, for instance, have remained largely vertical, while other units such as FCSD have elected to restructure themselves horizontally.

The new Xerox 2005 provides a slight variation to the more conventional redesign around core process groups. While it incorporates many features of horizontal organization (the formal organization structured around cross-functional teams, an integrated flow of activities without boundaries between functions, and multiskilled, cross-disciplinary teams, and so forth), Xerox represents an integrated system of "mini-businesses," some of which have organized cross-functionally around a section of the value chain of activities. The company has kept the research and sales sections of the value chain largely functional. Meanwhile, other activities—from product development through sales planning (including product planning, development, engineering, and manufacturing)—have become the focus of the various cross-functional business teams within the business groups under the executive vice president for business operations.

Horizontal design can extend across the boundaries of an individual company as well. The supply management organization of Motorola's SSTG illustrates that horizontality can extend even across company boundaries to integrate with suppliers and other elements in the value chain.

Such permutations of the horizontal structure are determined by the specific value proposition and performance challenges of the organization as well as the imaginations, the wills, and the needs of those responsible for analyzing, designing, and implementing the changes. Organizing around core processes rather than functions establishes a more natural fit between work and structure than the traditional vertical structure can achieve. Each functional department, after all, siphons off that portion of the work flow that it is designed to process, thus fostering in many organizations an attitude of "It's not my responsibility." The horizontal organization, on the other hand, integrates the process teams, opening up the sluices and enabling the work to flow vigorously but not uncontrollably.

Install Process Owners

To regulate that flow and coordinate the work of its core process teams, the horizontal organization establishes agents for oversight, control, and accountability. These are, of course, traditional characteristics of the vertical hierarchy, but they do not disappear when a company elects to go horizontal. Although the actual lines of reporting may be redrawn, there must remain a level of managerial responsibility even in the smallest and simplest core process group.

The responsibilities of "owning" a core process fall sometimes to one person, sometimes to an entire team or a small number of team members. In most cases, the burden of responsibility is borne by senior managers representing different activities in the core process. The precise configuration will depend on a number of factors, including the complexity of the process, the availability of experts in the process itself who can also demonstrate leadership abilities, and the willingness of team members to follow the instructions of the process owners or to set that agenda for themselves.

The owner or owners, however, must be willing to take responsibility for the entire end-to-end process (see sidebar 6). Managers cannot oversee only that part of the process that they happen to like the most or know the most about. Their regulations must apply to all or to none.

Ideally, the senior people who are process owners should themselves work as a process-owner team (see sidebar 7). They should aim for cooperation, not competition; for effective joint problem-solving, not one-upmanship; for added value to the end product, not salary increases for themselves alone. By actually participating as team members, these process owners benefit from the experiences and collective knowledge of the team, come to share values, and form realistic expectations about the amount and quality of work that can be performed by the various teams, as well the challenges to building and achieving effective team performance.

In Ford's Customer Service Division, four individuals along with a

6
Characteristics of the Process Owner

1. Predisposition to oversee and work with the teams within the process group

2. Experience as a senior manager—it is preferred that the process owner be a team of senior managers

3. Major equity in the process group

4. Clear understanding of activities and challenges in the core process

5. Knowledge of upstream and downstream activities, suppliers, and customers

6. Ability to influence people, to act as coach, to support the teams' efforts

7. Ability to personify values, particularly the adherence to continuous improvement and learning

team of senior managers have complete oversight over their respective core process groups. They stand between the top levels of FCSD management and frontline employees. In a horizontal organization such as Motorola SSTG's supply management organization, however, the senior managers on the process owner teams themselves have what they would call their senior staff or managers who make it part of their job descriptions to deliver the value proposition and keep the teams' focus on satisfying customers and maintaining the highest quality standards. But there is no managerial level between the process owner team and frontline teams.

Process ownership, therefore, depends largely on factors such as the demonstration of leadership, the ability to delegate authority as well as to work with both frontline employees and top managers, and a thorough understanding of the relationship between the value proposition and the

7
Process Owners' Responsibilities

1. Define performance objectives—in support of the company's overall value proposition—for the core process group.

2. Monitor team members' performance and resolve disputes.

3. Promote and drive continual performance improvement and effective collaboration throughout the core process group.

4. Develop process plans and budgets.

5. Serve as a process "champion."

6. Build a sense of shared objectives and support within the core process group; help members develop complementary skills and mutually beneficial working methods.

7. Evaluate and certify progress toward the goal.

8. Identify and remove bottlenecks and impediments to performance in the core process itself as well as any unhealthy resistance among team members (not all resistance is necessarily bad).

9. Represent all areas of activity along the core process.

10. Recognize and reward the good work of team members; help coach those who are having trouble meeting objectives, or in the worst case, remove or reassign them to other jobs.

work of the teams under one's direction. If the key objective of a horizontal transformation is to improve performance, then the architects of that structure must determine what lines of oversight and direction are best suited to the particular value proposition, the particular mix of human skills and experiences, and the various elements in the organization's value chain. It is much more difficult to build a house and then look for a place to put it than to adapt the architectural design to make the best use of the land on which that house will sit.

Make Teams the Cornerstone of Design

One of the primary assumptions about teams is that if two heads are better than one, 20 or so heads will be better than two. The validity of this assumption, of course, rests with the quality of the people who form the team in the first place, their willingness to devote themselves to fulfilling the needs of the team and to relinquish their individual desires to elevate themselves at the expense of others or the product they are working on. Its validity also rests on the organization's ability to design and support teams so that they perform at the highest and most efficient level possible. All teams do not function equally well, as the sports pages tell us every day (see sidebar 8). On the whole, however, if process owners and their advisors act wisely and purposefully, they can create teams of excellence which will be the principal building blocks of the entire organization and its new design.

With few exceptions, the complexity of the core process requires highly skilled teams with strong expertise and the confidence to be self-starters. If vertically structured organizations are immobilized by multiple hand-offs and delays for authorization from on high, horizontally structured companies will founder when teams lack the necessary skills and confidence to engage fully in the organization's core processes.

In the late 1980s and early 1990s, for instance, the Occupational Safety and Health Administration (OSHA) was an organization pulled apart by its attempts to satisfy various priorities while cost-conscious politicians attacked its budget at every opportunity. Both its internal bureaucracy and its position within the federal government helped create an unwieldy set of authorization channels: The organization simply had to please too many masters. During the early years of the Clinton administration, however, Secretary of Labor Robert Reich began holding "town hall" meetings with OSHA employees to hear their concerns about reinventing government and reorganizing OSHA in the wake of some 250,000 layoffs in the federal government. Reich appointed Joe Dear, well known

Requirements for High-Performing Teams

1. Membership of no more than 25 employees, although most teams number perhaps 10-15 members

2. Complementary skills

3. Commitment to a single purpose or performance goal

4. An attitude of mutual accountability (that is, no finger pointing)

5. Mutual respect for each other's expertise and contributions

Source: Jon R. Katzenbach and Douglas Smith, *The Wisdom of Teams*
(Boston: Harvard Business School Press, 1993), p. 45.

for his governmental reforms at the state level, to head up the changes at OSHA which were designed to improve OSHA's ability to make significant reductions in workplace injuries, illnesses, and deaths.

Dear asked Leo Carey and Kenneth Maglicic to lead a multifunctional, multilevel (that is, "diagonal slice") redesign team that focused on redesigning the 65 OSHA field offices, where approximately 1,500 employees worked. Merely setting a new set of standards for workers would not have adequately addressed OSHA's problems. As Dear explains, "Redesign is a great method for getting an organization to rethink how it performs its work. We were trying to break this rigid, hierarchical, change-resistant, bureaucratic culture and replace it with teams authorized to evaluate every aspect of field operations and to make whatever changes they needed, within the limits of the law."

In OSHA's new horizontal structure, an area director retains the authority of each area office and directs the work of two types of office teams: A strategy team takes responsibility for collecting data, identifying and prioritizing problems, analyzing causes, and proposing solutions; a response team handles reports of actual dangers, responds to workers' complaints, and takes account of safety and health violations in the workplace. Moreover, both types of teams are cross-trained and cross-functional, with both safety specialists and industrial hygienists, for example, residing on the same teams. Although such principles as cross-functional training, empowerment, and multiskilling do not show up on the organizational chart depicted in Fig. 2.2, they are essential means of developing the needed behavior and skills for teams to perform to their maximum potential—and continually improve on that performance in a horizontal organization.

Flatten the Hierarchy

"Breaking the bureaucratic culture," as Dear puts it, is an essential step in the transformation process. Too often, however, it has been equated with the wholesale elimination of managerial ranks. In both large and small companies, senior managers continue to make deep cuts in personnel as a quick-and-easy solution to their companies' problems. This "solution," however, just as often becomes a continuation of the problem.

As illustrated by all the case studies in this book, the purpose of the horizontal organization is *not* to do away with all managers below the CEO. Inevitably, companies that go horizontal will see some flattening of their hierarchies. The reasons for this are clear. First, the reengineering of core processes to deliver the value proposition requires the elimination of any work or activity that adds no value. Second, when decision-making authority is vested in frontline employees, they take over responsibilities typically held by middle managers. But a transformation to the horizontal organization does not necessarily mean a loss of jobs. Ron Goldsberry, general manager of FCSD, points out that the makeover to the horizontal in his division at Ford, although it resulted in some transfers and reassignments, it did not force the termination of *any* employee.

As we have seen in the case studies, some hierarchy remains even in the most radical of horizontal changes. People still need leaders to develop strategy, resolve problems with personnel and production, allocate resources, and hold employees accountable. Mintzberg's anatomy of managerial roles is by no means overturned by the company's decision to develop a horizontal structure; indeed, those roles—figurehead, leader, liaison, monitor, disseminator, spokesperson, entrepreneur, disturbance handler, and negotiator—are needed as much as ever.[5]

Mike Ockenden of Barclays Bank's Home Finance Division (HFD), for example, has intentionally expanded the province in which HFD employees act to solve customers' problems. Although their decision-making authority has vastly increased, Ockenden still at the end of the day remains in charge and has the final say on major capital investments, credit accounts, and loan approvals.

In some cases, traditionally placed managers are in line to become the owners of core processes. They will direct the work of the teams assigned to each process and keep watch over the team's activities, intervening when necessary to handle a personnel issue or help solve a problem with the supply chain. With their managerial skills, knowledge of market trends, and understanding of personnel procedures, those managers are often the best candidates to take control of cross-functional processes that create the value proposition. In other cases, some managers will need to remain in control of functional units or vertical processes, so long as they adopt the attitude of becoming true partners in process—that is, working side by side with the core process groups to deliver the value proposition.

In developing a change management strategy, it is important *not* to treat this reorganization initially or fundamentally as a traditional human resources issue. You should base your decision to decrease hierarchy on the identification of the core processes that deliver the value proposition, not on the individuals who have the most seniority at your organization or the best sales records. While those traits are important, the identification of core process owners should hinge on the question of who can best motivate and empower the people in the group, remove barriers to their work, and coordinate the team's work with that of other teams and stakeholders in the organization.

Before the design and implementation of the horizontal supply management organization at Motorola's Space and Systems Technology Group, as many as seven or eight levels of management might have been involved in the purchase of supplies. A senior buyer reported to a section manager who reported to a purchasing manager, and on up the line to the division manager. After reorganizing into horizontal process teams, the new supply management organization reduced these managerial levels to one or at most two: a process manager and, in certain non-exempt areas, a supervisor. "Other than those," says Larry Burleson, SSTG's vice president and director of operations and supply chain management, "there are no management levels." This decrease in hierarchy is possible largely because process teams absorb many of the former responsibilities of managers.

During the transformation itself, many companies find it necessary to install a steering committee to provide leadership, help set strategy, and facilitate the redesign process. As a change management tool, this steering committee can help break bottlenecks and overcome resistance from stakeholders if it occurs (and it probably will). As the hierarchy is flattened, the steering committee can act temporarily to make sure that the design teams are adequately staffed, thoroughly motivated, and provided with the resources they need to design a new organization that can do a superior job of delivering the winning value proposition. Above all, senior executives must keep clearly in their minds that the fundamental purpose of the move to a horizontal structure is *not the change itself but the delivery of the value proposition.* The organization must continue performing, even while the transformation is taking place.

Integrate with Customers and Suppliers

Organizing around cross-functional core processes, installing process owners, making teams the cornerstone of design and performance, and flattening hierarchy—all these design principles are confined primarily to elements *internal* to the organization. The fifth design principle asks you to make sure you look beyond the walls of your enterprise to those elements in the value chain that have a direct impact on the delivery of your value proposition. In particular, you need to ask how you can better integrate your customers and suppliers into the core processes that define the work you do and deliver the value proposition.

At Motorola, for instance, the supply management teams regularly meet with both suppliers and customers, thereby exercising control on both sides of the production process. Karen Chapman, a member of the mechanical commodity team within the supply management organization, notes that team members set up the metrics, assess risks, and gather the information they need to compare various suppliers in order to determine which ones to do business with.

We work with our suppliers and track what they are doing to decrease cycle time and focus on continuous improvement. We want to see what they are doing at their facilities to improve work with their subcontractors because how they work affects how we work. The quality of our suppliers' products, of course, affects the quality of our products, so if we can identify a problem they are having, we can develop a plan to help them correct it and keep it from happening again.

Karen Chapman, member of the mechanical commodity subteam, Motorola SSTG

Although it may initially seem like an intrusion into the organization's privacy, such close and direct work with suppliers and customers often pays for itself in short order. Inviting customers and suppliers into your facility—or, on the other side, sending your people out to visit their sites—increases your chances of delivering the right value proposition to the right customer. At GE Salisbury and Motorola, for example, others in the value chain have the opportunity to spell out exactly what products and services they can provide or need for themselves.

As we have seen in the case of Motorola's supply management organization discussed in chapter 5, certain suppliers work directly with company representatives on teams and meet face to face with end users or intermediate customers, tackling production issues such as improving cycle time and devising more coherent plans to manage risk. Motorola representatives alert suppliers to points in the process where they might need to handle parts with particular sensitivity or schedule an inspection with Motorola before completion of a project. In addition, every month Motorola sends primary suppliers a summary documenting metrics dating back as far as one year. The company evaluates each supplier's quality (in terms of defective parts per million) and rates each according to delivery criteria for the same 12-month period. After reaching mutual agreement with suppliers on goals for quality, price, and design, Motorola teams establish those goals as part of the company's Six Sigma continuous improvement process.

Likewise, Ford's Customer Service Division has fine-tuned its repair processes with teams responsible for parts design and availability and standardized services so that customers now receive better service for lower prices. According to Ron Goldsberry, FCSD's focus on being the world's best customer service organization has helped the division reduce prices in some cases by as much as 50 percent. It accomplishes this goal by managing its value chain with eagle-eyed presence. If customers indicate through surveys, for instance, that they are willing to pay X dollars for a repair, but no more, and if FCSD determines that the competition is offering that repair in that price range, then the various process teams at FCSD will work with suppliers to find the right parts at the right price, as well as negotiate with technicians over labor costs and with dealerships over profit margins until the unit has arrived at a competitive price for the repair. As Goldsberry puts it, he spends a great part of his time in just this kind of activity, helping his people manage the overall value chain in order to provide the best service at the best price to Ford's customers.

I spend a significant amount of my time making sure that we are aligned with the totality of Ford Motor Company as well as with our dealers and our customers.

Ron Goldsberry, vice president and general manager,
Ford Customer Service Division

No doubt, these five design principles, like the other principles discussed in chapter 12, will meet with no small degree of resistance when change managers introduce them. Typically, 10 to 25 percent of the people at any organization will be ready for change, in fact eager to embrace it. But at least half the employees in the organization are likely to have mixed feelings about the redesign and resist committing to it wholeheartedly until either some tangible results are available or a concerted, thoughtful effort is made to enlist their support. Perhaps another fourth of them will resist change, no matter how well the business case supports the need for the change. At OSHA, for example, Joe Dear found that approximately one in four employees actively resisted the changes and remained fully skeptical even after the results started coming in. As Dear notes, OSHA workers asked why bother to generate a lot of enthusiasm for a change that most of them would not be around long enough to see implemented. Such a "wait-and-see" attitude is not uncommon among employees at both public and private organizations undergoing a major change. Although it does present some anomalies—the average assistant secretary in most government agencies, for instance, lasts only about 18 months in that position—OSHA offers many lessons to change managers involved in the transformation of a public or private enterprise that needs to prepare for this resistance to change.

Formulating a horizontal design, especially one that you can then "sell" to the employees in your organization, requires rigorous thinking about the assumptions you and other managers in your organization hold about business processes, performance, and people. The truly horizontal organization is not simply comprised of teams of employees within certain business functions, such as customer service or human resources, any more than it installs just another level of management as "process owners." Having broken down the walls of many functions within an organization, horizontal teams must work productively and cooperatively with people still working in any remaining functions.

After determining that their company can profit from a horizontal structure, after all the planning and discussion, change managers need to make the case for an urgent shift to a newly transformed company and create a guiding coalition or steering committee of stakeholders who can help make that change. As we will see in the next chapter, this coalition can help introduce ways for empowering people through cross-functional training and multiskilling. Larry Burleson of Motorola SSTG's supply management organization succinctly describes the ideal attitude of managers toward empowering employees when he says, "To be a good manager in a horizontal organization, you have to be a person who gets fulfillment out of watching other people succeed."

12 PHASE THREE—INSTITUTIONALIZE THE APPROACH

HOW WILL YOU MAINTAIN MOMENTUM?

Football coaches can tell you how relatively easy it is to get their players to memorize the rule book and learn the plays, but how difficult it is to get them to execute the end sweep or the onside kick. Neither athletic agility nor behavioral changes happen by fiat.

It is no less difficult for the visionary CEO or a change management team intent upon restructuring an organization horizontally. Such a thorough makeover requires months, often years, of cooperative effort, some trial and error (no matter how well you plan for the transformation), a commitment to learn from the trials and errors, and a concerted effort to enlist and obtain support from top managers, from frontline workers, and from most everybody in between. After the initial burst of energy following your call for a horizontal makeover, how can you maintain the momentum to carry the organization through the months and years of incremental change?

In this chapter we look more specifically at some of the techniques you can use to persuade employees, managers, customers, suppliers, and other stakeholders to support the new horizontal structure. But these should be distinguished from the seven additional principles discussed in this chapter, principles that exist on an on-going basis for the life of the organization, not just during the brief period (which some organizations measure in years) when the changes are being implemented. One way of thinking about this distinction is to note that change management principles help you get from here to there, from inefficient bureaucracy to streamlined horizontal structure, whereas the seven additional principles address the behaviors, skills, and cultural issues that are necessary for a horizontal organization to succeed on an on-going basis. In particular, those seven principles underlying the transformation to the horizontal are as follows:

- Empower people by giving them the tools, skills, motivation, and authority to make decisions essential to the team's performance.

- Use information technology (IT) to help people reach performance objectives and deliver the value proposition to the customer.

- Emphasize multiple competencies and train people to handle issues and work productively in cross-functional areas within the new organization.

- Promote multiskilling, the ability to think creatively and respond flexibly to new challenges that arise in the work that teams do.

- Redesign functional departments or areas to work as "partners in process performance" with the core process groups.

- Measure for end-of-process performance objectives (which are driven by the value proposition), as well as customer satisfaction, employee satisfaction, and financial contribution.

- Build a corporate culture of openness, cooperation, and collaboration, a culture that focuses on continuous performance improvement and values employee empowerment, responsibility, and well-being.

These principles will help maintain, if not increase, the momentum you have initiated by organizing your organization around processes and teams. In contrast to the five principles discussed in chapter 11, each of which is concerned primarily with the *design* of the makeover, these seven are oriented more toward the *institutionalization* of the skills and behaviors that are required for a successful horizontal organization.

As we saw in chapter 11, the principles must work in tandem if the horizontal organization is to be successfully institutionalized. More than just "moving boxes" around the organizational chart, even more than doing the design in the first place, the institutionalization of the horizontal structure represents a challenge of developing the necessary values, behaviors, and attitudes in all employees so that they can work in tandem and increase their performance. Note that these are not so much sequential "steps" as they are a set of guidelines to organizational thinking, planning, and coaching.

That said, however, it is essential to note that underpinning the first five principles which focus on design is the fundamental need to organize around core processes rather than tasks or functions. Directed by the requirements of your value proposition, you must decide first what your organization's core processes are, redesign them, and restructure around them, before you can identify and build the appropriate teams, understand how best to integrate with customers and suppliers, decrease hierarchy, and install process owners. This chapter recognizes that mere "design" is not enough. To make organizing around core processes work, you must develop the necessary supportive skills and behaviors.

To get from "here to there"—that is, to manage the change itself—requires laying out to all stakeholders the vision, the urgency of the change, and its consequences. Resistance is sure to come from all corners, but you can stave off some of it—perhaps a great deal of it—by keeping people informed, inviting their comments, and listening to their suggestions. It is, after all, a cardinal principle of human nature that excluding people is one of the surest ways to build their distrust and resistance.

The key to unlocking the potential of the horizontal organization is giving people a stake in the change and an opportunity to design it. Then achieve performance improvements in the short term that demonstrate in concrete, measurable, and personally satisfying ways that the changes these people are involved in are actually working for them.

Joe Dear, former assistant secretary of labor for Occupational Safety and Health

---

Empower People

Although it has become one of the clichés of choice in the late twentieth century, the term *empowerment* has significant consequences for the horizontal organization. But for those consequences to have meaning, the notion of empowerment cannot be inflated with puffy promises and feel-good fabrications. When managers trust employees to evaluate the supply chain or redesign the steps in a core process, for instance, they enable those team members to make valuable contributions to the product or service the company offers its customers.

Empowerment lies at the heart of implementing and institutionalizing a horizontal makeover: It directs the kind and degree of training, multi-skilling, and performance measurement that the redesign team/change management team establishes. Without empowered employees, an organization has little hope of creating a corporate culture of continuous performance improvement and collaboration, which is necessary to deliver the value proposition successfully. After all, if employees do not have access to the tools and materials of production, including shared data and critical information affecting performance, they cannot make informed decisions and be held accountable for them.

Throughout his writings, Karl Marx faulted capitalism for fostering a sense of alienation from the process of work and its products. If, as Marx argued, people are defined by the work they do, then stripping them of any meaningful connection to their labor deprives them of their humanity, their sense of purpose and inclusion in the work they do.[1] Socialism, Marx's alternative, has in most of its manifestations proven equally unsuccessful in ennobling workers and increasing the care with which they do their work.

The traditional vertical hierarchy also failed, by and large, to engender the desired psychological, emotional, and creative connections between workers and the products they produced. Frederick Taylor and his followers could measure workers' productivity but not guarantee that those workers would be any more committed to what they produced and actually believe, as the Ford Motor Company proclaims, that Quality is Job 1. It has long been the assumption among enlightened business managers that workers fully and seriously committed to their work will, either for material or psychological rewards, take pains to ensure their work is of the highest quality. But the deep sense of "ownership" continues to elude both managers and workers in most vertical organizations. By entrusting employees to carry out many of the traditional duties of the manager, however, the horizontal organization offers an antidote to the dispiriting and demoralizing sense of alienation that plagues many a modern organization.

In vertical organizations, people often use information to control others and protect themselves or their turf, not to support the frontline employees and improve the company's performance. Patients shunted from one department to another in the local hospital or from one service representative to another at a large department store experience the nerve-fraying dysfunction of the vertical organization at its worst. In horizontal organizations, by contrast, information flows freely wherever it is needed. Information is the indispensable fuel that drives the value proposition and empowers people to do their best work.

Some kinds of information, such as the just-in-time (JIT) approach to inventory control from which it takes its name, can arrive "just in time." That is, team members do not need to concern themselves with inventory control until the moment they have to make decisions about setting priorities in production, substituting parts, responding to sudden changes in the market, and the like. Similarly, job training itself can take place just in time for employees to meet newly set performance objectives, especially when the organization has set "stretch" targets.[2]

This is what happened at OSHA, for example, when area offices identified short-term objectives critical to improved performance. Teams within each geographical area developed action plans for "moving the ball" and meeting their challenges within a specified eight-week period. One office, for instance, set a stretch target for a 50 percent reduction in response time to workers' complaints about unsafe conditions in the workplace. The team developed an eight-week action plan, received "just-in-time" training in process improvement and problem solving, and achieved its goals.

Key to this success, the OSHA workers had to have a *context*—a real-life situation—for mastering the skills they needed. When they recognized the immediate need, they knew that there was a significant purpose to their work. Placing the training in the context of meeting a performance goal that both the organization and the workers themselves consider important is an ideal way to achieve measurable results from the training. OSHA workers themselves could observe the cause-and-effect linkage between performing and obtaining the necessary skills at precisely the right moment. When OSHA workers, not to mention the public at large, saw this linkage, they recognized the immediate benefits of training as a key enabler of better performance. Accordingly, OSHA personnel found that their work had benefits in the ''real'' world, not just on someone's work completion chart. These workers, newly empowered, were actually protecting their fellow workers from serious injuries, even death.

Last Christmas we had customers clamoring for a new Xerox machine. When our supplier pointed out that one of its gears would freeze if not properly lubricated, a group of three Xerox engineers hopped on a plane for the West Coast and worked in a warehouse late on Christmas Eve, unpacking all the machines, lubricating the gear, and then repacking them for immediate shipment. Our engineers simply realized that there was a problem and they set out to fix it. Without asking anybody's permission, they took ownership of the situation, hired some people to help them with the unpacking and loading, and got the problem fixed.

Jim Lesko, president of Xerox Supplies Group

Contrary to one popular misconception, the horizontal organization does *not* transform people into ''generalists'' who are unable to deal with technical issues that arise during the process. As Larry Burleson, vice president of Motorola's SSTG, notes, ''In forming teams, you do not want your people to sacrifice their expertise in their specific areas. It's important that they're perceived as the experts.'' To accomplish this goal, the organization needs to engage in continuous training of its employees, not only because technology keeps changing, but also because people do. Actual instruction on the intranet, for example, takes place every day at Ford's Customer Service Division, where service technicians in faraway locations can receive the most up-to-date training in vehicle repair and service.

The horizontal organization has to allow its employees to have meaningful input into the agenda of the core process group itself. At Motorola, this input begins to be realized as early as the interviewing process for new employees. Purchasing agents and supplier managers from the teams, for instance, participate fully in those job interviews. Up until a few years ago, managers at Motorola conducted all the work in scheduling, hiring, firing, buying, and problem solving. Now, however, team members themselves take part in those activities, assessing the needs of the team to meet customer demands, and ultimately increasing the employees' sense of empowerment and satisfaction.

Successfully empowering people also depends on motivating them to take the initiative *at any point* in the work process, to solve problems wherever they occur, in order to keep performance on track. To achieve this goal, employees cannot function in the dark: Depending on the particular process, they must have direct, immediate access to information concerning things like materials availability, production status and breakdowns, customers' special requirements, and suppliers' costs (to name a few). For this reason alone, information technology has been a boon to horizontal organizations, both large and small. At GE Salisbury, for instance, team members have direct contact with suppliers and can make decisions on the spot about which parts to order and at what price. Increases in authority, properly supported, can have a direct bearing on rewards, both monetary and psychological, as employees at many horizontal organizations such as GE Salisbury can verify.

Use Information Technology to Support Process-Based Performance

"Nothing has changed the way we work," says Richard Sparks, manager of Motorola's production purchasing, "more than e-mail. That is the single biggest information technology tool Motorola has installed in the past 10 years."

While there may be pieces of information technology that are more sophisticated and costly, certainly there is nothing to compare with e-mail in the distribution of information to large numbers of people both inside and outside the organization. As Sparks explains, a Motorola purchasing agent and a supply management engineer can gather information from a supplier on the cost, lead time, and performance specifications for a certain product, then distribute that information to 50 people instantaneously so that they can evaluate the product and plan for contingencies.

At Ford's Customer Service Division (FCSD), problems with sharing information ran deep. Ninety percent of all warranty repairs are covered by approximately 600 defined operations. But at one time FCSD published a manual that detailed nearly 3,250 possible options for repair technicians and salespeople. The excessive duplication and complexity helped to create unnecessary costs and confusion for FCSD personnel, not to mention a lot of irritation and extra expense for Ford customers.

In part as a result of the dramatic increase in the number of errors in warranty claims, FCSD saw the need for improved ways to make the best use of information technology. Since there was no global transmission protocol, data from one operation could not be re-used efficiently by repair personnel in other locations. Additional inefficiencies delayed publication of the FCSD operations manual, which each local market had to see through a translation from the original English into a language technicians elsewhere could understand.

As part of its transformation process to a horizontal organization, FCSD created a common technology base that could support simultaneous vehicle launches accurately and swiftly. The process included common formats, automatic "translation" into local languages, and faster cycle times. FCSD also installed information technology to allow its personnel to complete competency testing and to receive online instruction either at other dealerships or through satellite transmission when face-to-face instruction is either impossible or impractical. In short, FCSD's transformation to a horizontal organization could never have been achieved without the foresight of managers who provided a robust and accessible information technology network on a global scale.[3]

Moving the change effort to center stage in the mind of each stakeholder is hardly conceivable without information technology, but it is essential to remember that IT is merely a tool, not the end in itself. As always for the design of the IT system, including the technology enablers chosen and the information provided, the proper end is the impact that technology will have on the organization's ability to deliver the value proposition. The new FCSD common technology was important not because the technology was "nifty," but because it helped reduce errors and cycle times, both critical parts of FCSD's value proposition. At Ford's service centers in Germany, for instance, customer satisfaction with repairs and cycle times went from a dismal last place to the number one ranking in that market, largely because of the best-practices operations processes that make widespread use of information technology.

Change managers or the steering committee in charge of the change management effort will need to weigh carefully both the kinds of information to be shared and the degree to which that information should be accessible. The impact on improving the company's ability to deliver on its value proposition should act as the "acid test." Through training and other means of helping employees develop the required skills and behaviors, managers can help employees accept wholeheartedly the new responsibilities that the horizontal organization will require of them. While not every piece of information need be shared with every team member, it is essential to provide the *right* information to the *right* people in the time frame needed to improve performance.

The organizations profiled in chapters 2 and 5-8 show that information technology is a central feature of the successful horizontal organization in at least four main areas:

1. IT makes information available on a "real-time" basis to monitor performance. GE Salisbury teams, for instance, use an electronic monitor, visible to all on the shop floor, to track their progress in meeting production requirements. On a daily, weekly, and monthly basis, the supply management organization of Motorola's SSTG utilizes leading-edge technology to supply information on defect rates, cycle times, and order fulfillment, all in the name of delivering a winning value proposition. Such examples demonstrate the varied uses that organizations are making of improved IT.

2. IT supplies the tools needed to solve problems critical to the value proposition. FCSD, for example, uses IT to identify problems and track the progress in solving them. According to Salvador Psaila, manager for Ford's Worldwide Technical Support Operations, FCSD has reduced the number of calls from its technical assistance centers by as much as 15 percent. With the new horizontally empowered teams, technicians can more easily locate the information

they need. At the same time, the cost of developing information for its global processes has declined by 5 percent, according to Psaila.

3. IT makes best-practice knowledge readily accessible. As we saw in chapter 8, Xerox's FIRST system provides information instantaneously at any time to salespeople in the field, thus enabling them to answer customers' questions and provide up-to-the-second information about new products and services.

4. IT enables team members to collaborate effectively, crossing traditional departmental or functional boundaries that in the past would have hindered their communication. Xerox uses "COLAB" software to power some of its IT systems, allowing users to send data to each other and place complex material on large, high-resolution computer screens. Participants can scribble, draw, or make notations that are visible to others on the system.[4]

These are a few of the ways that information technology gives people the power to do work that a few decades ago was unheard of. As e-mail has changed the way we communicate both personally and professionally, so larger, more complex IT systems are changing the way we do business.

Emphasize Multiple Competencies

As Hall, Rosenthal, and Wade point out in a 1993 *Harvard Business Review* article, many reengineering efforts fail because managers define too narrowly the processes to be redesigned. Limiting a process to its functional area—for example, accounting or human resources—is not the way to address the organization's primary problems, especially those that extend across functions. According to the authors of the study, the redesigned process "has little discernible impact on overall performance. Still more distressing, many managers . . . analyze improvements relative to the process being redesigned rather than the business unit as a whole."[5]

One implication of this argument is that many managers find it tempting to restrict process redesign to functional areas. Perhaps they are so tempted because the functional structure continues to dominate both their thinking and that of frontline employees. It is much harder to imagine how accountants or human resource specialists, for instance, can learn about each other's work to the extent that they develop at least an appreciation for what others do in their jobs. Developing that degree of cross-functionality in the horizontal organization demands a concerted effort from both top managers and workers. Ideally that effort should produce a group of committed team members who know and respect each other's work so well that with some agility they can move from one position to another, whenever the need arises.

In some cases, of course, developing true expertise and competency in a job really does require specialization: The challenge of maintaining and nurturing the competencies required for Xerox to attain a leading edge was an argument for keeping Xerox researchers specialized in areas of great technological complexity. In other cases, however, people can learn to master different kinds of work. Where the expertise challenges are especially daunting, this may not be possible. Other areas that are not so challenging can probably be readily mastered by others as part of multiple skills they possess. On teams such as those at OSHA or GE Salisbury, the expertise requirements are not so daunting that team members cannot master most of them themselves. But not all team members can be engineers like the specialists at Motorola SSTG. Hence, teams need to be open to new members (or visitors), often on an ad hoc basis. Engineers can absorb a lot of what procurement people do on the teams without compromising their own knowledge of engineering; thus, they can help the team develop solutions with suppliers or customers.

To encourage people to become committed workers ready to accept broader responsibilities, you have to give them the training they need to perform in or to manage horizontal processes. At GE Salisbury, employees are rewarded for improving their skills, either by taking classes at a local community college or by receiving on-the-job training at the plant. Members of Motorola SSTG commodity teams have access to online courses in both managerial and technical areas. Using CD-ROM technology, for instance, employees can brush up their skills with software such as Pro Engineer, Application Specific Integrated Circuits (ASIC), and Design for Manufacturing. According to Sandra Hopkins, manager of systems and software team and streamline purchasing, the purpose is to satisfy the company's need to give its people "a hands-on knowledge of managing intellectual property." In the age of sophisticated technology and communications, which allows Motorola to partner with its customers and suppliers, the company recognizes that it must train its own people to conduct such correspondence across secure lines.

It is easy to see this agility in action at a facility such as GE Salisbury, where workers team up to manufacture lighting panel boards. Although there are thousands of variations for a single board, people at GE Salisbury have learned each other's work so thoroughly that they are able to switch from team to team when production needs arise. As we saw in chapter 6, some 90 percent of GE Salisbury employees in the build-to-order process know how to operate approximately 90 percent of the tasks on the production floor. This is known as the "90 by 90" rule, and going beyond this degree of shared expertise would be impractical.

Team 4 at GE Salisbury works both inside and outside the actual manufacturing cycle. Their jobs require experience in negotiating and excellent communication skills so that they can talk directly with customers and suppliers, keep track of materials flow, and handle inventory problems. Accordingly, GE Salisbury provides the resources for these employees to receive training and certification so that they can take control of a higher order of activities such as purchasing, scheduling, and customer service.

As noted by the former plant manager about Team 4, "If there are 10 individuals, one acts as a master scheduler for the entire plant; three others are purchasers; four take on customer service responsibilities; one works in logistics; and another handles steel suppliers. Virtually all those people have conducted each other's jobs at one point because they have been thoroughly cross-trained." Not only does trading off responsibilities keep team members more actively engaged in their work, but it also ensures that the build-to-order process continues to function smoothly whenever team members are away from their jobs.

In the case of GE Salisbury's build-to-order process, the primary performance challenge is cross-functional (Team 4 offers a clear example), yet at the same time the direct production part of the process itself requires a high degree of technical proficiency not just in one area but in several. GE Salisbury's 90/90 rule says that 90 percent of frontline workers know how to perform 90 percent of the tasks. As Opal Parnell, automatic equipment (robotics) operator, puts it, "If I get caught up with my own work, I know of other jobs in the plant that need to be done, and I just go do them." Harold Driver agrees: "I can fill in for the robots or fill in at one of the other lines, even helping out on maintenance if necessary. That is, I can work either with or on the equipment, and I like that part of my job."

The degree of job rotation evident at GE Salisbury, however, will not necessarily be matched by every company adapting a horizontal structure. Nor does it spell the end of technical expertise. Even at GE Salisbury, teams have to meet requirements for technical competency in building the lighting panel boards. Beyond that, they must develop the personal skills they need to function well as team members working with customers and suppliers to build products to exact specifications.

Instilling this degree of cross-functional competency demands a concerted effort from everyone in the organization. Not only does the training permit job rotation, but job rotation itself helps broaden the workers' appreciation of the work's complexity. New hires at GE Salisbury attend day or night classes, depending on which shift they work, two or three times a week and enroll in as many as three classes each semester. In addition, all GE Salisbury associates receive Six Sigma training. Employees attend classes provided by the company to improve communication skills and team skills, learn how to work better with customers, sharpen their knowledge of business economics, and master new technical skills and problem-solving techniques.

Similarly, to review training offerings and sign up for on-the-job training, Motorola employees consult an online compendium equivalent in size to the telephone book for a medium-sized metropolis. At Ford's Customer Service Division, employees working on the Technical Support Core Process Group have unlimited access—either through multimedia, satellite, or intranet—to training that is *fully funded* by the company. According to Salvador Psaila, manager for FCSD's global technical support operations, employees simply secure their supervisors' approval for any training program they want to take. "To my knowledge," says Psaila, "there are no refusals."

Some companies devote a great deal of attention to one-on-one coaching techniques or apprenticeships. Others are relying more and more on computer-based, interactive training through an intranet system. At Xerox, for instance, the Field Information Research Systems Team (FIRST) shares its expertise and technical notes about products with field representatives equipped with laptop computers. Installed in October, 1995, the intranet site registers as many as 70,000 hits a month from Xerox salespeople and customers seeking solutions to document reproduction problems.

The principle that people should be trained in multiple competencies is integral to the success of the horizontal organization in three primary ways: First, it ensures that the company is able to keep its core processes functioning smoothly and efficiently even in emergencies or in instances when essential employees are away from their jobs. Second, it promotes the idea of *right-skilling,* the need to find people with highly developed skills to perform the tasks at hand, thus optimally matching the experts with new positions or job descriptions as they arise. Third, the principle underscores the importance of giving people a deeper sense of their contributions to the core process in which they are working, as well as their significance to the organization itself. In short, a sense of self worth adds dollars to a company's coffers.

We add new technical talent to our managerial ranks by finding someone in our engineering department or one of the functional areas who already has the expertise and the discipline. We usually do not hire our managers directly from among those newly recruited from colleges and universities.

Kris Krishnaswamy, engineering and quality manager
for operations and supply chain management at Motorola SSTG

Promote Multiskilling

Once change managers have begun the makeover to a horizontal design, they realize that the flow of activities necessary for delivering the value proposition requires various combinations of multidisciplinary skills. These are much different from those dictated by normal functional arrangements, where an employee skilled in financial planning or human resources, for instance, typically does not show deep concern for integrating the work of a core process. Put one of these people on a team committed to integrating the work of the core process group, and the range of activities that the employee must master grows by quantum leaps.

Readiness to find and assign the right people for each job arises naturally out of continually training people to learn new approaches to work, accept more responsibilities, and manage themselves in the delivery of the value proposition. This means thinking creatively to find new ways to do things since the job is to deliver the value proposition rather than fulfill a predetermined job description. Some organizations carry this principle one step further to emphasize employees' developing multiple skills to complete tasks, particularly on a just-in-time (JIT) basis in order to meet performance challenges. In the horizontal organization, unlike the vertical, multiple competencies should be the rule, not the exception.[6]

There is the obvious analogy to JIT inventory control, whereby a company contracts with suppliers to have parts delivered precisely where and when they are needed, for instance, in the manufacturing of an automobile or the building of a condominium. The goal of JIT skills training is to generate measurable improvements and performance in a short time, perhaps a few weeks. Managers begin by identifying the performance goals they need to reach. Either they or the process owners discuss the targets with team members, refining the goals as necessary and persuading employees that only a team effort can achieve so high a mark. Next, managers introduce training, in the form either of specialists who work with the teams to help them develop new skills or of technology that can help workers meet the goals. Just as information technology helps both supplier and customer keep tabs on the availability and shipment of parts needed in a JIT manufacturing process, so it can help promote the acquisition of needed skills when the team requires them. Challenged to meet performance standards, team members find JIT training an important asset in their work. Although not all skills, competencies, and understanding can be developed in a just-in-time manner—indeed, some tasks require a deep knowledge of products and customers—the competencies to perform these tasks may best be improved by classroom training, online training, or on-the-job coaching.

All horizontal organizations, as well as most vertical companies, set performance objectives and goals to help drive their improvement and present challenges to all employees. The difference between the two types of organizations, however, lies in the intention behind establishing those goals: Whereas vertically structured companies tend to focus on task specialization in the service of "functional excellence," horizontal organizations emphasize the delivery of products and services with added value in order to win customers. In the horizontal organization, information technology both directs the design of core processes by systematically capturing and analyzing customer data, and supports the use of that data in monitoring customer value and meeting performance objectives. As important as it is, however, information technology by itself can never take the place of employees committed to cooperating with each other across functional boundaries in order to deliver the best products to solve any problems their customers have.

At GE Salisbury, for instance, the emphasis falls not on the production of a fixed number of lighting panel boards, but on the timely delivery of the boards constructed precisely to the customer's specifications. As a direct result of revamping its build-to-order process, GE Salisbury has realized numerous savings, including a sixfold improvement in inventory turns and a 50 percent savings in variable costs. Equally impressive is the plant's output, which has doubled since the initial transformation that began in the mid 1980s.

It is essential, therefore, to let value for customers drive behavior, performance, and design in the horizontal organization. And in order to achieve that performance, you must integrate customer value into the daily activities and behavior of employees at all levels.

Xerox, for example, has instituted a sophisticated 360° review process for all managers, by which one receives evaluation data from peers, subordinates, and supervisors. The company focuses on eight "cultural dimensions," including one's proclivity to work with teams, an orientation toward decisive action, positive attitudes about empowering people, and the ability to engage in open and honest communications. The premise underlying this evaluation is that employees create the cultural values that affect the working environment, the common good of team members, and the "Xerox way" of working—all of which eventually determines the value that customers experience in the products and services they receive.

While pride in the team effort can help carry many projects to completion and increase value for customers, that by itself is usually insufficient to maintain the level of performance a company needs. Rewarding individual skills, or the acquisition of those skills, as well as contributions to a team effort, will require that managers recognize the direct relationship between performance and reward systems. At the General Electric plant in Bayamon, Puerto Rico, for example, employees are rewarded for the number of different jobs they master, the communication skills and business understanding they develop, and the contributions they make to the team effort.[7] In a truly horizontal organization, where teams reach *across* functional boundaries rather than merely *within* a stovepipe department, recognition for multiple competencies and contributions to the team is a major factor in institutionalizing the changes that the horizontal organization brings. The difficult part is ensuring that rewards are fairly distributed, that the review process is open, and that employees learn from it rather than view it as a burden.

Partners in Process Performance

Anyone who has worked in a traditional hierarchical system (that is, just about *all* of us) knows what happens to information when it moves up or down the ladder. As Tom Stewart observes, because hierarchical systems need to keep themselves orderly and functional, managers at any level can put their special spins on any piece of data that moves. "Information is edited, delayed, politicized, and sometimes destroyed."[8] Logic suggests that such attitudes toward the sharing of information render an organization *disorderly* and *dysfunctional* rather than the other way around.

In the horizontal organization, such attitudes about sharing information are anathema. Consider, for example, the case of Ford's Customer Service Division (FCSD). In its FCS2000 initiative, nearly 12,000 employees worldwide combine forces to serve over 15,000 Ford dealers on five continents. As we have seen in chapter 2, the new FCSD comprises four main core process groups, which interact on a global scale to provide best-in-class customer service. The new FCSD, depicted in Fig. 2.1, actually is a "hybrid" business unit within the Ford organization, and, as such, combines elements from both the horizontal and the vertical organizations.

Unlike their counterparts in a strictly vertical organization, the vertical areas under Ron Goldsberry work hand in hand with the core process groups to deliver best-in-class service. A customer service representative analyzes a Ford dealer's service program in one European city, for example, then goes online to study a similar dealership, say, in São Paulo, Brazil, which has experienced and solved a similar problem. Rather than attempting to reinvent the wheel, the representative uses the Brazilian dealer's solution to help craft a business plan for the European dealer. Many people support that effort: the human resource personnel who have hired, trained, and directed the European representative; the information technology systems personnel who have installed the IT system that enables the customer service representative to discover that the São Paulo dealer has had a problem similar to the European dealer's; and the financial planners who have evaluated the resources necessary for building such a system in the first place.

Salvador Psaila provides a more complex example in the need to provide dealers with technical assistance whenever they call in for it. Past experience with such calls has suggested perhaps seven or eight measures to address just about any technical assistance problem that arises. Equipped with an action plan for each measure, FCSD operators seek to identify the dealer's problem—for example, insufficient training to install a new type of brake system—and to provide a solution that will work in the interim. Each month, the data is collected and tabulated, analyzed as to root causes, and sent to strategists, designers, and the like who find some innovation that solves the general problem. "People spend more of their time," says Psaila, "working on a solution than on pointing fingers at those who may have caused the problem."

Measure for "End-of-Process" Performance Objectives

With only a handful of exceptions in the first 25-odd years of its existence (that is, 1970-1994), OSHA never developed a practice of using empirical data to define health and safety problems and to formulate intervention strategies to combat them. Until Dear and his associates began a thorough redesign of the organization, OSHA never set clear, results-oriented performance targets—for instance, to reduce the number of fatal falls in the construction industry by a given percentage. As the redesign began taking shape in 1994, Dear accurately predicted that there would have to be a "complete change in the mindset of OSHA officials as they conduct their day-to-day operations and the means by which they measure success."

Similar changes have taken place at Motorola SSTG. According to Sandra Hopkins, the organization has certainly driven down costs that, prior to its horizontal redesign, it had to add to the price it charged for its products. The overhead rate Motorola SSTG charges customers now stands at an all-time low. Moreover, it has consolidated the work of some 16 departments or vertical functions into its cross-functional supply management teams, thereby reducing the administrative costs of supply management by over 60 percent.

Quality, according to Larry Burleson, has also improved dramatically: In 1989, the rejection rate for suppliers' products hovered between 15 and 20 percent; today, it is less than 1 percent. Motorola's production varies between 5.8 and 6 sigma per month in terms of defective parts, up from 4 sigma just a few years ago. And its on-time delivery rate has improved from as low as 60 percent in 1989 to nearly 92 percent today. As Burleson sees it, this improvement is directly attributable to Motorola SSTG's implementation of a horizontal supply management organization.

While such tangible results make managers, customers, and shareholders happy, it is important that employees also take heart in them and experience a commensurate rise in the satisfaction they derive from their work. This is where the horizontal approach offers a marked advantage over its vertical counterpart. FCSD employee satisfaction rose by 20 percent in the first year after the horizontal restructuring took place. Other studies have shown similar results to corroborate the conclusion that when employees have a direct and tangible influence on the products or services they produce, they demonstrate greater commitment to and care for the work they do and the customers they serve.

As a group, the managers of Motorola's supply management organization teams report that the horizontal organization has encouraged them to grow in personal and professional ways: They have enhanced their managerial skills, increased their ability to solve problems, and taken more interest in facilitating the work people do.

Motorola's supply management organization uses both quarterly and yearly measures to provide its managers and team members feedback about their performance. Peer evaluations as well as reports from process owners or managers figure prominently in measuring how successfully employees are engaged in the work of their teams. Self-monitoring provides another valuable source of information about employees' responses to the team approach. But Burleson identifies an important area of improvement when he points to the decline in the number and kinds of questions he receives from employees. When teams are formed, people initially feel some insecurity with their newfound responsibilities; accordingly, they ask the manager or team leader to give them the answers to their questions and find solutions to problems, rather than working through these solutions themselves. As they develop their confidence, their tendency to seek immediate gratification from authority figures diminishes. Instead, they search their own experience and expertise for solutions to problems the team encounters.

Cooperation, Collaboration, and Continuous Improvement

A story told earlier bears repeating here. Mike Ockenden, managing director of Barclays Bank Home Finance Division, tells how one Friday afternoon at 3:30, the computer system crashes. Customers are waiting in line to hear the fate of their mortgage applications, in hopes that they can begin moving into their new homes over the weekend. Work in the office screeches to a halt. People on both sides of the customer service desk enter crisis mode.

Under these circumstances at your typical vertical organization, functional departments would close their books, send employees home for the weekend, and leave customers disappointed and frustrated. Maybe those unlucky people would have their applications approved on Monday (maybe not), no matter that most of them now will have to make other living arrangements for the next 48 hours. Not so at Barclays HFD, however. At this point in the story, the tone shifts because this crash on this Friday afternoon happens at Barclays HFD, a horizontal organization, where the corporate culture is collaborative, cooperative, and focused on continuous performance improvement.

Ockenden recounts that everybody in the office pulls together to find a solution to this problem within minutes of its occurrence. The call goes out, "This is how we're going to fix the problem and make sure our customers all move into their new homes this weekend," he says. Ockenden himself walks slowly and deliberately to the IT office, confronts the person in charge of the network system, and says, "John, I want to thank you for pointing out the biggest single weakness in our network systems, which can damage our relationship with our customers. Now that we know what it is, we can fix it so it won't happen again.''

The point of his remark, Ockenden says, is that at Barclays HFD a mistake is not necessarily a bad thing. It is bad only if it is not acted on as an opportunity for learning and improving, an invitation to fix a problem and keep it from happening again. Although implicit, the cultural values are clear in Ockenden's words and actions: Learn from mistakes; fix a problem once, but do not fix the blame; and try not to disappoint customers whose expectations you have raised. Such experiences are always opportunities for learning and improving.

In the organizational chart for the typical vertical company, a line of authority connects each silo to a higher authority, but rarely to each other. Inside one of those silos the only line of sight is up or down. Because such models of organizational life do affect the way we work, it is not surprising that the traditional corporate cultures have emphasized the values of proprietary information and restricted access to technology, as well as an increased narrowness of orientation. From protecting one's turf to hoarding information essential to smooth operations, it is a matter of control. Further circumscribing people and their work, each department establishes its own internal objectives or quotas, often without regard for what other divisions are doing. In such organizations, openness and cooperation are scarce commodities.

The alternative proposed by a horizontal organization such as Barclays HFD is a collaborative culture promoting continuous improvement in delivery of the value proposition. Both within and between core process groups, the goal is to allow information to pass unimpeded so that team members stay attuned to the needs of the process itself as well as to those of suppliers and customers. Instead of rendering information static and proprietary, the horizontal organization proposes that information be "actionable"; that is, employees throughout the organization can access it and act upon it at a moment's notice. The organizational design itself becomes actionable as well in that it directs the work that people do in their business unit, core process, operating unit, or their entire organization.

One of the best examples of this open, cooperative culture occurs at the GE Salisbury plant in North Carolina. Team members in the build-to-order process share information about the progress of their work at their daily 7:00 A.M. meeting, where they plan for that day's production and try to anticipate upcoming supply problems. The members of Team 4, it will be recalled, serve as problem-solvers—bringing in other employees, for example, to work on a production team when emergencies arise, choosing another supplier if parts are unavailable, collaborating with customers to find solutions to a production problem whenever it occurs. Equipped with the right information technology, a customer can send specific requirements for lighting panel boards directly to the GE Salisbury team, which can process the order, build and ship the product, and bill the customer in one smooth operation.

This efficiency would be impossible, were it not for the cooperative atmosphere that exists at GE Salisbury. As Ryerson noted, "Our production teams have formal communication every eight hours to integrate their work schedules and keep production on track."

How do you incorporate such openness and cooperation into your organization's culture? The creation of cultural values is an extremely slow process, often taking years, but its pace of acceptance can be hastened when top leaders adopt the values in tangible, personal ways and show by their actions that they have done so. Ron Goldsberry, FCSD general manager, sums it up this way: "You have to be a teacher. From a cultural standpoint, all this horizontal organization around processes is new to most people. I have to make certain that we do not lose sight of our priorities, particularly our focus on customer service. I try to teach people a new point of view, a new focus on processes and shared responsibilities." That is no easy task, given that FCSD today is a global business unit within a large organization, with operations in various countries, each of which has a set of cultural values unlike any found elsewhere.

You can also hasten the adoption of values relevant to the horizontal organization by removing resistance, either by persuasion or through directly trying to remedy some of the "skill" or "will" gaps that may underlie resistance to the new values, or, if necessary and only as a last resort, through dismissal. The message has to go out that the train is departing the station and all riders have to be on board. Every organization has its resistors, people who oppose any change and even sabotage the effort to make improvements. The less vehement can be persuaded by incentives to change the way they do their jobs, but the most strenuous and persistent objectors will have to be replaced or given the chance to leave on their own accord. When most organizations begin the transformation process to a horizontal approach, employees are given the option of adapting to the new core processes and accepting increased responsibilities or either finding another position within the organization or leaving it altogether.

The key point to remember in building an open and responsive culture is that success depends on integrating *all* the design principles simultaneously rather than piecemeal. It makes no sense to ask frontline people to take on extra responsibilities if the company does not or cannot provide the adequate technology, resources, and incentives to facilitate and reward their work.

The open, collaborative corporate culture required for a successful horizontal makeover and continuous performance improvement is geared to help people attain their highest potential as creative and productive employees focused on delivering the value proposition. It is a culture conducive to promoting a greater sense of satisfaction with the work they do to bring that proposition to fullness and to make sure that customers are delighted with it. As Jim Lesko, president of the Xerox Supplies Group, puts it, "Every year we measure employee satisfaction by asking people how they rate themselves as members of the entire organization, as members of a group or team, and as individuals. Employee satisfaction is not just a survey we take, however; it is part of our bonus scheme and part of our core objective."

Continuous performance improvement is an additional feature that distinguishes the horizontal organization from many versions of reengineering which limit themselves to a "one-shot" change, a quick fix. Too many of these efforts leave organizations gasping for breath and employees struggling to explain the violent turns in their livelihoods. Unlike reengineering, a transformation to the horizontal organization is intended to give workers autonomy, task significance, identity, and skill improvement, all of which contribute to their sense of well being and job satisfaction. Accordingly, they pledge a higher degree of commitment to their work. And when that happens, job performance rises dramatically. The benefits, therefore, are spread among three recipients: The workers themselves who report they are happier in their jobs; the customers who report they are more satisfied with the organization's products and services; and the company itself, which sees its revenues and reputation improve.

Phase III of building your own horizontal organization, in sum, focuses on the implementation of those principles that help institutionalize the skills and behaviors required for a horizontal organization to be successful. The change management team has to make it clear to all stakeholders that their involvement and participation are essential to success. In addition, the team needs to engage people actively in the change effort. Team members may secure representation on the steering committee, design, change management, or roll-out teams, or leverage their participation in performance-based problem-solving efforts that help institutionalize the new skills of the organization as well as improve performance. Their involvement in the actual effort improves performance, as illustrated by the OSHA example. The success of the venture depends on maintaining or increasing performance levels, cooperating and collaborating with others, and ensuring employees' sense of satisfaction with the work they do. You can purchase the best IT system in the world, talk endlessly about strategy and vision, and redesign the structure of the organization, but if you do not develop the skills and behaviors, the corporate culture that values openness and collaboration, your chances for success will be greatly diminished.

As outlined in this and the preceding chapters, the 12 principles must be applied in an integrated fashion in the change management process. They cannot be implemented in isolation, in hopes that a little effort expended here or there will somehow magically reform the entire organization. Both top executives and process owners, as well as team members throughout the organization, have to keep their sights on improving performance, not being satisfied with some one-shot salvo that sputters off into a change of little import.

Above all, change managers must have the confidence to allow others to take charge, share authority and responsibility, and in fact take responsibility to make sure the others are fully supported and enabled to deliver the value proposition. Great leadership is often most clearly seen in the willingness and the follow-through to plan thoughtfully and develop the capability in others to be empowered and held accountable for meeting performance goals. ''Willingness'' is a first step, but not enough by itself: The follow-through is critical.

EPILOGUE
THE ROAD AHEAD
ANTICIPATING AND AVOIDING PROBLEMS
AND SEIZING OPPORTUNITIES

To reiterate an earlier theme, this book offers no silver bullet, no magic potion, no quick-fix, no crepe-lined bandwagon to jump on as the parade passes by. The hard truth is that business solutions to organizational problems—how to achieve maximum performance and make continual improvements in the value proposition, while empowering workers and increasing their sense of accomplishment and satisfaction—require time, effort, commitment, and inspired leadership. In the rush to find the quick fix, managers often allow their expectations or their sense of what is required to become unrealistic. Common sense often gets lost.

If this book could deliver only one message, it would be this: Any transformation of the old vertical hierarchy has to be undertaken with serious intent, full but realistic expectations, an eagle-eyed focus on continuous performance improvements, a deep concern for the well-being of employees, and a willingness to involve all stakeholders from the beginning by sharing with them the vision, the responsibilities, and the rewards of the horizontally structured organization. Simply redesigning core processes, in hopes that the rest of the organization will somehow take care of itself, makes about as much sense as pouring half the concrete foundation for a new skyscraper and then trying to erect the floor supports and joists.

There is no bullet, silver or otherwise, in the horizontal organization. I am convinced, however, that the principles of the horizontal organization establish a firm ground upon which to build your new organization, whether public or private, or transform the one you now manage. The principles of the horizontal organization can be applied equally well to the most bureaucratic of government agencies as they can to the most entrenched departments of a private enterprise.

The experiences of those involved in horizontal makeovers show us that change leaders require months, if not years, to do the groundwork, prepare the foundation, and then finish putting the new structure and supports in place. If Rome was not built in a day, why should we expect anything less for some of the major institutions of modern society?

Thorough planning and thoughtfulness, however, should never be confused with lethargy. Overly cautious change leaders who act with the speed of a glacier run a great risk of communicating indecisiveness and lack of discipline, the very messages that will derail a transformation of such importance. To succeed, leaders have to convey that sense of urgency, without which employees and other stakeholders are likely to view the makeover with increasing skepticism or remain utterly confused and bewildered. If done right, the transformation to the horizontal organization proceeds with deliberate speed, consideration, and discipline.

Let us have no illusions about such a change: It is analogous to a journey in which the destination keeps moving. Although the travel will become steadier the longer and farther you go, the road is sure to have its rough places and smooth. With the certain occurrence of more competitors, unpredictable market conditions, new regulations, and innovations in the way business is conducted, you must be always on the lookout for changes that will require you to adjust, refine, and improve your company's strategy, core processes, and all the other organizational enablers of performance. Above all, you must be vigilant for ways to enhance your organization's performance, both short-term and long-term.

The horizontal organization itself will not solve every business problem, of course. It is not proposed as a panacea, nor should a change management team treat it as a temporary solution to long-range problems. As illustrated by the six organizations discussed in this book, the horizontal component of any one business will display certain basic similarities (e.g., organized around process), while also exhibiting differences in specific application from that of its competitor or a similar company in another industry. The design, in other words, has to be tailored to fit each organization, taking into account its value proposition, goals, and the capabilities of its people. Uniting all stakeholders under a single vision, integrating them with the right systems and business enablers into a new entity focused on continuous performance improvement, will challenge even the most intrepid of leaders. But in their promotion of innovative solutions, change managers can show a deft hand at motivating people both inside and outside the organization to collaborate to make the new organization a reality.

Paul Allaire, CEO of Xerox, says there is an inevitable tension between the horizontal and the vertical aspects of a company and that people have to work at finding the right mix for their organization. This tension can manifest itself in any number of ways. For example, performance objectives may not dovetail precisely at first. As functional departments, however, learn to partner with process owners and core process groups, the newly designed horizontal company will begin to see positive results in performance. Recall that the Xerox Corporation began seeing impressive results of its horizontally organized business groups, including significant growth in new markets, close to 170 new products launched between 1991 and 1996, greater customer satisfaction, and a three-fold increase in earnings per share. In the public sector, OSHA has recently enhanced its image by moving away from the "numbers game" that only emphasized enforcement and to an approach that still enforces when necessary but now places an increased emphasis on proactively solving problems to prevent injuries, illnesses, and deaths. Where possible, OSHA acts today as more of a partner to businesses in a concerted effort to improve working conditions and save lives. Although these success stories are repeated in various industries, both in the public and in the private sectors, managers should be aware that such changes and results have to be won with hard work and dedication.

Moreover, in order to ensure the success of the change, management needs to have in place all the "major change" fundamentals for a performance-based transformation to succeed. These include the willingness to commit the energy and resources that will provide the support needed to enable core process teams to work collaboratively, and the discipline to both perform analyses systematically and follow through to execute and "quality control" change initiatives. Moreover, they need the courage to hold themselves accountable for the results of their decisions, just as empowered employees in the horizontal organization must be ultimately accountable for the results of their actions.

The opportunities for a successful transformation are limited by short-sightedness, lack of commitment, unrealistic expectations, and the failure to follow through systematically over the long term. We recall also that, as Dichter, Gagnon, and Alexander point out, major change initiatives often fail because leaders too narrowly focus the change initiatives: They concentrate only on one or two of three axes—top-down, bottom-up, and across the organization—not on all three simultaneously.[1] For the change effort to have maximum benefit, company leaders have to show both in words and actions that they are fully committed to an *integrated* change effort along all three axes.

In an article for *Harvard Business Review,* John Kotter offers his analysis of eight errors that leaders typically make in directing major transformations. Managers, according to Kotter, frequently fail to establish a sense of urgency, assemble a group powerful enough to lead the change effort, create and communicate a vision, empower others to act, recognize and reward short-term wins, reenergize the change effort periodically, and establish clear connections between the behavior and success.[2] None of these failures needs to occur, however, in an organization where managers have systematically completed the "up-front" work to prepare for the change, created a specific and inspiring strategy, and persuaded stakeholders to lend their support to the effort. If those leaders remain disciplined and systematically carry out the initiatives, they can help ensure the success of the change effort.

Managers should not hesitate to experiment with assigning various people to core process teams as they look for that perfect combination of talents and skills that will enable them to deliver the value proposition. As Thomas Stewart points out in a recent book, experts exist here and there throughout the traditional vertical hierarchy. The trick is to bring them together in creative ways, to give them the information they need, and to help them communicate with experts in other areas. And information technology has an essential part to play in this transformation. As Stewart succinctly argues, "the network's edge is that it can deliver information just in time, not just in case."[3]

The most important element in a successful redesign, of course, is the people in your organization. Yes, it is difficult to change people's attitudes, patterns of behavior, old habits, and mindsets; but it is not impossible. To accomplish that goal, managers need to help employees understand why a change of behavior and attitude is necessary and what rewards they can reasonably expect for their wholehearted participation and contributions to the value proposition. Furthermore, management can provide high-quality support to help employees develop the skills required to be successful in the new organization and do a superior job in delivering value to customers.

As we have seen in the case of OSHA and other organizations, change always brings resistance. But resistance is not always a bad thing, not if it comes in an environment that can tolerate different points of view and new approaches to solving old problems. The best managers—and this is particularly true for a change management team—have to be willing to live with uncertainties, the most significant of which is that they cannot anticipate all the problems that the organization will encounter in its shift to the horizontal. A delicate balance is needed here, for management must deal effectively and swiftly with any resistance or problem that deeply threatens the change effort. Although they do not have all the answers "pre-programmed," change managers still must work to anticipate and solve problems in such a way that their decisions are consistent with and support the objectives of the horizontal organization.

Although a horizontal design is not suited for every company, if your organization experiences volatile markets, seeks to develop a distinguishing value proposition that depends on meeting cross-functional challenges, needs to offer consumers added value for their loyalty, and wants to provide employees with ever-increasing satisfaction about the work they do, then the horizontal approach can help you achieve these objectives. The innovative and collaborative thinking that goes into planning, organizing, and directing a change to the horizontal offers managers and employees an opportunity to create a vibrant, agile, and flexible organization for the twenty-first century. Carefully planned and orchestrated, the new, more horizontal approach will find support among all stake-holders: Shareholders will appreciate the bottom-line benefits that come with competitive success; employees will find a more meaningful, satisfy-ing workplace; and the company, along with its suppliers and customers, will experience the benefits of being able to continually improve its ability to add value and perform.

The change cannot come by fiat. It cannot come only from top man-agement, any more than it can arise only from the bottom of the vertical hierarchy. Both the change effort itself and the new organization born from the old must have full top-down, bottom-up, and cross-functional commitment. If done right, the integration of the fundamental principles of the horizontal organization will inspire the people in your organiza-tion, supercharge their performance, and create a winning value propo-sition that lifts your organization far above the competition.

NOTES

CHAPTER 1

1. See Frank Ostroff and Douglas Smith, "The Horizontal Organization," *McKinsey Quarterly*, no. 1 (1992): 149.

2. Stephen Salsbury, *The State, the Investor, and the Railroad: The Boston & Albany, 1825-1867* (Cambridge: Harvard University Press, 1967), 186-87. See also Alfred D. Chandler, Jr., *The Visible Hand: The Managerial Revolution in American Business* (Cambridge: Harvard University Press, 1977), 96-97.

3. Salsbury, *The State, the Investor, and the Railroad*, 187.

4. Chandler, *The Visible Hand*, 98.

5. Cf. the Pennsylvania Railroad, which developed an organizational structure similar to that of the Western Railroad. That structure was modified in 1857, as specified in a document entitled "Organization for Conducting the Business of the Road" (Philadelphia: Crissy and Markley, 1858).

6. Frederick Winslow Taylor, *The Principles of Scientific Management* (New York: Harper and Brothers, 1911), 34-35.

7. Taylor, *Scientific Management*, 70.

8. See, for example, Paul R. Lawrence and Jay W. Lorsch, *Organization and Environment: Managing Differentiation and Integration* (Boston: Harvard Business School Press, 1986). Illustrating the multiplicity of approaches, Henry Mintzberg identified almost 20 years ago what he calls five basic structural configurations: "the simple structure, the machine bureaucracy, the professional bureaucracy, the divisionalized form, and the adhocracy." See Henry Mintzberg, *The Structuring of Organizations: A Synthesis of the Research* (Englewood Cliffs, N.J.: Prentice-Hall, 1979), 301.

9. Cf. Jim Rohwer, *Asia Rising: Why America Will Prosper as Asia's Economies Boom* (New York: Simon and Schuster, 1995), who notes that over half of Asian population alive today is under the age of 25, destined to be a formidable force in the workplace of the twenty-first century (42-43). Despite those increases, however, the number of qualified and skilled workers may well decline.

10. See, for example, John A. Byrne, "The Horizontal Corporation," *Business Week*, December 20, 1993, 80-81; James Brian Quinn, *Intelligent Enterprise: A Knowledge and Service Based Paradigm for Industry* (New York: Free Press, 1992); Peter F. Drucker, "The Coming of the New Organization," *Harvard Business Review* 88.1 (January-February 1988): 45-53.

11. The concept of the "value proposition," discussed more fully in Chapter 3, has become a staple of business management. In *The Discipline of Market Leaders* (Reading, Mass.: Addison-Wesley, 1995, xiv), Michael Treacy and Fred Wiersema define the term as "the implicit promise a company makes to customers to deliver a particular combination of values—price, quality, performance, selection, convenience, and so on." See also Francis J. Gouillart and James N. Kelly, *Transforming the Organization* (New York: McGraw-Hill, 1995, 174-76), who present three rules for developing a value proposition: (1) Select customers as far down the value chain as possible to avoid being squeezed out by intermediate customers; (2) develop a greater sense of customer intimacy; and (3) listen to customers' complaints and suggestions, but avoid relinquishing the decision about what will actually constitute the added benefits of the product or service (174).

12. Cf. Michael Hammer and James Champy, *Reengineering the Corporation: A Manifesto for Business Revolution* (New York: HarperBusiness, 1993), 35-47.

13. Gene Hall, Jim Rosenthal, and Judy Wade, "How to Make Reengineering Really Work," *Harvard Business Review* (November-December 1993): 119-31.

14. For a discussion of the relationship between structure and strategy, particularly in efforts to downsize companies, see Michael D. Hitt, Barbara W. Keats, Herbert F. Harback, and Robert D. Nixon, "Rightsizing: Building and Maintaining Strategic Leadership and Long-term Competitiveness," *Organizational Dynamics*, September 22, 1994, 18-32. In a study of 65 major U.S. companies, the authors found that the most successful efforts grew out of executives' clear visions and ability to articulate and set strategy.

15. Steven F. Dichter, Chris Gagnon, and Ashok Alexander, "Memo to a CEO: Leading Organizational Transformations," *McKinsey Quarterly*, no. 1 (1993): 104.

16. Treacy and Wiersema, *Market Leaders*, 137.

17. Although this is far from an exhaustive list, among the most important sources are the following: R.E. Walton, "From Control to Commitment in the Workplace," *Harvard Business Review* (March-April 1985); Peter Drucker, "The Coming of the New Organization," *Harvard Business Review* (January-February 1988); J. Richard Hackman and Greg R. Oldham, *Work Redesign* (Reading, Mass.: Addison-Wesley, 1980); Hammer and Champy, *Reengineering the Corporation;* Robert Reich, *The Next American Frontier* (New York: Times Books, 1983); and Edward E. Lawler, III, Susan Albers Mohrman, and Gerald E. Ledford, Jr., *Employee Involvement and Total Quality Management: Practices and Results in Fortune 1000 Companies* (San Francisco: Jossey-Bass, 1992).

18. As discussed throughout the book, functions and core process groups are two distinct options available when making a choice about how to formally assign people to departments. These choices and their benefits—e.g., role clarity—make sense when work is of sufficient duration that it is feasible to formally define departments. However, there are situations where an organization might want its people to be able to reach across departments or even company boundaries and work collaboratively to solve problems on an instantaneous or "real-time" basis. In these situations, work may be of insufficient duration to make sense to formally define departments. These are situations in which network organizations or network approaches present themselves as additional options.

19. Robert S. Kaplan and David P. Norton, "The Balanced Scorecard: Measures That Drive Performance," *Harvard Business Review* (January-February 1992): 71-79. See also Kaplan and Norton's *The Balanced Scorecard: Translating Strategy into Action* (Boston: Harvard Business School Press, 1996), especially 24-40.

CHAPTER 2

1. "Xerox 2005 Transformation: Our Strategy, Our Organization, and the Way We Work," unpublished Xerox internal document, May 1997, 5.

2. Henry Mintzberg, *The Structuring of Organizations: A Synthesis of the Research* (Englewood Cliffs, N.J.: Prentice-Hall, 1979), 69-70.

3. Adam Smith, *An Inquiry into the Nature and Causes of the Wealth of Nations*, ed. Edwin Cannan (Chicago: University of Chicago Press, 1976), 8.

4. Henri Fayol, *Industrial and General Administration*, trans. J. A. Coubrough (Geneva: International Management Institute, [1930]), 19.

5. Ibid., 19-20.

6. Frederick Winslow Taylor, *The Principles of Scientific Management* (New York: Harper and Brothers, 1911). See, for example, Taylor's comments on "gang workers," who unloaded ore for less than five cents a ton (73-77).

7. Cf. Mintzberg, *The Structuring of Organizations*, 69-74.

8. Ford Customer Service Division, "FCS2000 Info Exchange Global Bulletin," 8.

9. Joseph S. Nye, Jr., reports that in 1964, nearly three-quarters of the American public said that they "trusted the federal government to do the right thing most of the time." During the last decade, less than a fourth of the public responded with such a positive assessment of the government. See *Why People Don't Trust Government*, edited by Joseph S. Nye, Jr., Philip D. Zelikow, and David C. King (Cambridge: Harvard University Press, 1997), 1, 80-81.

10. Philip Dine, "Talent, Trumka Battle Over Safety," *St. Louis Post-Dispatch*, October 31, 1997, p. 7C; "Ergonomics Can Cut Worker Health Costs," *Toronto Star*, September 22, 1997, p. C3.

11. Al Gore, *Gore Report on Reinventing Government: Creating a Government That Works Better and Costs Less* (New York: Times Books, 1993).

12. As stated in the text OSHA recognized, of course, the essential impossibility of eliminating *all* preventable injuries, illnesses, and deaths. It was felt, however, that by setting the bar high that it would stretch the organization to innovate and require the introduction of new approaches and techniques. And it was viewed that this innovation was what was required for the agency to significantly improve its capabilities and achieve a dramatic reduction in injuries, illnesses, and deaths.

13. See Mark H. Moore, *Creating Public Value: Strategic Management in Government* (Cambridge: Harvard University Press, 1995), 70-71. Moore rightly argues that public-sector managers, no less than their private-sector counterparts, must develop a strategy that is "substantively valuable . . . legitimate and politically sustainable . . . and operationally and administratively feasible" (71).

14. A 1993 survey conducted by *Occupational Hazards* determined that respondents by a three-to-one margin thought OSHA needed reform (they were less in agreement on exactly what the reform should be). See Stephen G. Minter, "Voting for a Change at OSHA," *Occupational Hazards* 55.9 (September 1993): 93-95.

15. Occupational Safety and Health Administration Act (Public Law 91-596, Section 1 [December 29, 1970], as amended by Public Law 101-552, Section 3101 [November 5, 1990]).

16. Vice President Al Gore, Address at Harvard's 343d Commencement, June 9, 1994, reprinted as "The Cynics Are Wrong," *Harvard Magazine* 96.6 (July-August 1994): 28-32, especially 30.

CHAPTER 3

1. In contrast to the fragmented work of the vertical hierarchy, one of the primary characteristics of the horizontal organization is maximizing the integration of work. In some situations, through redesigning work processes and information systems, individual employees acting as "case managers" can carry out the complete work of a core process. Successful examples can be found, for instance, in customer service operations in some insurance companies and banks. See Thomas H. Davenport and Nitin Nohria, "Case Management and the Integration of Labor," *Sloan Management Review* 35.2 (January 1994): 11-23. More typically, however, carrying out the work of a core process entails more activities and requires a greater range of skills than one person can supply.

2. Henry Mintzberg, *The Structuring of Organizations* (Englewood Cliffs, N.J.: Prentice-Hall, 1979), 106.

3. Grouping may also take place by product, service, customer, geographic location, or work shift. However, subgrouping within these groups has traditionally been by function or functional specialty.

4. Irving DeToro and Thomas McCabe, "How to Stay Flexible and Elude Fads," *Quality Progress* 30.3 (March 1997): 55-60. For a more detailed discussion of core processes, see Robert B. Kaplan and Laura Murdock, "Core Process Redesign," *McKinsey Quarterly*, no. 2 (1991): 27-43.

5. For a further discussion of teams, see Jon R. Katzenbach and Douglas K. Smith, *The Wisdom of Teams: Creating the High-Performance Organization* (Boston: Harvard Business School Press, 1993). In addition, this definition of "team" seems to square with Michael Schrage's idea of "creative collaboration," a term he prefers to what he sees as the overly politicized and nearly meaningless notion of *team*. See his *No More Teams! Mastering the Dynamics of Creative Collaboration* (New York: Doubleday, 1989; rev. ed. 1995), xi-xv. While one may agree that the term is frequently misused today, that is not a compelling argument for avoiding it altogether.

6. Ron Ashkenas, Dave Ulrich, Todd Jick, and Steve Kerr, *The Boundaryless Organization: Breaking the Chains of Organizational Structure* (San Francisco: Jossey-Bass, 1995), 33.

7. Executives and managers will still perform many of the same roles they always have. In his classic work on management, Henry Mintzberg described 10 such roles: figurehead, leader, liaison, monitor, disseminator, spokesperson, entrepreneur, disturbance handler, resource allocator, and negotiator. See his *The Nature of Managerial Work* (New York: Harper & Row, 1973), 59.

8. See Frank Ostroff and Douglas Smith, "The Horizontal Organization," *McKinsey Quarterly*, no. 1 (1992): 151-52.

9. J. R. Hackman and G. R. Oldham, *Work Redesign* (Reading, Mass.: Addison-Wesley, 1980), 166.

10. Jerald Greenberg and Robert A. Baron, *Behavior in Organizations: Understanding and Managing the Human Side of Work* (Upper Saddle River, N.J.: Prentice Hall, 1997), 166.

11. Ibid., 168

12. Michael Hammer and Steven A. Stanton, *The Reengineering Revolution: A Handbook* (New York: HarperBusiness, 1995), 3.

13. Thomas J. Peters and Robert H. Waterman, Jr., *In Search of Excellence: Lessons from America's Best-Run Companies* (New York: Warner Books, 1982), 9-11.

14. The more thoughtful observers and theorists on reengineering have called for the need to go beyond merely redesigning processes if the reengineering effort is to be successful. See James Champy, *Reengineering Management: The Mandate for New Leadership* (New York: HarperBusiness, 1995); Gene Hall, Jim Rosenthal, and Judy Wade, "How to Make Reengineering Really Work," *Harvard Business Review* (November-December 1993): 119.

15. See Guillermo G. Marmol and R. Michael Murray, Jr., "Leading from the Front," *McKinsey Quarterly*, no. 3 (1995): 18-31. The authors argue that high-performance companies must be driven by leaders who have a superior understanding of the business environment and can wed strategy to a simple structure based on core processes. In addition, such companies must exhibit world-class skills and have well-developed "people systems" with strong support and "bench strength" (28).

16. Jeffrey Pfeffer, *The Human Equation—Building Profits by Putting People First* (Boston: Harvard Business School Press, 1998), 165.

17. Ibid., 11; James A. F. Stoner, R. Edward Freeman, and Daniel R. Gilbert, Jr. *Management*, 6th ed. (Englewood Cliffs, N.J.: Prentice Hall, 1995), 328.

18. For thoughts about alternatives to downsizing, see Pfeffer, *The Human Equation*, 182-94; Alan Downs, *Corporate Executions: The Ugly Truth about Layoffs—How Corporate Greed Is Shattering Lives, Companies, and Communities* (New York: AMACOM, 1995), especially 162-65.

19. On linking best practices, knowledge, and skills across the organization, see Sumantra Ghoshal and Christopher A. Bartlett, *The Individualized Corporation: A Fundamentally New Approach to Management* (New York: HarperBusiness, 1997), 214-15.

20. Michael Hammer, *Beyond Reengineering: How the Process-Centered Organization Is Changing Our Work and Our Lives* (New York: HarperBusiness, 1996), 130.

21. Pfeffer, *The Human Equation*, 165.

CHAPTER 4

1. Max Weber, *The Theory of Social and Economic Organization*, trans. A. M. Henderson and Talcott Parsons (New York: Oxford University Press, 1947), 337.

2. Henry A. Mintzberg, *The Structuring of Organizations* (Englewood Cliffs, N.J.: Prentice Hall, 1979), 301. See also David A. Nadler and Michael L. Tushman, with Mark B. Nadler, *Competing by Design: The Power of Organizational Architecture* (New York: Oxford University Press, 1997), 143.

3. See Nadler and Tushman, *Competing by Design*, 143-44.

CHAPTER 5

1. The term *Six Sigma* refers to the use of standard deviation, usually represented by the Greek letter σ (sigma) to measure the spread of variability of items from the mean in a typical bell curve. Used as a measure of risk, one standard deviation in normal distributions includes approximately 68 percent of the outcomes. If two sigmas or standard deviations are taken, the measure jumps to almost 95 percent of outcomes. Motorola's famed Six Sigma standard aims to achieve near 100 percent perfection, with only 3.4 defects per one million parts produced.

2. Motorola press release, May 5, 1997. See Motorola website: www.motorola.com.

CHAPTER 8

1. "Xerox 2005 Transformation: Our Strategy, Our Organization, and the Way We Work," Stamford, Connecticut: Xerox Corporation, May, 1997.

2. See, for example, Michael E. Porter, *Competitive Advantage* (New York: Free Press, 1985); Robert B. Kaplan and Laura Murdock, "Core Process Redesign," *McKinsey Quarterly*, no. 2 (1991): 28-29.

3. Mary J. Cronin, "Knowing How Employees Use the Intranet Is Good Business," *Fortune*, July 21, 1997, 103. See also Kate Maddox, "The Work Connection," *Information Week*,

September 16, 1996, 98ff., and Beth Schultz, "Documenting the Xerox-Wide Web," *Intranet Magazine*, July 1996, 35-38.

CHAPTER 9

1. See, for example, John P. Kotter, "Leading Change: Why Transformation Efforts Fail," *Harvard Business Review* (March-April, 1995): 59-60. Kotter says that in his study of over 100 companies that undertook major transformations, all in an effort to cope with uncertain markets, he witnessed a few successes, a number of failures, and a lot "in between, with a distinct tilt toward the lower end of the scale" (59).
2. Cf. Guillermo G. Marmol and R. Michael Murray, Jr., "Leading from the Front," *McKinsey Quarterly*, no. 3 (1995): 18-31.
3. Michael E. Porter, *Competitive Strategy: Techniques for Analyzing Industries and Competitors* (New York: Free Press, 1980), 3-33.
4. Steven F. Dichter, Chris Gagnon, and Ashok Alexander, "Memo to a CEO: Leading Organizational Transformations," *McKinsey Quarterly*, no. 1 (1993): 101.
5. John Kotter, *Leading Change* (Boston: Harvard Business School Press, 1996), 26.
6. Marmol and Murray, "Leading from the Front," 19.
7. Dichter, Gagnon, and Alexander, "Memo to a CEO," 90-100.
8. Ibid., 91.
9. Ibid., 97-100.

CHAPTER 10

1. Mark H. Moore, *Creating Public Value: Strategic Management in Government* (Cambridge, Mass.: Harvard University Press, 1995), p. 65.
2. Ibid., 66.
3. Marcus Aurelius, *Meditations* 4.36, trans. Whitney J. Oates (New York: Modern Library, 1940), 513.
4. Francis J. Gouillart and James N. Kelly, *Transforming the Organization* (New York: McGraw-Hill, 1995), 45.
5. Ibid., 49.
6. James C. Collins and Jerry I. Porras, "Building Your Company's Vision," *Harvard Business Review* 74.5 (September-October 1996): 65-77, especially 66.
7. Moore, *Creating Public Value*, 71. Moore points to two other tests as well: The strategy must be "legitimate and politically sustainable." That is, the enterprise must be able continually to attract both authority and money from the political authorizing environment to which it is ultimately accountable. And "it must be operationally and administratively feasible in that the authorized, valuable activities can actually be accomplished by the existing organization with help from others who can be induced to contribute to the organization's goal" (71).
8. U.S. Department of Labor, News Release USDL: 97-457, December 17, 1997.

CHAPTER 11

1. See Frank Ostroff and Douglas Smith, "The Horizontal Organization," *McKinsey Quarterly*, no. 1 (1992): 148-68, especially 152-66, for the original set of ten principles.
2. See Robert B. Kaplan and Laura Murdock, "Core Process Redesign," *McKinsey Quarterly*, no. 2 (1991): 28-29.

3. See Thomas Davenport and Nitin Nohria, "Case Management and the Integration of Labor," *Sloan Management Review* 35.2 (January 1994): 11-23. In small organizations, and occasionally in large ones as well, there are certain situations in which there may be a core process that one individual handles in its entirety. More often, however, the amount of activities and skills required to carry out the work of core processes requires multifunctional teams—each preferably no more than 20 or 25 people—who share performance objectives, possess complementary skills, agree on an approach to the work, and support each other in a positive environment or culture. See also Jon R. Katzenbach and Douglas K. Smith, *The Wisdom of Teams: Creating the High Performance Organization* (Boston: Harvard Business School Press, 1993), 54.

4. Core process groups, as discussed elsewhere, are formally structured around core processes. Teams within the core process group may be focused on carrying out the work of a core process along different dimensions, including product, geographic region, or customer segment. For example, at Motorola, the individual commodity teams each carry out the complete work of the supply-management process for a particular commodity. The response teams at OSHA carry out the work of the response process within a particular geographic region.

5. Henry Mintzberg, *The Nature of Managerial Work* (Englewood Cliffs, N.J.: Prentice-Hall, 1979), 69-70.

CHAPTER 12

1. Karl Marx, *Selected Writings*, ed. Lawrence H. Simon (Indianapolis: Hackett Publishing Company, 1994), 58-68.

2. Certainly just in time training is not the best choice for developing every type of skill or competency. For example, classroom training may be the best choice for developing detailed customer or industry knowledge. In addition, please see 215-18 of this text for approaches helpful for building cross-functional competencies important in horizontal organizations.

3. See also Rahul Jacob, "The Struggle to Create an Organization for the 21st Century," *Fortune*, April 3, 1995.

4. Michael Schrage, *No More Teams* (New York: Currency Doubleday, 1989), 98.

5. Gene Hall, Jim Rosenthal, and Judy Wade, "How to Make Reengineering Really Work," *Harvard Business Review* (November-December 1993): 119-31.

6. Frank Ostroff and Douglas Smith, "The Horizontal Organization," *McKinsey Quarterly*, no. 1 (1992): 162-63.

7. Ibid., 166.

8. Thomas A. Stewart, *Intellectual Capital* (New York: Currency Doubleday, 1997), 185.

EPILOGUE

1. Steven F. Dichter, Chris Gagnon, and Ashok Alexander, "Memo to a CEO: Leading Organizational Transformations," *McKinsey Quarterly*, no. 1 (1993): 91.

2. John Kotter, "Leading Change: Why Transformation Efforts Fail," *Harvard Business Review* (March-April 1995): 59-67. On the need for creating a vision for the company, see James C. Collins and Jerry I. Porras, "Building Your Company's Vision," *Harvard Business Review* (September-October 1996): 65-77.

3. Thomas A. Stewart, *Intellectual Capital: The New Wealth of Organizations* (New York: Doubleday, 1997), 185.

INDEX

A

Accountability: and anticipating and avoiding problems, 232; and changes in workplace, 7; and corporate culture, 228; and design formulation, 194, 198, 199; diffusion of, 7; and empowerment, 208; and features of horizontal organizations, 62, 63; and guidelines for change, 159, 163, 165; and hierarchy, 63, 199; and horizontal organizations as actionable alternatives, 84; and institutionalization of change, 159, 208, 228; and process owners, 194; and setting directions, 184; and structure, 14; of teams, 14, 62, 198. *See also specific organization*

Adjunct teams, 192

Administration: Fayol's principles of, 28–29

Alexander, Ashok, 15, 158, 232

Alienation, 64, 208, 209

Allaire, Paul, 19, 20, 71, 130–31, 132–33, 135, 137, 141, 142, 146, 170–71, 179–80, 231

Analysis: and anticipating and avoiding problems, 232; and design formulation, 156; of environment, 168–74, 180; and failures of reengineering, 214; and guidelines for change, 153–56, 159–60; and setting directions, 153–56, 168–74, 176, 180

Argonaut Insurance Company, 53–54

Aspirational goals: and anticipating and avoiding problems, 232; and benefits of horizontal organizations, 22; and charting horizontal organizations, 15; and corporate culture, 175; and design formulation, 156–57, 189; and empowerment, 209; and guidelines for change, 155–57; and institutionalization of change, 209; and setting directions, 155–56, 168, 174–76, 183; and strategy, 15; and structure, 15. *See also specific organization*

Authority: and basic principles of horizontal organizations, 190; and commonali-

Authority (*continued*)

ties among horizontal organizations, 186; of core process groups, 188; and corporate culture, 225, 228; and design formulation, 186, 188, 190, 195, 199; and empowerment, 211; and hierarchy, 199; and institutionalization of change, 206, 225, 228; and process owners, 195

B

"Balanced scorecard" for performance evaluation, 21–22

Balancing change, 159–65

Baldrige awards, 132

Barclays Bank: accountability at, 119, 125, 126; aspirational goals at, 116, 157, 175–76; authority at, 121, 126, 200; "Being the Best" initiative at, 116; commitment to change at, 116, 147, 176; competition at, 123; continuous improvement at, 124, 127–28; core processes at, 119, 157, 192–93; corporate culture at, 121, 126, 127, 175, 224–25; customers of, 116, 118, 126, 128, 175; decision making at, 122, 124, 200; democratization at, 121, 175; design formulation at, 157, 192–93, 200; efficiency at, 116, 120; empowerment at, 119, 123–24, 127, 175–76; feedback at, 124; and guidelines for change, 156, 157; hierarchy at, 116, 121, 122–25, 200; as horizontal organization, 114; Human Resources at, 122–23, 125–28; as hybrid organization, 20, 120, 121; institutionalization of change at, 224–25; job satisfaction at, 123, 127; leadership at, 121–22, 123, 126–27; loyalty at, 118; managers at, 121, 122, 123, 124, 126, 175; multiskilling at, 118, 123–24, 125; networks at, 122; organization chart for, 119, 120; performance evaluations at, 126, 175; performance measures at, 120, 126–27; performance objectives at, 119, 120, 121, 126, 157; personal development system at, 126; problems at, 116; process owners at, 121, 122; responsibility at, 120, 121, 122, 123–24, 125, 176; results of horizontal organization at, 119–22; rewards at, 126; setting directions at, 175–76; skills/expertise at, 119, 122–24; strategy at, 117, 121, 125, 126, 157; structure at, 117,

157; teams at, 118, 119–20, 121–24, 125, 127; training at, 122–24; value proposition of, 116–19, 121, 128, 157; vertical organization at, 115–16, 119, 120, 121

Best-practice databases, 20, 71

Bethlehem Steel Company, 5–6

Bottom-up change, 160–64, 232, 234

Bureaucracy, 67–68, 73–74, 84, 113–14, 199. *See also specific organization*

Burleson, Larry, 91, 93, 94, 98, 99, 100, 201, 204, 210, 223–24

C

Capital structure management, 67

Carey, Leo, 46, 47, 198

Chandler, Alfred, 5

Change: balancing of, 159–65; bottom-up, 160–64, 232, 234; and characteristics of twenty-first-century organizations, 20–21; commitment to, 147–48, 153, 157, 159, 180, 181; as constant, 183; in core process groups, 84–85; cross-functional, 160–65, 232, 234; and errors of leaders, 232; as failure, 22, 151–52, 164, 232; guidelines for increasing success in, 152–66; importance of, 230–34; and integration of basic principles, 234; involvement of people in, 151–52, 207, 229; "language" of, 9, 161; laying groundwork for, 178–83, 230; leadership for, 151–65; main objective of, 179, 183; phases in, 151–66; questions to ask when considering, 153–55; resistance to, 152, 159, 196, 201, 203–4, 207, 226–27, 233; road map for, 165–66; and setting directions, 170, 171, 178–83, 184; and strategy, 171; top-down, 160–64, 232, 234; and transformation triangle, 160–64; and vertical organizations, 170; in workplace, 7–9. *See also* Design formulation; Institutionalization of change; Setting directions; *specific organization*

Change teams. *See* Steering committees

Chapman, Karen, 100, 201–2

Collins, James C., 175

Commitment: and anticipating and avoiding problems, 232; and change in organizations, 147–48; and corporate culture, 227; and design formulation, 157, 190; and guidelines for change,

153, 157, 159; and institutionalization of change, 159, 205, 215, 220, 223, 227; of leadership, 22–23, 181, 190, 232; and multiskilling, 215, 220; and performance measures, 223; and performance objectives, 223; and setting directions, 153, 181. *See also specific organization*

Communication, 15, 165, 175, 179–81, 182, 183, 230, 232, 233

Compensation, 64. *See also* Rewards; *specific organization*

Competition, 170, 176–78, 183, 234

"Complete solutions," 18

Continuous improvement, 66–67, 189, 196, 199, 208, 224–28, 229, 231

Control, 85, 186, 194

Core process groups (CPG): and anticipating and avoiding problems, 232; authority of, 188; benefits of, 82–83; as characteristic of horizontal organizations, 59–62, 66; and commonalities among horizontal organizations, 188–89; and corporate culture, 225; and decision making, 188; definition of, 62; and design formulation, 185–86, 188–89, 192, 194, 196, 200; and empowerment, 210; example of, 78; and functional areas, 26–27, 77–78; functions of, 76; and generic picture of horizontal organizations, 79, 80, 81, 82; and hierarchy, 188, 200; in hybrid organizations, 26–27; and institutionalization of change, 206, 210, 218–19, 225; members of, 78, 84–85, 232; and organization charts, 76; and performance objectives, 188; and process owners, 188; and reengineering, 66; responsibility in, 194; rotation of members in, 84–85; and skills/expertise, 71, 188, 192, 218–19; teams comprising, 81; uniqueness of individual, 185–86; and value propositions, 188. *See also specific organization*

Core processes: and anticipating and avoiding problems, 229–30; and basic principles of horizontal organizations, 23, 189; and benefits of horizontal organizations, 6–7, 10, 11–12, 15; and characteristics of horizontal organizations, 59–62; and corporate culture, 226, 227; and design formulation, 157, 185, 189, 190–93, 197,

199, 200, 201; and empowerment, 73–85; example of, 76; functions of, 7, 76; and generic picture of horizontal organizations, 77–82; and guidelines for change, 157, 160–65; and hierarchy, 199, 200; and horizontal organizations as actionable alternatives, 82–85; and hybrid organizations, 192–93; identification of, 77; and institutionalization of change, 207, 218, 220, 226, 227; and multiskilling, 218, 220; and organization charts, 74–77; organizing around, 89–101; and performance objectives, 192; and responsibility, 192; and selection of horizontal organizations, 18–19; and setting directions, 168, 177, 179, 183; simple process distinguished from, 7; and skills, 191–92; and strategy, 13–14, 16, 17–18; and structure, 16, 17–18; and suppliers, 201; and teams, 62, 191–92, 197; test for, 191; in twenty-first-century organizations, 13–14; uniqueness of, 56, 76, 77, 185, 191; and value propositions, 76, 192. *See also* Core process groups; Process owners; *specific organization*

Corporate culture, 11, 24, 168, 175, 206, 208, 224–28. *See also specific organization*

Creativity, 6, 10, 24, 206, 219, 227

Cross-functional change, 160–65, 232, 234

Customers: and anticipating and avoiding problems, 234; and basic principles of horizontal organizations, 10, 11, 24, 190; and basic requirements for high-achieving companies, 67; and benefits of horizontal organizations, 21, 23, 234; and changes in workplace, 7, 8; and characteristics of horizontal organizations, 59, 60–62, 64, 70, 71, 82; and core processes, 201; and corporate culture, 225, 227–28; and design formulation, 190, 201–4; as focus of horizontal organizations, 18–20, 74; and guidelines for change, 165; and horizontal organizations as actionable alternatives, 83; and horizontal organizations as balanced organizations, 21–22; and institutionalization of change, 206, 215, 217, 220, 223, 225, 227–28; internal and external, 61–62, 71; loyalty of, 39–40; and multiskilling/expertise,

Customers (*continued*)
70, 71, 215, 217, 220; and performance evaluations, 223; and performance objectives, 223; and selection of horizontal organizations, 18–19; and setting directions, 169–70, 176, 177; and strategy, 16; and structure, 16; and value propositions, 176, 201; and weaknesses of vertical organizations, 6. *See also specific organization*

D

Deal, Tim, 110
Dear, Joe, 46, 47, 48, 49, 50, 54, 55, 178, 180–81, 197–98, 199, 204, 207, 222
Decision making, 10, 24, 63, 84, 188, 190, 199, 206, 208. *See also specific organization*
Design formulation: and accountability, 194, 198, 199; and analysis, 156; and anticipating and avoiding problems, 232; and aspirational goals, 156–57, 189; and authority, 195, 199; and bureaucracy, 199; and commitment, 190; "contingency approach" to, 6; as continuum, 26; and continuous improvement, 189, 196, 199; and control, 194; and core process groups, 185–86, 188–89, 192, 194, 196, 200; and core processes, 157, 185, 189, 190–93, 197, 199, 200, 201; and corporate culture, 225; and customers, 201–4; and decision making, 199; and empowerment, 199, 204; and guidelines for change, 151–53, 155, 156–57, 165–66; and hierarchy, 199–201; and hybrid organizations, 192–93; and institutionalization of change, 190, 220, 225; and integration of basic principles of horizontal organizations, 227; and leadership, 156–57, 190, 194, 195, 199, 200; and managers, 194, 199–200, 204; and organization charts, 189, 199; and partners in process, 200, 204; and performance evaluations, 196; and performance measures, 157; and performance objectives, 156–57, 188, 192, 196, 198; as phase in change, 147, 151–53, 155, 156–57, 165–66; and problem solving, 194, 199; and process owners, 188, 189, 194–97, 200; and productivity, 189; and resistance to

change, 196, 201, 203–4; and resource allocation, 199; and responsibility, 186, 189, 192, 194, 199; and rewards, 196; and setting directions, 168, 177, 178–83; and skills/expertise, 185–86, 189, 191–92, 196, 197, 198, 199, 220; and steering committee, 201, 204; and strategy, 156–57, 168, 189, 199, 201; and structure, 186; and suppliers, 190, 201–4; and teams, 185–86, 188, 190, 191–92, 194–95, 197–99, 200, 201; terminology for, 9; and training, 199; and value propositions, 156–57, 185, 188, 189, 190, 192, 195–96, 199, 200, 201; and vertical organizations, 188–89, 192, 194, 197, 200
Design team. *See* Steering committee
Dichter, Steven F., 15, 158, 232
"Diffusion teams," 70
Discipline, 79, 194
Divisions: horizontal organization of, 115–29
Downsizing, 67–70, 199
Driver, Harold, 104, 112, 217

E

E-mail, 211–13, 214
Efficiency, 5–6, 8, 9, 73, 74, 85. *See also specific organization*
Employees: altering psychological state of, 64–65; and anticipating and avoiding problems, 233, 234; and aspirational goals, 156; and basic principles of horizontal organizations, 10, 11; and benefits of horizontal organizations, 15, 21, 22, 23, 234; and changes in workplace, 7–8; and characteristics of horizontal organizations, 61–62, 63–65, 66; commitment of, 22, 215, 220, 223, 227; and guidelines for change, 151–52, 156; and hierarchy, 63–65; and horizontal organizations as balanced organizations, 22; quality of life for, 66; and reengineering, 67; and specialization, 29; in vertical organizations, 4, 6, 29. *See also* Downsizing; Empowerment; Teams; *specific organization*
Empowerment: and accountability, 208; advantages of, 12; and anticipating and avoiding problems, 232; and aspirational goals, 209; and authority, 211; and basic

principles of horizontal organizations, 10, 11, 24; and benefits of horizontal organizations, 148; and characteristics of horizontal organizations, 64, 65; and continuous improvement, 208; and core process groups, 210; and core processes, 73–85; and corporate culture, 11, 208, 228; and design formulation, 199, 204; and generic picture of horizontal organizations, 77–82; and guidelines for change, 157, 159, 165; and hierarchy, 64; and horizontal organizations as actionable alternatives, 82–85; and information technology, 209, 211; and institutionalization of change, 157, 159, 206, 208–11, 228; and motivation, 211; and organization charts, 74–77; and performance measures, 208; and problem solving, 211; and process owners, 209; and productivity, 208; and rewards, 211; and selection of horizontal organizations, 19; and skills/expertise, 208, 210; and strategy, 16; and structure, 16; and teams, 199, 210; and training, 208, 209, 210; and value propositions, 208; in vertical organizations, 208, 209. *See also specific organization*

Environment, 168–74, 176, 180, 183

European natural resources company: as change failure, 151–52, 164

Evaluation. *See* Performance evaluations; *specific organization*

Expertise, 26, 60, 70–72, 192, 197, 210. *See also* Multiskilling; Skills; Specialization

F

"Faith capital," 22

Fayol, Henri, 28–29

Feedback, 64, 65, 165

Financial contributions, 11, 24, 67, 234

Flanagan, Pat, 122

Flexibility, 10, 21, 56–57, 70, 171, 206, 233–34. *See also specific organization*

Ford Customer Service Division (FCSD): accountability at, 35–36, 43; aspirational goals of, 31, 156; authority at, 186; business development at, 32, 33, 35–36, 192; commitment to change at, 180; and commonalities among horizontal organizations, 186; communication at, 180; core process groups at, 186, 188;

core processes at, 31, 32–39, 42, 163, 191, 192, 193; customers of, 30–43, 169, 180, 203, 212, 213; decision making at, 39, 42; design formulation at, 186, 187, 188, 191, 192, 193, 194–95, 203; efficiency at, 31, 39, 188; empowerment at, 39, 210; "Ford 2000" initiative at, 30–31; and guidelines for change, 156, 163; human resources at, 41–44, 222; as hybrid organization, 40–41, 42, 186, 193, 221–22; information technology at, 212–14, 222; institutionalization of change at, 212–13, 217, 221–22; job satisfaction at, 39, 40–41, 223; key processes at, 32–39; managers at, 43, 212; organization chart of, 187; partners in process at, 186, 221–22; parts supply and logistics at, 32, 36–37, 39, 192; performance evaluations at, 35–36, 39–44; performance measures at, 39–41, 223; performance objectives at, 30–43, 163, 186, 188, 223; problem solving at, 192, 213–14, 222; problems and weaknesses at, 29–31, 180; process owners at, 186, 191, 194–95; "pulse" surveys at, 40–41; and resource allocation, 31; responsibility at, 32, 35–36, 186; setting directions at, 169, 180; skills/expertise at, 32, 41–44, 192, 217; strategy at, 17–18, 31, 32–29; structure of, 17–18; suppliers for, 32, 203; teams at, 32, 36–37, 41, 42, 186, 191, 192; technical support at, 32, 38–39, 192; training at, 38–39, 217; transition team at, 31, 32, 36; value proposition at, 17–18, 31, 32, 33, *34*, 37, 39, 188, 192, 212–13; vehicle service and programs at, 32, 37–38, 192; and vertical organizations, 193

Ford Motor Company, 208. *See also* Ford Customer Service Division (FCSD)

Fragmentation, 83, 90, 102

Functional areas, 11, 26–27, 59–60, 77–78. *See also* Hybrid organizations; Vertical organization

Functional goals, 6

G

Gagnon, Chris, 15, 158, 232

Gasaway, Roger, 103

General Electric: as hybrid organization, 20

192, 233–34; and change, 21, 147–48, 153; characteristics of, 6–7, 11–13, 15, 16, 17, 18, 58–72, 74, 82; charting a, 15–18; commonalities among, 186, 188–89; and design formulation, 185–204; divisions organized as, 115–29; entire company organized as, 130–48; external versus internal focus in, 59; as flatter not flat, 63; flexibility of, 21, 56–57, 70; generic picture of, 77–82; humane nature of, 69; measures of success in, 11; and operating units, 102–14; and organizing around core process, 89–101; permutations of, 192–93; "pure," 25–26; purpose of, 66, 199, 201; as successful, 166; theory of, 21–23; and uniqueness of organizations, 25, 56, 58, 185–86, 231; vertical organizations compared with, 16–17, 111, 188–89, 192; weaknesses of, 197. *See also* Design formulation; Hybrid organizations; Institutionalization of change; Setting directions; *specific topic*

Hoyler, Horst, 33, 34, 35, 187

Hybrid organizations, 19–20, 21, 25–27, 78–79, 82, 153, 192–93. *See also specific organization*

I

Incremental thinking, 155

Information, 6, 209, 211, 213, 221. *See also* information technology (IT)

Information technology (IT): and anticipating and avoiding problems, 233; and basic principles of horizontal organizations, 10, 24; and characteristics of horizontal organizations, 65–66; and empowerment, 211; importance of, 213–14; and institutionalization of change, 206, 211–14, 220; and managers, 213; and organization charts, 75; and performance objectives, 10, 24; and problem solving, 213–14; and reengineering, 65–66; and responsibility, 213; and selection of horizontal organizations, 18; and skills, 213, 220; and steering committee, 213; and structure, 17–18; and training, 213; and value propositions, 212–13. *See also specific organization*

Institutionalization of change: and accountability, 208, 228; and anticipating and avoiding problems, 233; and aspirational goals, 209; and authority, 206, 225, 228; and basic principles of horizontal organizations, 206–7; and commitment, 205, 215, 220, 223, 227; and continuous improvement, 208, 224–28; and core process groups, 206, 218–19, 225; and core processes, 207, 218, 220, 226, 227; and corporate culture, 206, 208, 224–28; and creativity, 219, 227; and customers, 206, 215, 217, 220, 223, 225, 227–28; and decision making, 206, 208; and design formulation, 190, 220, 225; and empowerment, 206, 208–11, 228; and guidelines for change, 151–53, 155, 157–59; and hierarchy, 221; in high-performance companies, 159; and information technology (IT), 206, 209, 211–14, 220; and integration of basic principles of horizontal organizations, 227, 228; and job satisfaction, 206, 218, 223, 227; and leadership, 151–53, 155, 157–59, 228; and managers, 213, 219, 221, 223, 228; and motivation, 211; and need for follow-through, 228; and paralleling of old and new organization, 158; and partners in process, 206, 221–22; and performance, 220–21; and performance evaluations, 221, 222–24; and performance measures, 206, 208, 222–24; and performance objectives, 159, 206, 219–20, 222–24, 228; as phase in change, 147, 151–53, 155, 157–59, 205–28; and problem solving, 211, 213–14, 222, 224, 228; and process owners, 209, 219, 228; and productivity, 208; and reengineering, 227; and resistance to change, 159, 207, 226–27; and responsibility, 206, 213, 215, 219, 224, 226, 227, 228; and rewards, 220–21, 227; and sense of urgency, 207; and skills/expertise, 206, 207, 208, 210, 213, 214–21, 228; and steering committee, 208, 213, 228; and suppliers, 215, 217; and teams, 210, 215, 224, 228; and training, 206, 208, 209–11, 213, 215–16, 217, 219; and value propositions, 206, 207, 208, 212–13, 218, 219, 225, 227, 228

Iridium Project (Motorola), 98–99

Morris, Steve, 123

Motivation, 65, 155, 159, 211, 231

Motorola Space and Systems Technology Group (SSTG): accountability at, 94–95; aspirational goals of, 90, 156; authority at, 94–95; bureaucracy at, 90, 95; commitment to change at, 147; core process groups at, 97, 188–89, 202; core processes at, 91–92, 93–96, 192–93; corporate culture at, 98; cost reduction at, 100, 223; customers of, 90, 93, 96, 181, 195, 201–3, 216; decision making at, 92, 93–94, 99; design formulation at, 186, 188–89, 192–93, 195, 200–203, 204; empowerment at, 92, 93–95, 100, 101, 210–11; feedback at, 223; functions of, 89; and guidelines for change, 156; hierarchy at, 91, 94, 200–201; hiring at, 211; as hybrid organization, 20, 99; information technology (IT) at, 96–97, 99, 211–12, 213, 215; institutionalization of change at, 210–12, 213, 217, 218, 223–24; Iridium Project of, 98–99; job satisfaction at, 95, 100; managers at, 93, 95, 96, 218, 223; motivation at, 94–95; performance evaluations at, 95, 97, 223–24; performance measures at, 95, 223–24; performance objectives at, 95, 99, 223–24; problem solving at, 91, 92–94, 99, 100, 101, 223, 224'oblems at, 89; process owners at, 91, 92, 93, 95, 195, 223; productivity at, 181; quality control at, 97, 181, 195, 202–3, 223; resources at, 96; responsibility at, 90, 91–92, 94–95, 192, 224; rewards at, 95; and setting directions, 181; Six Sigma at, 97, 181, 203; skills/expertise at, 92, 93, 98–99, 186, 215–16, 217, 218; strategy at, 93, 95, 96; suppliers of, 90, 91, 92–93, 96–98, 100, 188–89, 193, 201–3, 216, 223; teams at, 70, 91, 92–95, 96, 97–98, 99, 100, 186, 188–89, 192, 215–16, 223, 224; training at, 92, 94–95, 99, 215–16, 217; value proposition of, 90, 91–93, 95, 100–101, 181, 186, 195; as vertical organization, 89–91, 99

Motroni, Hector J., 132, 141

Multi-competencies. See Multiskilling

Multiskilling: and basic principles of horizontal organizations, 10, 24; benefits of, 217–18; as characteristic of horizontal organizations, 59, 60, 61–62, 64, 82; and commitment, 215, 220; and core process groups, 85, 218–19; and core processes, 192, 218, 220; and creativity, 219; and customers, 215, 217, 220; and design formulation, 192, 196, 199, 220; and downsizing, 70; and empowerment, 208; and hierarchy, 64; and horizontal organizations as actionable alternatives, 85; and information technology, 220; and institutionalization of change, 206, 208, 214–21; and job satisfaction, 218; just-in-time, 219; and managers, 214–15, 219, 221; and performance, 219–21; and problem solving, 12; and process owners, 196, 219; and responsibility, 215, 219; and rewards, 220–21; and selection of horizontal organizations, 19; and suppliers, 215, 217; and training, 215, 217, 219; and value propositions, 218, 219; in vertical organizations, 220. *See also* Skills; *specific organization*

Murray, R. Michael, Jr., 158–59

N

Networking, 71, 233

Non-value-added work, 23, 67–68, 122, 190, 199

O

Ockenden, Michael, 115, 116, 117, 121, 123, 124, 125–28, 175, 200, 224–25

Oldham, G. R., 64

O'Mahony, Gregory, 117

Operating units: as horizontal organizations, 102–14

Organization charts: and adaptation of horizontal organizations, 74; and core processes, 74–77; and design formulation, 185, 189, 199; and empowerment, 74–77; functions of, 3–4, 14–15, 74–77; for horizontal organizations, 15–18, 74–77; and information technology, 75; and performance objectives, 75; and uniqueness of organizations, 56, 185; and value propositions, 76; for vertical organizations, 1, 82, 225. *See also specific organization*

OSHA (U.S. Department of Labor Occupational Safety and Health

OSHA (*continued*)

Administration): and anticipating and avoiding problems, 231, 233; aspirational goals of, 47, 48, 155, 178, 209; Atlanta office of, 53–54, 178; authority at, 198; bureaucracy at, 45–46, 47, 56, 197; commitment to change at, 147; communication at, 180–81; core processes at, 48; culture of, 228; decision making at, 54; design formulation at, 197–99, 204; employees at, 48–49, 50, 52–53, 54–55, 197–98; empowerment at, 50, 52, 55, 209–10; funding for, 45, 47; and guidelines for change, 155; as hybrid organization, 20; impetus for change at, 47–49, 197; institutionalization of change at, 209–10, 215, 222, 228; job satisfaction at, 54–55, 65, 228; managers at, 52–53, 180–81; "numbers game" at, 45, 231; organization chart for, 51, 52; overview of, 44–47; performance evaluations at, 65; performance measures for, 45, 222; performance objectives at, 209–10, 222; and politics, 48; poultry partnership with, 178; problem solving at, 48, 52, 209, 231; problems at, 45, 47; productivity of, 49; as public sector model of horizontal organizations, 43–44; redesign team at, 49, 50–53, 54, 55, 181, 198; resistance to change at, 204, 233; setting directions for, 177–78, 180–81; skills/expertise at, 52, 71, 209–10, 215; strategy of, 50, 52–53, 178, 198; structure of, 44; teams at, 52–43, 52, 54, 65, 71, 197–99, 209; training at, 209–10; value proposition of, 44, 46–47, 48, 49, 177–78

P

Parallel teams, 192
Parnell, Opal, 113, 216–17
Partners in process: as basic principles of horizontal organizations, 24; and characteristics of horizontal organizations, 71; and design formulation, 186, 200, 204; and empowerment, 78; and hierarchy, 200; and institutionalization of change, 206, 221–22; and skills/expertise, 71; and uniqueness of organizations, 27. *See also* Hybrid organizations; *specific organization*

Performance: and basic requirements for high-achieving companies, 67; importance of focus on, 72; and institutionalization of change, 220–21; as main objective of change, 183; and multiskilling, 220–21. *See also* Performance enablers; Performance evaluations; Performance measures; Performance objectives

Performance enablers, 21, 165–66, 179, 231, 232. *See also specific enabler*

Performance evaluations: and "balanced scorecard," 21–22; and basic principles of horizontal organizations, 24; and characteristics of horizontal organizations, 65; and design formulation, 196; and institutionalization of change, 221, 222–24; of managers, 138–39; peer, 113, 126; and process owners, 196; and setting directions, 184; and technical expertise, 71. *See also* Performance measures; Performance objectives; *specific organization*

Performance measures: benefits of having, 157; and characteristics of horizontal organizations, 64; and charting, 15; and commitment, 223; and customers, 223; and design formulation, 157; and empowerment, 208; and grouping, 59; and guidelines for change, 157; and institutionalization of change, 206, 208, 222–24; and job satisfaction, 223; and managers, 223; performance objectives as, 182–83; and problem solving, 224; and reengineering, 66; and responsibility, 224; and setting directions, 177, 182–83; and teams, 224. *See also specific organization*

Performance objectives: and basic principles of horizontal organizations, 10, 11, 24, 159; and changes in personnel, 84–85; and characteristics of horizontal organizations, 59, 60, 62; and commitment, 223; and core process groups, 188; and core processes, 192; and corporate culture, 228; and customers, 223; and design formulation, 156–57, 188, 192, 196, 198; and distinction between core and simple processes, 7; and functional areas, 26; and generic picture of horizontal organizations, 79, 81; and guidelines for change, 156–57, 159; and hierarchy, 62;

and horizontal organizations as actionable alternatives, 84–85; and information technology (IT), 10, 24; and institutionalization of change, 157, 159, 206, 219–20, 222–24, 228; and job satisfaction, 223; and managers, 223; and multiskilling, 219–20; and organization charts, 75; and performance evaluations, 82; as performance measures, 182–83; and problem solving, 224; and process owners, 196; and responsibility, 224; and setting directions, 171, 182–83; and strategy, 14, 17–18; and structure, 17–18; and teams, 14, 81, 198, 224; and value propositions, 11, 24; in vertical organizations, 220; and weaknesses of vertical organizations, 6. *See also specific organization*

Porras, Jerry I., 175

Porter, Michael, 156

Problem solving: and anticipating and avoiding problems, 233; and characteristics of horizontal organizations, 62, 63, 71; and corporate culture, 228; and design formulation, 194, 199; and empowerment, 211; and expertise, 71; and guidelines for change, 165; and hierarchy, 63, 199; and horizontal organizations as actionable alternatives, 85; and information technology, 213–14; and institutionalization of change, 211, 213–14, 222, 224, 228; and networks, 71; and performance measures, 224; and performance objectives, 224; and process owners, 194; and resistance to change, 233; and selection of horizontal organizations, 19; speed of, 18–19; and strengths of horizontal organizations, 15; and structure, 14; teams as integral to, 12, 62. *See also specific organization*

Process owners: and accountability, 194; and authority, 195; and basic principles of horizontal organizations, 23, 189; and benefits of horizontal organizations, 148; and characteristics of horizontal organizations, 59, 62–64, 68; characteristics of, 195; and continual improvement, 196; and control, 194; and core process groups, 188; and corporate culture, 228; and design formulation,

188, 189, 194–97, 200; and discipline, 194; and downsizing, 68; and empowerment, 209; functions of, 63–64; and generic picture of horizontal organizations, 81; and hierarchy, 62–63, 194, 200; and horizontal organizations as actionable alternatives, 85; and institutionalization of change, 209, 219, 228; and leadership, 194, 195; and multiskilling, 196, 219; and performance evaluations, 196; and problem solving, 194; and resistance to change, 196; and responsibility, 194, 196; and rewards, 196; team of, 81; and teams, 194–95, 196, 197; and value propositions, 195–96. *See also specific organization*

Productivity, 5–6, 12, 29, 59, 72, 159, 189, 208

Psaila, Salvador, 213–14, 217, 222

Public sector, 20, 56, 177–78. *See also* OSHA

Q

Quality control, 179, 181–82, 232. *See also specific organization*

R

Reengineering, 11–12, 65–67, 77, 214, 227

Reich, Robert, 47, 197

Research and development, 67, 77, 78. *See also specific organization*

Resources, 59, 165, 168, 186, 199, 232

Responsibility: and anticipating and avoiding problems, 229; and basic principles of horizontal organizations, 24, 189; and benefits of horizontal organizations, 148; and characteristics of horizontal organizations, 62, 64, 69; and commonalities among horizontal organizations, 186; in core process groups, 194; and core processes, 192; and corporate culture, 226, 227, 228; and design formulation, 186, 189, 192, 194, 196, 199; and generic picture of horizontal organizations, 81; and guidelines for change, 163, 165; and horizontal organizations as actionable alternatives, 84, 85; and information technology, 213; and institutionalization of change, 206, 213, 215, 219, 224, 226, 227, 228; of leadership, 179; of

Responsibility (*continued*)
managers, 111–12, 186, 194; and
multiskilling, 215, 219; and performance
measures, 224; and performance
objectives, 224; and process owners, 194,
196; and selection of horizontal
organizations, 19; and setting directions,
179; and social contract, 69; of teams,
62, 81; in vertical organizations, 192. *See
also specific organization*
Rewards, 79, 83, 196, 211, 220–21, 227,
232, 233. *See also specific organization*
Reyneri, Nelson, 65
Rickard, Norman E., Jr., 138, 139
Right-skilling, 218
Road map: drawing the, 165–66
Rosenthal, Jim, 12, 214

S

Sacks, Joel, 55, 178, 181
Sales and service delivery process. *See*
Barclays Bank
Scientific management, 5–6, 29, 74, 84, 208
Setting directions: and accountability, 184;
and analysis, 168–74, 176, 180; and
anticipating and avoiding problems, 232;
and aspirational goals, 168, 174–76, 183;
and change, 170, 171, 178–83, 184;
checklist for, 183–84; and
communication, 175, 179–81, 182, 183;
and competition, 170, 176–78, 183; and
core processes, 168, 177, 179, 183; and
corporate culture, 168, 175; and
customers, 169–70, 176, 177; and design
formulation, 168, 177, 178–83; and
environment, 168–74, 176, 180, 183; and
flexibility, 171; and guidelines for
change, 151–56, 165; and laying
groundwork for change, 178–83; and
leadership, 151–56, 165, 174–75, 179,
181; and performance evaluations, 184;
and performance measures, 177, 182–83;
and performance objectives, 171, 182–83;
as phase in change, 147, 151–56, 165,
167–84; and public sector, 177–78; and
responsibility,
179; and staking a claim, 176–78; and
strategy, 168, 171, 177, 183, 184; and
value proposition, 168, 176–77, 183. *See
also specific organization*
Shareholders, 21–22, 23, 234

Simple process, 7
"Single noble purpose," 22
Skills: and characteristics of horizontal
organizations, 66, 67, 70; and core
process groups, 188; and core processes,
191–92; and corporate culture, 228; and
design formulation, 185–86, 189, 191–92,
197, 198; and downsizing, 70; and
guidelines for change, 159; and
information technology, 213; and
institutionalization of change, 159, 207,
213, 228; mismatching of, 70; and
reengineering, 66, 67; right, 218; and
setting directions, 179; and teams, 197,
198. *See also* Expertise; Multiskilling
Smith, Adam, 28
Smith, Douglas K., 191, 198
Social contract, 69
"Soldiering," 5
Sparks, Richard, 211–12
Special interests, 14
Specialization, 28–29, 215, 225. *See also*
Expertise
Speed, 18–19
Staking a claim, 176–78
Stanton, Steven, 66
Steering committee: and anticipating and
avoiding problems, 232, 233; and
corporate culture, 228; and design
formulation, 201, 204; and
empowerment, 208; and hierarchy, 201;
and information technology, 213; and
institutionalization of change, 158, 208,
213, 228; and resistance to change, 233;
and setting directions, 184
Stewart, Thomas, 232–33
Stewart, Tom, 221
Strategy: and aspirational goals, 15; and
change, 171; and characteristics of
horizontal organizations, 63, 66, 67; and
commonalities among horizontal
organizations, 186; and core processes,
13–14, 16, 17–18; definition of, 177; and
design formulation, 156–57, 168, 186,
189, 199, 201; and empowerment, 16;
and functions of general managers, 79;
and generic picture of horizontal
organizations, 79; and guidelines for
change, 156–57, 161; and hierarchy, 63,
199, 201; importance of, 13–14; and
performance objectives, 14, 17–18; and

reengineering, 67; and setting directions, 168, 171, 177, 183, 184; and structure, 13–18, 66; in twenty-first-century organizations, 13–18; and value propositions, 13–14, 16–18. *See also specific organization*

Stretch goals. *See* Aspirational goals

Structure: and accountability, 14; and aspirational goals, 15; and changes in workplace, 9; and characteristics of horizontal organizations, 66, 67; and core processes, 16, 17–18; and customers, 16; and design formulation, 186; and empowerment, 16; and horizontal organizations as actionable alternatives, 85; importance of, 9–10, 12, 14; and information technology, 17–18; and innovation, 14; as internal environment, 168; and leadership, 14; and performance objectives, 17–18; and problem solving, 14; and reengineering, 67; and roles, 14; seven S's of, 12; and strategy, 13–18, 66; in twenty-first-century organizations, 14–18; and uniqueness of organizations, 25, 186; and value propositions, 16–18. *See also specific organization*

Style, 67, 151–52

Suppliers: and anticipating and avoiding problems, 234; and basic principles of horizontal organizations, 10, 24, 190; and benefits of horizontal organizations, 234; and characteristics of horizontal organizations, 61–62, 70; and core processes, 201; and design formulation, 190, 201–4; as external environment, 168; and institutionalization of change, 215, 217; and skills/expertise, 70, 215, 217; and value propositions, 201. *See also specific organization*

T

Taylor, Frederick Winslow, 5–6, 29, 74, 84, 208

Teams: accountability of, 14, 62, 198; adjunct, 192; advantages of, 12; and basic principles of horizontal organizations, 10, 23, 24, 190; and benefits of horizontal organizations, 148; and characteristics of horizontal organizations, 59, 62, 65, 66, 70–71;

characteristics of, 62; and core processes, 62, 191–92, 197; and corporate culture, 228; and design formulation, 185–86, 188, 190, 191–92, 194–95, 197–99, 200, 201; "diffusion," 70; and empowerment, 199, 210; and generic picture of horizontal organizations, 81; and guidelines for change, 159; and hierarchy, 62, 200, 201; and institutionalization of change, 159, 210, 215, 224, 228; linked, 192; mutual respect in, 198; parallel, 192; as peers, 188; and performance measures, 224; and performance objectives, 14, 81, 198, 224; as problem solvers, 12, 62; of process owners, 81; and process owners, 194–95, 196, 197; and reengineering, 66; requirements for high-performing, 198; responsibilities of, 62, 81; rotation of members in, 81, 104, 108, 109, 110, 217; and selection of horizontal organizations, 18–19; selection of, 62, 66; as self-managing, 59, 62; size of, 62; and skills/expertise, 70–71, 197, 198, 199, 210, 215; and training, 199; in twenty-first-century organizations, 13, 14; and vertical organizations, 197. *See also* Core process groups; Employees; *specific organization*

Thoman, Richard, 133

Top-down change, 160–64, 232, 234

Torres, Chris, 39–40, 41

Training: and basic principles of horizontal organizations, 24; and characteristics of horizontal organizations, 65, 69; and design formulation, 199; and downsizing, 69; and empowerment, 208, 209, 210; and guidelines for change, 165; and information technology, 213; and institutionalization of change, 206, 208, 209–11, 213, 215–16, 217, 219; just-in-time, 209; of managers, 112; and multiskilling, 215, 217, 219; and teams, 199. *See also specific organization*

Transformation triangle, 160–64

Transition/change team. *See specific organization*; Steering committee

Traube, Brett, 95, 97

Traver, Jeff, 169

Turecki, Ron, *34*, 36, 187

Twenty-first-century organizations: and anticipating and avoiding problems, 233–34; and appropriate use of horizontal organizations, 233–34; basic questions about, 9–10, 20; and change as constant, 20–21; characteristics of, 20; conceptualization of, 9–13; strategy in, 13–18; structure in, 14–18; teams in, 13; and virtuous circle, 72

U

Urgency, sense of, 179, 183, 204, 207, 230, 232

U.S. Department of Labor Occupational Safety and Health Administration. *See* OSHA

V

Value propositions: analysis for, 153, 176; and anticipating and avoiding problems, 232, 233, 234; and appropriate use of horizontal organizations, 233; and basic principles of horizontal organizations, 11, 24; and benefits of horizontal organizations, 21, 22, 23, 234; and characteristics of horizontal organizations, 59, 60, 61–62, 63, 66, 67, 68–69; and charting horizontal organizations, 16; and core process groups, 188; and core processes, 76, 192; and corporate culture, 225, 227, 228; and customers, 176, 201; definition of, 16; and design formulation, 156–57, 185, 188, 189, 190, 192, 195–96, 199, 200, 201; and distinctions between horizontal and vertical organizations, 16–17; and downsizing, 68–69; and empowerment, 208; as fundamental purpose of horizontal organizations, 201; and guidelines for change, 153, 156–57, 163; and hierarchy, 63, 199, 200, 201; and horizontal organizations as actionable alternatives, 83, 84; importance of, 13, 16–18, 176–77; and information technology, 212–13; and institutionalization of change, 206, 207, 208, 212–13, 218, 219, 225, 227, 228; and multiskilling, 218, 219; and organization charts, 76; and performance objectives, 11, 24; and process owners, 195–96; in public sector, 177–78; and

reengineering, 66; and setting directions, 168, 176–77, 183; and strategy, 13–14, 16–18; and structure, 16–18; and suppliers, 201; in twenty-first-century organizations, 9, 10, 13–14; and uniqueness of organizations, 56, 185, 231; in vertical organizations, 16. *See also specific organization*

Vertical organizations: alienation in, 64; appropriate conditions for choosing, 8–9, 26; and change as constant, 7–9, 170; characteristics of, 3, 4, 9, 12, 72, 83, 194, 225; corporate culture in, 224, 225; and design formulation, 188–89, 192, 194, 197, 200; efficiency in, 73; employees' roles in, 29; empowerment in, 208, 209; evolution of, 4–6; hierarchy in, 194, 200; horizontal organizations compared with, 16–17, 111, 188–89, 192; limitations of, 14; organization charts for, 1, 82, 225; performance objectives in, 220; in public sector, 56; responsibility in, 192; skills in, 220; special interests in, 14; and specialization, 29; strengths and weaknesses of, 4, 6, 7–8, 12, 192; value propositions in, 16. *See also* Hybrid organizations

Virtuous circle, 72

W

Wacker, Sally, 41, 42–43
Wade, Judy, 12, 214
Ward, Sue, 127
Weber, Max, 73–74, 84, 85, 113
Welch, Jack, 103
Western Railroad, 4–5
Wilson, Steve, 124
Wong, Cindi, 92, 96
Workers. *See* Employees; Empowerment; Teams
Workplace, 7–9, 65. *See also* Environment

X

Xerox Corporation: accountability at, 137, 145; analysis at, 179; anticipating and avoiding problems at, 231; aspirational goals of, 130–31, 143, 155; authority at, 135–36, 145; Baldrige awards for, 132; bureaucracy of, 131; business development group at, 182, 231; commitment to change at, 147;

communication at, 179–80; as company-wide horizontal organization, 128–29; as composite of mini-businesses, 133–36, 170, 193; core process groups at, 193; core processes at, 192, 193; corporate culture at, 137, 139, 143, 220, 227; customers of, 132, 133, 135, 136–37, 138, 141, 142, 143–44, 145–46, 169–70, 172, 179, 182, 214, 220; decision making at, 133, 137, 141–42, 145; design formulation at, 192, 193; empowerment at, 133, 135, 137, 139, 143, 145, 146, 210; environment at, 220; expertise at, 71, 136, 140, 141, 217–18; FIRST at, 140–41, 214, 217–18; flexibility of, 136, 143; and guidelines for change, 155; as horizontal organization, 131–39, 142–47, 170; human resources at, 182; as hybrid organization, 19–20, 26, 129, 133, 136, 139–42, 193, 231; information technology at, 146, 214, 217–18; institutionalization of change at, 210, 214, 215, 217–18, 220, 227; Japan 50/50 at, 140; job satisfaction at, 138–39, 143, 182; leadership at, 137, 179–80, 182; loyalty at, 182; managers at, 135, 136, 137, 138–39, 143, 144–45, 220;

motivation at, 182; multiskilling at, 135, 137, 143, 215, 220; networks at, 140–41, 143; organization chart of, 134; partnerships at, 141–43; performance evaluations at, 137, 138–39, 145, 220; performance measures at, 138, 220; performance objectives at, 26, 135, 138, 145, 231; personal copier success story at, 143–47; problem solving at, 132, 143, 144, 217–18; problems of, 130–31, 179; process owners at, 135, 210; productivity at, 182; quality control at, 26, 182; research and development at, 71, 140–43, 215; responsibility at, 131, 135, 137, 139, 143, 144–45, 192; results at, 142–43, 231; rewards/compensation at, 137–38, 139, 145; setting directions at, 169–74, 179–80, 182; strategy at, 144, 171–74; structure of, 131, 133–36, 144; suppliers of, 136, 144, 172; teams at, 133, 135, 136–37, 139–40, 143, 144–45, 146, 192; tensions at, 142; training at, 137, 217–18; value proposition of, 26, 132–33, 182; as vertical organization, 130–31, 139–42; Xerox 2000 initiative at, 171–74; Xerox 2005 initiative at, 26, 132–33, 135, 171–74, 182, 193